Political Auditing

Manifesto for Rescuing Democracy

Attention Authors

Manas Publications is fighting a war to tell the world that India can win the battle not only by the bullet but also by pen. There is no dearth of intellectuals in our country, but their knowledge is confined to them only. No sincere effort has been made by any other publisher to channelise their knowledge in national interest, which is why the talent of large number of intellectuals remain latent. An author always gives the raw material in the shape of a manuscript and it is the job of the publisher to convert it into a beautiful book. Manas always motivates the intellectuals by publishing their manuscripts since more than four decades and would like to publish your manuscript too. If you or your colleagues have any manuscript ready for publication or are working on it, kindly contact us with a detailed synopsis and list of contents for its best publication. If you wish, we can also suggest you a suitable title for writing related to your area of expertise. Manas is known for its publishing quality and commitments. We take utmost care in production and give wide publicity to the book as well as its author through our national and international distribution network.

Political Auditing

Manifesto for Rescuing Democracy

Gopal Chowdhury

Manas Publications
(We Convert Fighters into Writers)
New Delhi-110002 (INDIA)

MANAS PUBLICATIONS
(Publishers, Library Suppliers, Importers & Exporters)
4402/5-A, Ansari Road (Opp. HDFC Bank)
Darya Ganj, New Delhi-110 002 (India)
Off. (23260783, 23265523, Res. (23842660
Fax: 011-23272766
E-mail: manaspublications@vsnl.com
manaspublications@yahoo.com
manaspublications@gmail.com

ISBN 978-81-7049-418-8
₹ 595/-

Designed at
Manas Publications

Printed in India at
Harmain Offset Press, Delhi
and published by Mrs Suman Lata for
Manas Publications, 4402/5-A, Ansari Road
(Opp. HDFC Bank),
Darya Ganj, New Delhi-110 002 (INDIA)

CONTENTS

PREFACE

The book is a manifesto to establish democratized (or popular) and institutionalized Political Auditing for rescuing democracy from the clutches of oligarchy and its subversion by the vested interest. The democracies world over are urged to institutionalize and democratize political auditing to salvage it from the rule by the few, for the few and of the few. If the political actors world over refuse to institutionalize it, the civil society is urged to form their political audit groups on popular basis, and liberate democracy from the 'Iron Law of Oligarchy'.

Despite the triumph of the liberal democracy over socialism, the former has resulted into a system where people have been marginalized, and powers in its all manifestations have come to be concentrated into few hands, what has been termed as 'Iron Law of Oligarchy'. In its glorious history of more than two and half millennia, the democracy has never encountered such existential problem as it is confronting now. Not even during black days of Interwar period (the period between First World War and Second World War) when the combined onslaught of Hitler and Mussolini was threatening very existence of democracy world over.

Then the enemies of democracy were visible, now they are invisible. The globalization has globalized the arc of the antagonists of democracy and liberalization has further strengthened the mutual bonds. The situation has become so confusing that it is difficult to decide which one is strengthening the democracy and which is preparing its burial ground. The free market economy has further exacerbated the situation for democracy. The amalgamation of market economy and the liberal democracy has undercut its very basis – equality and social justice – causing widespread poverty, hunger, unemployment and inequality.

It is ironic that capitalism gets its very life support such as capital, raw material at lower rate, tax and custom holiday, all sorts of concessions, a conducive and supportive government, and various kinds of infrastructural and non-infrastructural sustenance at the cost of tax payers. Whenever the crisis hit the world, the stimulus packages are given to very those stakeholders of the capitalism who cause the burst, while average recession-hit taxpayers, whether in India or USA or Europe are left to fend for themselves as happened during recent crisis.

However, it is not so that capitalism, the political economy of democracy or liberal democracy, in its globalized and liberalized avatar has not contributed to the humanity. It has done commendably, heralding growth and development, even though the wealth and resources have been monopolized by handful of corporations, billionaires, few countries and two-three million of investors across the world. In spite of this feat, capitalism has created more problem than it has solved – concentration of wealth in few and fewer hands, inequitable growth, imbalanced development, rampant exploitation of human beings and natural resources, global warming threatening very existence of life on earth, growing poverty and unemployment.

However, the book is not outright critique of democracy and its political economy – capitalism. Democracy and capitalism is only good option among the worst alternatives of communism, mercantilism, Chinese brand of socialism, Fabianism, authoritarianism, dictatorship, etc. What is needed is a balanced course correction and equitable growth, and distributive justice should be factored in, to offset the deviation and distortion that has set in.

Through the case study of Indian democracy and its political economy, the book analyses the state of democracy world over. The main problem of democracy is that it has been highjacked by neo-liberals and has been used to further their interest. The campaign for making democracy safe for capitalism, which started in post Second World War period, and later picked up by neo-liberals has done more harm to democracy than anything else. In making democracy safe for capitalism, the very basis of democracy – equality and social justice – has been sacrificed at the altar of untrammelled growth and development. The ideal situation should have been two-way interface – both being made safe for each other.

However, the book through case study of Indian democracy in particular and that of democracies as existing in world in general comes to conclusion that lack of popular participation and proper representation, particularly the 'First-past-the-post' or 'winner-take-it-all' has been behind the subversion of democracy and its highjacking by oligarchy. The lack of transparency and responsibility has been its collaterals. This can be rectified through democratized (popular) and institutionalized political auditing.

This book is different in the sense that it has developed democratized (based on popular method or indirect election) parameters to do the political auditing of each and every aspect of public life. It seeks to institutionalize political auditing based on indirect election so that it could act as permanent mechanism of check and balance. This would bridge the representation hiatus that exists in most of the democracies based as these are on 'first-past-the-post' or 'winner-takes-it-all' voting system on one hand, it would encourage political participation on other. This would certainty enforce accountability and transparency lacking in the democracies across the world, and has been the main cause behind its subversion.

This would certainty provide new direction to democracy and discourse on democracy, factoring in much needed course correction.

I am thankful to JNU – my Alma metier; its faculty, its democratic traditions and sensitive students, and its surreal environ which is in quite contrast to outside world. I am not less thankful to the teeming billions of poor, hapless, exploited and underfed Indians and those of other countries who inspired me to do something for them, even if it is on ideational level.

Finally, I am thankful to Almighty God, Yadavraj Krishna, my Ma and Papa and my family, and invisible Indians whose very life patterns and philosophy are steeped in democratic traditions, inherited down from the time when even word, 'democracy' was not coined.

Gopal Chowdhury

FOREWORD

The Book titled as *Political Auditing* can be gainfully categorized as a manifesto which posits the fundamentals of the theory and praxis of Political Science and Political Studies in the crucible of the realm of political economy. Despite the venality and the negative crassness which has crept inside the dynamics of the Indian Political system, the country and its humdrum mortals go on unabated with an unflinching faith in the modicum of the praxis of Democracy and polity. With India having reached its "Geriatric sixty", the mandarins need to have a delving inside what all ails the framework and the praxis of Democracy in the Indian Union.

The present work elucidates upon a few poignant themes which also ought to serve as grave reminders as to what cleaning up and resuscitation of the Indian political system is required through the writing lance of Shri Gopal Chowdhary. The democracies world over are urged to institutionalize and democratize political auditing to salvage it from the rule by the few, for the few and of the few. If the political actors world over refuse to institutionalize it, the civil society is urged to form their political audit groups on popular basis, and liberate democracy from the Law of Oligarchy. The notion which the anointed President Abraham Lincoln advanced before the World Polity in the context of the American Political system portends the notion of, "Democracy by the People, of the People and for the People" which has been convolutedly presented by a mediocre practice to the Neanderthal levels of, "Democracy for the Few, by the Few and of the Few". Which is a grave cause of concern for the Indian denizens as it is here that a political economist can have a say into the brass-tacks of the whole debate and can have an indelible impact upon the body politic of the besieged Indian nation State.

Though the Indian political firmament rekindled the hope for an age of egalitarian norms and the era of untrammeled social justice, through the pen and the deeds of our founding fathers, still, the ending of the Organic State of the young and entophytic Indian Republic stymied the tide of political and social morality. The advent of nepotism, favouritism and political legerdemain of the crassest genre vitiated the sound moral fabric of the nation and thus emerged the advent of the "criticality" of the Indian State, wherein, double dealing and political one upmanship in the form of a want of accountability and transparency and Governmental fiscal prudence led to the dirtying of the turf of Indian Politics. It is here that a political leveller is the need of the hour whether be it the advent of the Lokpal debate or the need of the system of Political auditing which is being practised in some parts of the international polity and can serve as a panacea for the beguiled and robbed Indian nation. The antagonists of the Indian democratic firmament were visible, now they are invisible. The advent of the gurgling lore globalization has globalized the arc of the antagonists of democracy and liberalization has further strengthened the mutual bonds. The scenario is so baffling that one needs to strive hard in order to decide which one is strengthening the pillars of democracy and which is having a deleterious impact upon the political system.

The Book finally asserts the socio-political theme that the battle against Fabianism and Socialism might have been won but the notion of the crediting of justice to the marginalized and the left out classes of the Indian society and polity remains a task unaccomplished which is where lies the academic significance of this work. The immense accuracy and objectivity with which the book takes up cudgels against the untrammeled growth of Neo-Liberalism and its corporate avatar needs to be comprehended as one of the immense contributions of the author, which is not a novae thesis but still constructs a new personalized narrative about the challenges being faced by the Indian polity in toto. Thus the core and primary preoccupation of the work remains the one of a disgust against the concentration of wealth in few and fewer hands, inequitable growth, imbalanced development, rampant exploitation of human beings and natural resources, global warming threatening very existence of life on earth, growing poverty and unemployment. The work is eruditely orchestrated with a great deal of useful and reader worthy information to enthrall the uninitiated.

Manan Diwedi

Assistant Professor, IIPA, New Delhi

Former Assistant Professor of Gujarat University

Section One

Prologue

"There has come into fashion a strange and easy manner of suppressing the revelation of history, of invalidating the commentaries of philosophy, of eluding all embarrassing facts and gloomy questions".

Victor Hugo in *Les Miserable*

"As for us we respect the past here and there, and we spare it above all provided that it consents to be dead. If it insists on being alive, we attack it and we try to kill it."

V H

It appears to be an unprecedented time in the history of mankind. The riches and wealth have never been so galore for few people and countries, while bare minimum facilities are eluding the masses. The technology and growth has attained it zenith, while values and morals have plummeted to its nadir. Despite breathtaking pace of development, communication and digital revolution, globalization, liberalization, freedom, liberty and democracy, all round decay and downslide has set in. It is the time of deceit, exploitation, contradiction, imbalanced and uneven growth, sleaze and moral decay. "...... No degree of progress allows one to ignore that never before, in absolute figures, have so many men, women and children been subjugated, starved or exterminated on the earth."[1]

It is the time when Time and space has shrunk and in that proportion collective and individual morality, character, integrity and values seem to have stooped to the lowest level. It will not be an exaggeration when it is termed as nadir of the human development, despite all the growth, development, and technological breakthroughs. For some, for chosen few people, classes, sections, societies, communities and countries, it may be the zenith, but for the majority life is what has been termed as a 'burning inferno' or "…. Nasty, brutish and short"[2].

Democracy, the best system among the worst forms of government[3] seems to be passing through a crucial period. Autocracy, plutocracy, oligarchy, dynastic rule and what not is being perpetrated in the name of democracy without any apparent risk. As the state apparatus world over is having massive propaganda, money, resources, and muscles power at its beck and call, it can camouflage a dynastic or one family rule or oligarchy with democracy apparently. Despite being the dominant form of governance for almost three fourth countries of the world, it is passing through a period which can make it or break it, if the distortion, maladies and deviation which have gripped it world over are not rectified. "The calamity of the Information age is that toxicity of data increases much faster than its benefits"[4]. This has further exacerbated the problem for democracy which has been subverted without any substantial protest and movements.

The crisis of democracy can be best expressed with one euphemism: 'Why people, why people, why people?'[5] Though it is parody of a well-known definition of democracy, 'of the people, by the people and for the people', it sums up the malady which has afflicted democracy. The people, who are the very basis of democracy and in fact its very *raison de etre* seem to have been relegated to periphery, while a few rich, few families, few groups or cliques or their vested interests have grabbed the center. The simmering tension within a rather calm exterior of democracy betrays the fact that one or other democratic countries is plunging into civil war or political unrest or instability of government or coup or dictatorship, or at the best credibility deficit.

The ominous signal of crisis that has gripped democracy is emanating from the four corner of the world. Be it USA—the land of liberty and freedom or India—the land of ancient village republic or Europe—the cradle of democracy or Africa or West Asia—graveyard of democracy. While the 'Ersatz Capitalism' in which losses are socialized and profits are privatized is throttling the very foundation of Democracy in USA[6] where fundamentals have already been eaten by termites of 'crony Capitalism', the 'Predatory Capitalism', the amalgamation of democracy and the free market economy is going to be nemesis for Indian democracy. This rather heady mix of democracy and the free market economy has moved all motivation towards profit. Apart from strengthening the neo-liberals, it is making rich richer and poor poorer.[7]

The cradle of Democracy – Europe – is suffering from ebbing interest in participatory democracy and what is eating up the very foundation of democracy in USA – Ersatz Capitalism—seems to be hollowing the Continental democracies as well. "….The criticism began almost immediately after polls closed in the recent elections to European Parliament. Fewer had turned out than ever: a third of Brits and Dutch, under quarter of Poles and less than 20 per cent Slovaks....”[8] Moreover, European democracy, as is the case in India and other developing countries is characterized by what a ‘19th century’ Russian said that Europe’s democracies were moderated by corruption. Japan had corruption moderated by democracy’.[9] As for Africa and West Asia, democracy is like intersection from where four options sully forth – dictatorship, civil war, theocracy and dynastic rule—leading to civil war, genocide, fratricide and outright suppression.

The present state of democracy in world over, including India is pregnant with future of uncertainty and doomsday. When it fails, what is termed as the last hope for humanity, then what will happen? After democracy, what will happen to hopes, aspiration and dreams of billons of people? “What happens once democracy has been used up? When it has been hollowed out and emptied of meaning.”[10] The future without democracy is darker than that of with democracy. Moreover, it may result into the very end of ‘end of history’, throwing whole world in abyss and listlessness. All civilizational and cultural developments and achievements may be at risk of being plundered by savagery and barbarism of mayhem, plunder and violence. There may be ‘end’[11] of “End of history” on which democracy has been or being used for all non-democratic things that make democracy hollow if not manifestly then latently sure.[12]

For chosen few people, sections, groups, families, communities, societies and countries, it seems to be a virtual heaven granted on the earth. They have power, money, and loads of information, bank balance, and assets, islands, chartered planes and choppers, incessant flow of wine, women and all luxuries. These chosen few appear to have monopolized power, government, business, industries, trade, wealth, media and all means of communications. They have got almost substantial control over the lever that controls individual, community, society, country and world. What is rather appalling to note is that this ‘iron law of Oligarchy’ has taken over almost all genuine and sham democracies and developed and developing countries in its vicious grip?

It is a time when politics has become business and business politics.[13] It is a time when politicians control more businesses and industries than businessman or industrialist.[14] ‘It is no secret that many parliamentarians have varied business interests. But the Rajya Sabha (Upper House) has tried to fend off a Right to Information application seeking information on commercial dealings and shares held by members.’[15]

On the other hand, business and business houses wield more power than politicians. Even if their control is indirect or covert or in form of courtesy call (for public consumption), they have more political leverage than the politicians.[16] They are the powerful oligarchs who decide who will win the next election or who will be the prime minister or what policies are likely to be followed in their respective businesses or industries.

Monopoly or dynastic tendencies have come to characterize every walk of life and arenas of society. Be it political, economic, social, cultural, and educational, one or few families or groups are monopolizing everything. While in some cases as in politics, it is being highlighted, in another case nobody dares to rake up the issue. The monopolistic (or Dynastic problem) tendency seems to be obvious in politics, economy and media. Although it is there in other fields as well, yet it is not as manifest in these fields as in politics, economy and media.

How the dynastic or monopolistic tendencies have gripped our public life is best reflected by one family or group or class or caste domination in politics. One family or one group or sub-group or one caste or class in almost all political parties, contrary to popular beliefs that only one leading national party is having this malady, have been ruling the roost. Even the parties that claim to be ideology-driven and cadre-based are not immune from this tendency. There is a long lineage of leadership by one family, group or caste, albeit hidden or in guise of ideological claptrap, running deep into veins and arteries of political parties.

Apart from individual or group of families ruling the roost in political arena, there is no dearth of such dynastic or monopolistic tendency in business, industry, trade, media, film, etc. What is more worrying that these dynastic or monopolistic tendencies are being transformed into 'cartelization' which is more dangerous and certainly not in public interest? It may give rise to powerful oligarchs who may threaten the very existence of democracy and the country.

A democratic country like India got the glimpse of this foreboding when steel and cement cartels continued to defy the political actors despite their warnings of stringent actions if they did not heed their order (not jacking up the prices of cement and steel).[17] Lately, the political actors have publicly admitted their inability to control or rein in spiralling prices of essential and other commodities. Though the onus of this has been put on market forces, it is just an alibi to hoodwink the people in believing that the government is in control. The fact is that it is the 'cartels' in all segments of business and industry that are milching the people in cahoots with politicians and state apparatus.

As if it were not sufficient and proverbially speaking, adding salt to injury, there are certain individuals or family or group that is monopolizing right from the manufacture of needle to aero plane, from salt to high-tech car and from mobile to refinery. It is the replica of what is happening in politics and other fields. Even in the USA, the torchbearer of liberty and free market, there is bar from owning more than one type of industry or business. This rule applies to even American media as well whereby one person or a group owning newspaper cannot enter the field of television or Radio and vice versa. This is the case in most of the developed countries where liberal capitalism is in vogue.

The dynastic or monopolistic tendency is very anti-thesis of 'Circulation of Elite'[18] which is a condition for success of democracy or political economy in any country. The circulation of elite (leaders) in government or business or for that matter in any other field ensures new initiatives, endeavours and freshness resulting into a just and vibrant system. Like blood circulation, it keeps the system healthy and resurgent, bringing new idea, new initiatives, vigour and vitality and propelling the system to ever new heights. Moreover, it reinforces democracy by giving representation to every group, class, caste or section of the society.

How this monopoly or dynasty or cartelization or oligarchy, affects the society, there is eon of proofs. India is reigning proof of this undemocratic tendency. The 2009 National Election Survey, for instance, reveals that when asked if it was okay for sons and daughters to contest from seats held by their parents, nearly 60 per cent said it was undemocratic.[19] Even after thousands of year's civilizational history and more than six decades of Independence from colonial rule, we are still stuck up in backwardness, starvation, poverty, inequality, injustice and exploitation. "Despite several years of breakneck growth, India fails far short in protecting its own people from poverty. Some 230 million (23 crore) Indians suffer from chronic hunger, a number that has grown……"[20]

II

There is, however, stark difference among different Indian agencies compiling the data of poverty. While official figure puts the poverty rate at 26.10 per cent of the total population of the country for the Year 1999-2000 as compared to 44.48 per cent in 1983-84, the latest figure of poverty is pegged down to 28 per cent of the population.[21] Now the Planning Commission has come out with a new criteria of calculating poverty that is based on consumption, not on calories as was the case earlier. According to this new criterion, the number of poor has pegged down to 37 per cent.[22] Even this figure is disputed by the Saxena Panel that maintains the total figure of poverty as 50 per cent of the total population of the country. And that too this figure has been compiled on paltry sum of Rs. 1000 for urban poor and Rs. 600 for rural poor.[23]

An eminent economist of the country has made a survey on the earnings of Indian populace. The result is just shocking that cannot be penned down exactly: 84 crore (840 million) people in India have a daily earning of Rs 20. This is though not exact then approximately near what Saxena Panel has reported. It implies that there are 84 crore people who are eking their precarious existence below poverty line. Moreover, out of 20 crore (200 million) families in India, 14 crore (140 million) families have no access to drinking water. As if it is not enough, there is external debt of Rs 34 lac crore and it is going upward, ensnaring future Indian generations into debt trap.[24]

If the Saxena panel report's calculation of number of poor, which is 50 per cent of our population and it comes to approximately 61 crore is added to the 23 crore case of chronic hunger as reported by UNICEF, it comes to 84 crore people suffering from poverty as calculated by Arjun Sengupta. The other day the National Commission on Enterprises in Unorganized Sector has estimated that 78 per cent of Indians are being forced to survive on less than Rs 20 a day, based on consumer expenditure.[25] Whatever cynics may say about this mind-boggling number of people wallowing in degrading clutch of poverty, it is a fact that cannot be denied. And it is shame not only on us as citizen of India but also on our civilizational heritage, our system and ruling elites.

Expenditure data from the National Survey organization's 61st Round (2004-05) showed that the rural and urban per capita cloth consumption, real food expenditure, and calories intake have all declined from their already low levels since 1993-94. This country remains a Republic of hunger with a larger population of ordinary people being relentlessly pushed down to worst nutritional status.... The proportion of rural population unable to access 2,400 calories daily climbed from 75 per cent in 1993-94 to a record high of 87 per cent by 2004-05. The corresponding percentages for urban India, where the nutrition norm is lower at 2,100 calories are 57 per cent and 64.5 per cent respectively.[26]

The overall poverty in world is not less shameful and it is a challenge to our globalised and liberalized world. Out of a total world population of 6.785 billion as on September, 2009,[27] there are 3.4 billion poor people subsisting on an income of less than $2[28]. Added to this number of poor and destitute world over is another 84 million who joined the dehumanizing state of poverty due to global crisis hitting the world from 2007 onwards[29]. If one takes into account the hidden poverty in the USA and Europe, and unreported number in Asia and Africa, it would come to two-third of the total world population. And if the cut off line of poverty is raised to less than $3 per day, it would come to three fourth of total world population living in poverty.

However, the recent poverty index developed and applied by the Oxford Poverty and Human Development Initiative (OPHDI) with UNDP support has found 1.7 billion people living in poverty, out of 5.2 billion surveyed across 104 countries. The report underlined the gaping hole in the official estimation of poverty: there are more poor people in eight Indian states—42.1 crore in Bihar, Chhattisgarh, Jharkhand, Madhya Pradesh, Orissa, Rajasthan, Uttar Pradesh, and West Bengal than in the 26 poorest African countries combined—41 crore. Half of the world's poor live in South Asia (51 per cent or 84.4 crore), whereas one quarter in Africa (28 per cent or 45.8 crore) are poor.[30]

Globally, inequality has widened even with a Black American as the President of United States. (Gupta, 2009). Japan's poverty rate, at 15.7 per cent is close to the Organization for Economic Cooperation and Development's figure of 17.1 per cent in the US....(Fickler, 2010). The global divides between rich and poor countries are shocking and it continues to be growing despite globalization and liberalization. While a child born in Europe—Norway—is going to be alive 30 years longer than a child born in Nigeria, Africa. The average income of Norway is 85 times the average income of Niger.[31] Apart from it, the number of people going to bed hungry is growing in the age of plenty and surplus where even pets are being overfed. 'The number of hungry passes one billion this year (2009). What is lamentable is that there is shortage of fund as only $2.6 billion is available for its budget of $6.7 billion.'[32]

The problem of globalization must be seen in right perspective as majority does not seem to be sharing the enthusiasm of a few. Globalization is a business to share the means of material comforts among few prosperous men (nations), not the culture of sharing the common maladies. There is one picture that haunts us—one information system, one market with unified production line, licence to open factory or shop without any hassle. The whole world is a common market. Roughly this is the meaning of globalization for the rich nations or persons. There is not even the remotest possibility of every one being equal in sharing the riches of the world. In such a situation, globalization is a cruel reality which is favoured only by those who have everything or there is possibility of such unlimited luxury.[33]

After disintegration of the Soviet Union and wave of democracy sweeping across the erstwhile communist rules, capitalism had a field day aftermath the ebbing of cold war. In the aftermath euphoria of unipolar world that threatens to turn into 'multipolar' one, (for some it is already a multipolar world order with one power playing the role of referee) capitalism virtually has been running amok piggy riding the globalized and liberalized world. In this euphoria and gung ho when it was turned into first as 'crony capitalism'[34] and then in the wake of recession and stimulus package to very those stakeholders (Big banks, financiers, industries, business houses and cartels) who caused such burst of bubble, then it slide to 'ersatz capitalism'[35] (which socialize the losses and privatize the profit). The 'end of history', 'the theory of everything' or 'unified theory' provided capitalism and neo-liberals moral and political support which slowly and steadily turned into complacency and aura of indispensability, leading to the current crisis.

This has undercut the very basis of democracy—equality and social justice, causing widespread poverty, hunger, unemployment and inequality. It is ironic that capitalism got its very life support—capital at lower rate, tax and customs holiday or concession of all sorts, a conducive and supportive government and all sorts of infrastructural and non-infrastructural supports – at the cost of tax payers. When crisis hit the world, the stimulus package was given to those very stakeholders who caused the burst, while the average recession-hit taxpayers whether in India or USA or Europe were left to fend for themselves.

However, in its new avatar of globalized and liberalized mode, capitalism has delivered good growth and development. It has done so in many ways, even though the wealth of whole world has been monopolized by a handful of corporations, billionaires, few countries and one or two million investors across the world. Over the past quarter century, the global economy has doubled every 10 years, growing from $31 trillion in 1999 to $ 62 trillion in 2008. Recessions have become tamer than ever before, averaging eight months rather than two years. More than 400 million people across Asia have been lifted out of poverty. Between 2003 and 2007, average income worldwide grew at a faster rate – 3.1 per cent – than in any previous period of recorded history. In 2006 and 2007—the peak years of the boom—124 countries of the world grew at 4 per cent a year or more.[36]

Despite this feat achieved by capitalism, it has created more problems than it has solved—concentration of wealth in few and fewer hands, inequitable growth, imbalanced development, rampant exploitation of human beings and natural resources, global warming and destruction of bio-diversity, growing poverty and unemployment, and what not. The rest has been done by the heady amalgamation of capitalism and democracy. However, this is not to contend that the days have been numbered for Keynesian model of development and capitalism. Despite all its drawbacks, capitalism like democracy is only the good option available to a political economy among the worst choices of communism, mercantilism, Chinese brand of socialism, Fabians, authoritarian rule, dictatorship and benevolent dictatorship. However, equitable growth and distributive justice should be factored in, to offset the deviation and distortion that has set in.

That is why Francis Fukuyama, in his book, 'The End of History and the Last Man,' (1992) has maintained that liberal democracy as developed in Western countries is the last point of humanity's intellectual development and growth. The liberal democracy will continue to be only form of governance for posterity. "What we may be witnessing is not just the end of the Cold War, or the passing of a particular period of post-war history, but the end of history as such: that is, the end point of mankind's ideological evolution and the universalization of Western liberal democracy as the final form of government."[37]

It is better to trade some comforts and luxury for freedom rather than trade freedom for bread and butter. Capitalism has thrived on this credo. But freedom is a very hollow concept when faced with gut-wrenching poverty and hunger. This freedom is rendered useless when there is all round poverty, hunger and exploitation. The neo-classic failed to anticipate it, while parroting the oft-repeated jargon of capitalism that free market would result into a just and equalitarian society. What they missed to realize was that profit and motive for profit is infinite, while ground on which profit can be realized is finite.

In the heyday of globalization and liberalization, we have forgotten the credo of Gandhian philosophy of good means for good end. In the mad race for profit and accumulation of wealth and assets, the means has been conveniently discarded, while end has become everything. The result is before us: asymmetrical world where almost three-fourth of populace is wallowing in hunger and poverty, while the rest is enjoying all comforts and luxuries of the world. Is this modern age or ultramodern world or clone of medieval age minus the claptraps of feudalism?

More broadly, the fundamental crisis we face is globalization itself. We have globalized the economies of nations. ….. But our politics remains national.[38] This is very convincing theoretically, yet it seems to be a far possibility in the distant future. The people and their representatives world over are not willing to part even with petty interest, the dismantling of national, political, geographical and regional boundaries. These are very difficult task, if not impossible one. This ideal can be achieved only with major upheavals—engineered by Nature or some sort of 'shock therapy'. However, there have been some discourses regarding the emergence of the 'postnational society' in opposition to the globalization debates. The term 'postnational' is different from what is being promoted by corporations and the self defined 'global civil society' which is nothing but spaces above 'global civil society'. (Menon, 2009)

Habermas has been leading voice in propounding the theory of "postnational constellation". He has conceived a world citizenship in the context of Europe construed in opposition to the imperialist design of US. He makes a distinction between the US "enforcing the global implementation of human rights as part of the national mission of a world superpower and European vision of enforcement of a politics of human rights aimed at establishing the rule of law in international relations". (Habermas, 1999) However, from the perspective of global south in an unequally structured global economy, the distinction between US hegemony and European hegemony does not appear to be a significant one. (Menon, op.cit.)

The Eurocentric alternative to the postnationalism has not found much support from outside Europe for obvious reason. A different view is the idea of the 'global civil society' that has been put forward by Daniele Archibugi who has pitched for the idea of "cosmopolitcal democracy". He seeks to apply the principles of democracy at international level by arguing that democracy must transcend the borders of single states and assert itself on a global level. There would be a world parliament, peace assemblies and the International criminal court that would seek to establish 'global civil society'. It would not include the states as the representative; the peoples would act as member of this global society. However, if any action is to be taken against the states, the existing nation states would act as actors. The actions to be taken against the erring states must be corroborated by the world citizens in the assembly But the world citizens are not to be considered as agent in themselves in the form of cross-border political movement or mass struggles. (Archibugi, 2003)

There is another proposal for postnational world order which takes into account the crossborder initiatives by propounding the prospect of the globalization from below. (Appadurai, 2001) The globalization from below is based on the conflation of the political movements with state or any supranation funded non-governmental organizations (NGOs) and transnational networks (TAN) which are 'part movements, part networks, part organizations'. The successful TANs may offset the most volatile effects of runway capital and the reason that these are unable to do so because of their (TAN) alienation from different world organizations (*ibid*). However, this 'organizing from below is a fragile process which cannot be sustained in the wake of joint onslaught of state, global capital and NGOs itself. (Mertes, 2002) Nevertheless, the debate seems to have stuck up to the position that democratic politics should avoid becoming enclosed in representations such as the nation state that has been historically associated with emancipatory projects and struggles for citizenship, but now have become obstacles to their revival, preventing their permanent reinvention (Balibar, 2004).

Nevertheless, there is still hope for democracy and capitalism. The only hope for democracy is more democracy and democracy in real sense of the term. And for capitalism, more capitalism in the form of benevolent capitalism suffused with some equalitarian and egalitarian credos where 'losses are not socialized and profit not privatized.' It is hoped that various stakeholders of democracy and capitalism would heed the hidden message emanating from plethora of crises, ranging from political, economic, humanitarian, regional, national and international. Because 'no system—capitalism, socialism, or whatever (other system may be) can work without a sense of ethics and values at its core.'[39]

Although such diagnosis is laudable, it must be supplemented with some concrete measures. Otherwise the vicious circle of boom and bust would continue to haunt us, while in the name of democracy all type of farce would be perpetrated. Every time the crisis hits, the neo-classics come with firefighting measures, rather than some long lasting solution to the problems. If there is enough ground for some types of control or government intervention or introduction of any regulator, the neo-classics and their vast apparatus world over start parroting the oft-repeated jargon: the free market would take care of any deviation resulting from interplay of market forces, and the free play of market forces would result into a just and equalitarian society.

It must, however, be noted that globalization has aggravated socio-economic disparities and food deprivation in India as it has done the world over. The uneven distribution of wealth, unemployment, opportunities of corruption through purchase of shares, etc. have led to the 'rich getting richer' and 'the poor getting poorer' phenomena. India's top industrial houses are purchasing prestigious firms in foreign countries and their wealth has increased manifold due to facilities of investment, loan, incentives and export credit, facilities and other such undeclared benefits. But India's poor in the village have a reduced intake of cereals; pulses are out of reach of 70 per cent of people. India is ranked 128th in the human development Index Report published by the UNDP.[40]

Much water has flown down the major rivers of the world since capitalism and democracy have become dominant systems of political economy. Yet the ground realities seem to have remained the same, with some minor changes. In some respects, situations have become explosive: the imbalances of all sorts have become endemic, poverty and hunger has become permanent features and social justice has been reduced to a totem pole.There must be some institutional mechanism, backed by popular mandate, to check the vested interests from overshadowing democracy.

Moreover, 'the re-emergence of a specter from the darkest period of modern history argues for a different, indeed strident, response. Economic nationalism—the urge to keep jobs and capital at home—is both turning the economic crisis into a political one and threatening world with depression. If it is not buried forth, the consequence will be dire.'[41] Hence, there arises the need for political auditing, backed with popular mandate and institutionalized mechanism Lest, there may be danger of the 'End of the End of the History' project.[42]

Endnotes

1 Derrida, J., *Violence and Metaphysics: An Essay on the Thought of Emmanuel, Writing and difference*, Chicago: University of Chicago. 97-192

2 The Contractualist like Hobbes has observed about the human life as existing before the onset of State and government.

3 Aristotle, *Politics*, trans. H. Rackham : London,1977

4 Taleb, Nassim Nicholas, *The Best of Procrustes Philosophical Aphorisms*, Allen Lane/ Penguin, 2010.

5 An anonymous Indian amateur comedian made this observation during a TV show in 2008.

6 Stiglitz, Joseph E, '*America Socialism for the Rich*', Project Syndicate, 2009

7 Aleaz, Bonita, 'The praxis of Democracy'. *Statesman*, 30 Aug, 2009

8 Moravcsik, Andrew, 'Ignore the Skeptics: EU Democracy is doing just fine', *Newsweek*, June 29th, 2009

9 *The Economist*, July 18th 2009, p.68

10 Roy, Arundhati, "*Listening to Grasshoppers: Field Notes on Democracy*". Hamish Hamilton, 2009

11 Gat, A, 'The End of the End of the History', *Foreign Affairs*, July/August, 2007

12 Fukuyama, Francis, '*The End of History and the Last Man*', 1992.

13 ET, Editorial '*Too Little, Prime Minister: Reform Political Funding* , 5.02.2010.

14 Comparative Analysis of assets declared by politicians during filing of nominations for two successive election to Lower House (Lok Sabha) and State Legislative Assemblies, *The Times of India* and other national newspapers (March-April 2009)

15 Dhawan, Himanshi, 'RS won't disclose biz (business) dealings of MPs', *The Times of India*, dated 31.12.2009.

16 The Funding patterns of national political parties by the leading industrialists and business houses reveal who has how much control over policy and decision makers.

17 *TOI* and *Hindu* (Feb.) FM warns against Cartelization. Feb, 2009

18 Pareto, Vilfred, *The Mind and Society [Tratto Di Sociologia Generale] Harcourt*, Brace. 1935

Eisernan, G, "Pareto, Vilfred (1848-1923)", *International Encyclopedia of the Social and Behavioral Sciences*, 2001, pp 11048-11051

19 Sen, Ronojoy, " Why Dynasties Flourish", *The Times of India*, September16, 2009

20 Unicef Report, as Quoted in *The Economist*, London, June 6th 2009

21 Planning Commission of India, Report and Economic Survey, 2008

22 Approach Paper of Planning Commission, 2009-10 and news reports in various dailies on 08.12.2009

23 Saxena Panel Report, 2009

24 National Commission on Enterprises in the Unorganized Reprot, 2009 as quoted in *The Economic Times*, 01. 01.2010

25 As quoted in *The Economic Times*, page no 2 dated 1.1.10

26 *Frontline*, Volume 25, Issue 06:15-28 March 2008

27 US Census Bureau: World Pop clock Projection

28 Rural Development Institute website

29 The United Nations Department of Economic and Social Affairs Estimate, 2010 as quoted in *The Times of India*, dated 10.02.10.

30 UNDP Human Development Report, 2010.

31 Human Development Report, 2009, published by UNDP

32 UN World Food Program Report, 2009

33 Kishore, Krishn, '*First Stop of Struggle Odyssey*', Shilpayan, New Delhi, 2009.

34 Stiglitz, Joseph E, *op. cit.* p 3

35 Stiglitz, Joseph E, *op. cit.* p 3

36 Zakaria, Fareed, Newsweek, 22 June, 2009

37 Fukuyama, Francis, *op. cit.* p 4

38 Zakaria, Fareed, *Newsweek*, 22 June, 2009

39 Zakaria, Farid, *ibid*

40 Sharma, L.N, 'Democracy and Development in South Asia', *Indian Journal of Public Administration*, vol LV. No 4, October-December, 2009

41 *The Economist*, February 7th 2009, p. 9

42 Gat, A, 'The End of the End of the History', *Foreign Affairs*, July/August, 2007

References

Appadurai, Arjun (2001) "Grassroots Globalization and the Research Imagination" in Arjun Appadurai (ed.) *Globalization*, Duke University Press: Durham and London

Archibugi, Daniele ed. (2003) *Debating Cosmopolitics*, Verso: London.

Balibar, Eritenne (2004) *We the People of Europe?* PrincetonUniversity: Princeton

Fickler, Martin (2010) NYT News Service as quoted in *TheTimes of India*, dated 23 April, 2010

Gupta, Dipanakar (2009) Asian Age, 27.12.09

Habermas, Jugen (1999) '*Bestiality and Humanity: A War on the border between Law and Morality*' translated from the German, Franz Solms-Laubach, Die Zeit 54, 18 April , 2010

------------------ – (2005) 'Interpreting the fall of a Monument' in Max Pensky (ed.), *Globalising Critical Theory*, Rowan and Littlefield, New York

Habermas, Jugen and Jacques Derrida (2005) "February15, or, What Binds European Together: Plea for a Common Foreign Policy, Beginning In Core Europe" in Daniel Levy, Max Pensky and John Torpey (ed.) *Old Europe, New Europe, Core Europe Transatlantic Relations After the Iraq War*, Verso: London and New York

Menon, Nivedita (2009) *Thinking through the Postnation, Economic and Political Weekly*, Vol XLIV No 10

Mertes, Tom (2002) "*Grass-Roots Globalism*", New Left Review, 17, September-October

Section Two

Democracy at Crossroads

"…… No degree of progress allows one to ignore that never before, in absolute figures, have so many men, women and children have been subjugated, starved or exterminated on the earth."

Derrida

"For rich and strong, by rich and strong, of rich and strong in the name of poor and weak people."

Anonymous

Globalization and liberalization has thrown up new challenges before political theory in general and that of democratic or liberal one in particular. What should be the response of the political scientists and theorists towards globalization? What functions and structures, institutions and organizations would emerge or perish? And what transformations and changes have to be made in the existing theories, ideas and institutions, political behaviour and culture in general and that of democracy in particular? What forms or contents the national, international and local government would take to meet the challenges and changes arising from globalization and the emergence of the uni-polar world or multi-polar world with leading power feeling the heat of emerging powers? These are some of the questions and challenges that political theory in general and that of democratic one in particular would have to factor in, to deal with globalization and the new realities arising thereof.

The evolution of political science testifies to the fact that political theory is always concerned with current problems and challenges of the time as existing at a particular period. As a political theory is generally the outcome of the existing political, social, economic and cultural situations in a certain period of time, it helps us in understanding many aspects of a particular phenomenon such as democracy or its dynamism. Apart from reflecting on the socio-economic situation prevailing at a particular time, it also presents a depth analysis of the political facts.

Liberalism and Marxism, the binary in political arena has dominated the political theory until now. Modern political theory consists of an array of trends, streams of thoughts and schools of thought such as liberalism, liberal democracy, Marxism, positivism, empiricism, behavioural and post behaviouralism and other related theories. This binary modern political theory has been the most dominant theory of the twentieth century and its influence has spilled over to new millennium. The modern political theories may be categorized mainly into two streams: Liberal, including, individualistic, liberalism and pluralism, and Marxist including idealist, collectivist and socialist. However, both have failed to resolve the basic problems of the mankind.

Despite the triumph of the liberal democracy over socialism, the former has resulted into a system where people have been marginalized, and powers in its all manifestations have come to be concentrated into few hands, what has been termed as 'iron law of oligarchy'. Similarly, Marxist or the socialist state, despite its all tall claims of the freedom from hunger and exploitation, has turned into a centralized system and failed to emancipate people from the basic problems of the modern times. However, the New Right and New Left Movements have come to the fore to fill up the vacuum created by the apparent failures of these two main streams of political theory. Even these new binary movements seem to have been ingrained in the postmodernism.

The term 'postmodernism' was first coined by French philosopher and literary theorists, Jean-Francois Lyotard, when he published his paper 'The Postmodern Condition: A Report on Knowledge' in 1979. He proposes what he calls an extreme simplification of the "postmodern" as 'incredulity towards meta-narratives'. These meta-narratives, more often than not called as 'grand narratives, are grand, large-scale theories and philosophies of the world, such as the progress of history, the knowability of everything by science, and the possibility of the absolute freedom. He argues that we have ceased to believe that narratives of this kind are adequate to represent and contain us all. We have become alert to difference, diversity, the incompatibility of our aspirants, beliefs and desires and for that reason postmodernity is characterized by an abundance of micronarratives.[1]

Among the meta-narratives are reductionism and teleological notions of the history such as those of the Marxism, reductionism, totalitarianism, etc. These have become untenable, as per Lyotard, by technological progress in the areas of communication, mass media and computer science. Techniques such as artificial intelligence and machine translation show a shift to linguistic and symbolic production as central elements of the postindustrial economy and related postmodern culture, which had risen at the end of the 1950s after the reconstruction of Europe. It resulted into the language-games without an overarching structure, leading to the destruction of its own metanarratives by modern science.[2]

The postmodernism in the arena of the political theory has emerged due to the failure of the two main streams of the two modern political theory – Liberalism and Marxism or Socialism. The postmodernism is a critique of the liberals for their obsession with abstract idea and values. It criticizes them for their abstract ideas like universal rights and universal theory. Such abstractions and gesticulations have no practical values. The postmodernists lay emphasis on the right of the specific groups such as tribal, socially and economically backward classes and regions, women, blacks, ethnicity and minorities. The postmodernist discards the 'metanarratives' and universalism as these are unable to provide the coherent and meaningful narratives. It is impossible to construct a coherent narrative, or story, about what is really taking place without including contesting and contradicting narratives, and still have a "true story" from the perspective of the 'sovereign subjects' who can dictate the values pertinent to the 'meaning' of the situation. In fact, it is possible here to deconstruct the idea of meaning.[3]

Postmodernism is one of several subjectivist approaches to the study of social phenomena, usually emphasizing the interpretation of language as used with a setting or context. As such postmodernism questions the validity of 'scientific' approaches to political science or public administration or other subjects, and indeed, questions the meaningfulness of the concept of objective knowledge. In other words, the postmodernism has emerged in reaction to modernism or failure of modernism in providing 'a coherent' and sensible narratives to social and political phenomena. Modernism contains assumptions associated with particularaism, scientism, technologism and enterprise, whereas postmodernism contains assumptions associated with imagination, deconstruction, deterritorialization, and alterity.

Imagination counters the limit of rational bureaucracy based on rule observance. Deconstruction of texts, events, and symbols reveals how the 'reality' is socially constructed, thereby enabling new perspectives. Deterritorialization refers to radical changes in the structure of thinking under postmodernism, opposing such rationalist concepts as central planning and other authority-based structures. Alterity refers to empathy with new focus on socially excluded and oppressed groups.[4]

Thus, the major theme in postmodernism is subversion, the commitment to undermine dominant discourse. The subversion theme—variously described as deconstruction, radical indeterminacy, anti-essentialism, or anti-foundationalism—whether in politics, art, architecture, literature or philosophy—seeks to demonstrate the inherent instability of seemingly hegemonic structure, that power is diffused throughout society, and that there are multiple possibilities of interpretation or explanations.[5]

This has factored a paradigm shift in the study of political and social phenomena. Moreover, the rejection of meta-narratives has meant in many ways an end of one uniform solution, which can be seen as rejection of macropolitics—a common critique against and often also a position of, postmodern politics. It has been stated that such a rejection of macro politics and of uniform solutions might lead and have led to the politics of ethnicity or identity instead. An example of this has been put forth in the tragedies on Balkans and other ethnic or identity based civil war or protest movements.[6]

Postmodern politics are seen to be the politics of single issues and single-issue movement which will lead to a consensus rejection. And indeed there is a confrontation between Habermas and Lyotard—where Habermas is a frivolous supporter of consensus politics and Lyotard has rejected any form of meta-narratives and saw consensus politics as an attempt to create just that (Bertens, 1995). Consequently, it has given rise to the New Social Movements, questioning the various forms of domination based on race, caste, colour, language, gender.

It has factored the growth of the Identity Politics, which has acquired significance in the realm of the political theory. Consequent upon the emergence of the identity politics, there has been a substantial shift from micro to macro, social and economic issues to culture specific one. The basic premise of the identity politics is that people identify themselves to a culture-specific group, which is at disadvantage or exploited or the marginalized as compared to privileged and dominant groups such as imperialist countries, developed countries, white groups, upper castes, male, etc.

Epistemologically speaking, the postmodern political theory has resulted into the negation or rejection of three methodological tenets of modern political theory: universalism, reductionism and essentialism. While universalism is associated with the liberal doctrine of whole against the parts, the reductionism is associated with Marxist theory, which reduces a single factor such as economic to the cause or primary reason behind a phenomenon or problem. The essentialism emphasizes the importance of the comprehending the general essence of the phenomenon rather then appearance of it.

The postmodernist puts emphasis on particularism as against universalism, and the factoring of the several causes behind a phenomenon as against the reductionism. It stands for the study of the masses rather than elite or the classes in Marxist sense of the term. It emphasizes the importance and the significance of the subaltern realities and study of these.

Globalization has presented, in broader sense, two challenges to the identity politics. The first challenge to the identity politics is as to which aspect of the identity would be given primacy and which would be ignored among the wide range of identities available in the globalizing world. For example, a black has not only a racial identity, but also there pertaining to the occupational or the professional group, community, regional, linguistic, ethnic, and other such identities. Though the postmodernists are concerned about the racial identity factoring the problems befacing the black groups, the significance of other identity would depend upon the nature and direction of the globalization and the market forces. It is the same in the case of women group.

However, the questions remain as to what would happen to the multifarious desire and wants that globalization has whetted up? Will it be able to satisfy these wants and desires? Would it result into the realization of the 'idea of good life' as discussed and debated by the score of thinkers and political theorists for centuries, right from Plato and Aristotle to the realist and surrealist of the modern times? What would happen to the most cherished goals and ideals of the mankind – liberty, equality, justice and freedom?

It is being articulated that the political theory in general and that of liberal democracy in particular may acquire the character of synthesis of liberalism and Marxism. While the national, global and local factors would affect the nature of political theory in the globalized era, in broader perspective it would reflect some type of amalgamation of macro and micro, local and global, national and sub-national, universal and particular, unity and diversity and order and disorder. Thus, postmodern politics has given rise to many debates afresh, such as Welfare vs. Minimal State, Monism vs. Pluralism and Globalization vs. Isolationism.

The debate of the Welfare vs. Minimal state in the arena of the political theory as started by the libertarian like Nozick may be intensified in the wake of the new emerging realities of the globalized world. With the rise of the libertarianism in 60s, the very concept of welfare was questioned. The libertarianism prefers the voluntary cooperation between individuals in a free market to that of the coercion of the state. They are very skeptical of the role played by the state. They stand for the minimal state activity and maximum individual initiative. They deny the state even right to interfere in the name of the community. The state, according to libertarians, has no right to act on behalf of the community, and to trample the liberty and freedom of the individuals in the name of common goals.

The libertarianism denies state the right to redistribute wealth, interfere in the cultural and social sphere of the people, and help the agricultural sector and small firms. It wants the state to limit itself to the protection of individual freedom and maintenance of law and order. Thus, their view on the state activity resembles that of early classical Liberalism.

Although libertarianism stands for the formal equality of all before law, yet it is least bothered about the inequalities resulting from the free play of market forces. They maintain that poverty and equality are handled by the free play of market forces and the private initiative and charities would deal with the problem of poverty and inequality. They believe that the personal liberty and freedom are best guaranteed by the inviolability of private property, and limiting the size of government and scope of state intervention.

The libertarians are against any collective initiative and are dead against the collectivist ideology. For them, individual and liberty is an end in itself and it cannot and should not be curtailed or infringed in the name of the collective goals. They see with disdain the growing state activities and consider it as not good for the enjoyment of the liberty and freedom. Thus, they do not accept the main political developments of the Twentieth century, which is the continued growth in the size and activities of the state. Even in new millennium, the size and activities of the state have not reduced, in fact after the terrorist attacks across the world, it has grown bigger and libertarians would certainly not like it.

Another debate that is related with welfarism and certainly anti-democratic is that welfare activities of the state leads to the dependency. It is argued that excessive dose of welfare activities make citizens dependent and lethargic, killing the individual initiative. It breeds the culture of dependency. Another criticism of it is that it provides hollow citizenship as it does not give individual claim on the resources of the county.

Meanwhile the pluralist has risen in revolt against the sovereignty of the state and believes that it should be discarded altogether. In a democratic system, there are many types of associations that compete with each other to get their demands accepted or purpose served. As democratic system is based on individual freedom and choice, it provides a fertile ground for associations. As each of these associations competes with other, the State has to act as a referee. It has to decide and accommodate these competing interests and demands in such a way as to provide stability and cohesion to society. At the same time, it has to meet the aspirations and demands of various other associations.

It is because of this role that State is called a 'Super Association'. Though there are some writers, particularly those belonging to Social Contract theory of the Origin of State, who view state as association with political objectives. Even though the state is an association, it is more powerful and has wider jurisdiction within its territory. Its membership is compulsory, having coercive power at its command through which it commands loyalty and obedience. While an individual may become the member of as many associations as he wants, such vast option is not available in case of membership of a state. An individual can be member of only one state at one time. If he wants to become member of other state, he will have to forego the membership of original state.

Moreover, the scope and activities of state is much wider than associations. Associations have limited scope and activities. This has undermined the sovereignty of the state in the traditional sense, but it has brightened up the prospect of 'postnational global society' or the 'Cosmopolitan democracy'.

However, one has to take into account the other aspect of the modernity and post-modernity. The priori assumptions of modernity must be demolished and authoritarian strands in our society should be located. And it is not just to be found in the accidents of personalities or even in the structures of colonialism and capitalism, but in the dark heart of modernity itself. It is modernity which keeps us underdeveloped by imposing a tyrannical homogeneity, by uprooting people, by preventing us from blooming in our own idiosyncratic ways.[7]

There has been intense debate going around in respect of modernity and postmodernity. While some political scientists such as Michael Foucault have termed it as 'an enigmatic and troubling postmodernity', Habermas has criticized postmodernist thought for 'excessive pessimism, misdirected radicalism and exaggeration'. Taking dig at the postmodernism and its main tenet of end of modernity and enlightenment project, he maintains that the Enlightenment is "unfinished project", and should be corrected and complemented, not discarded. In one of the most scathing attack on postmodernism, Fredric Jameson has termed it as "the dominant cultural logic of late capitalism" (1991).

Noam Chomsky, the famous linguist, has put forward the view that postmodernism is meaningless as its contribution to the analytical or empirical knowledge is nothing but confusing the discourse of various streams of knowledge. Critic Timothy Bewes called postmodernity as "an historical blip", a "cynical reaction" against Enlightenment, and against the progress of the modern project. While James Fowler views postmodernity as characterized by the "loss of conviction", which is supported by Grenz and Seindder who maintain that it is period of pessimism contrasting with modernity's optimism, art critique Robert Hughes terms it as "kitsch", a turning way from fundamental deep structure and uncompromising progress.

Habermas sees postmodern conditions as self-deception over the uncompleted nature of modern project. He argues that without critical and rational traditions society cannot value the individual and social structure would tend towards totalitarianism. From his perspective universalism is the fundamental requirement for any rational criticism and to abandon this is to abandon the liberalizing reforms of the last two centuries. Postmodernists including Lyotard and Stanley Fish see Habermas as desiring to rationalize universalism and argue that the entire critique rests on the modernists' insufficient faith in social mechanisms.[8]

Michael Foucault criticizes postmodernism as it breaks with the utopian and transcendental nature of "modern" critique by calling universal norms of the Enlightenment into question. Giddens (1990) rejects this characterization of modern critique by pointing out that a critique of Enlightenment universals were central to philosophers of the modern period, most notably Nietzsche. What counts as "postmodern" is a stake in political struggles where method of critique is at stake in political struggles where the method of critique is at issue. The recurring themes of these debates are between essentialism and anti-foundationalism, universalism and relativism, where Nietzsche, Lacan, Foucault, Derrida, and Butler have been labeled "postmodernism", not because they formed a historical intellectual grouping but because they are seen by their critics to reject the possibility of universal, normative and ethical judgments.[9]

I

Democracy and Postmodernism

As postmodernism in political science means the use of postmodern ideas in discipline, the postmodernism in democracy in general and liberal democracy in particular denotes the postmodernist ideas and approaches as being used in the discourse on democracy. The major theme in postmodernism.... is subversion, the commitment to undermine dominant discourse. The subversion theme – variously described as deconstruction, radical indeterminacy, anti-essentialism or anti-foundationalism seeks to demonstrate the inherent instability of seemingly hegemonic structures that is power diffused throughout the society and there are multiple possibilities for undermining the dominant discourse.[10]

Stanley Aronowitz has observed that by now nearly everyone agrees that the shift in sensibility that Nietzsche mentioned about a century ago has finally arrived. Postmodernism, the name given to this shift is marked by the renunciation of foundational thought; of rules governing art, and of the ideological 'master discourse' Liberalism and Marxism Above all, postmodernism is 'a condition of life' and it affects democracy and democratic tradition even if it is 'conditions of epistemic uncertainty and anti-foundationalism'.

How postmodernism has affected democracy, and liberal democracy at large, to speak in postmodernist term, there is no single 'metanarratives', but a lot of 'narratives'. Since there is no universal truth, only points, counterpoints, and motley of ideas and counter ideas, and every viewpoint is true, there cannot be any 'decisive', 'dominant' or 'metanarratives' regarding how postmodernism has affected democracy or vice versa. However, the different viewpoints can be discussed and all points and counter points, ideas and counter ideas can be perused, to find its effects on democracy and liberal democracy. Even this cannot be final truth, but a motley of truths, all having equal epistemological values (Aronowitz, 1987).

Nevertheless, the postmodernism has provided new ground for liberal democracy to diversify itself, free itself from the clutches of elites, oligarchs and mercenaries and messianic claptrap of left and right that have filled up the space, left vacant from demise of binaries and universal truth or 'metanarratives' or 'grand theories'. It has given new shift to the liberal democracy by turning its attention to the marginalized, downtrodden, minorities of all hues and shades, Black, Dalits (lower caste of Indian hierarchical social order), women, etc.

However, in a melee of globalization, liberalization and 'flattening of the world', 'collapse of grand or metanarratives' opposite has happened. The marginal groups have been further marginalized; the poor, downtrodden and minority groups have been left out, while 'iron law of Oligarchy' has further tightened its grip on society and polity. Feminist movement has been derailed through objectification and commoditization of roles in name of economic independence or the empowerment of womanhood in general language. Historically democracy has been considered as a means to an end. Some ancient states such as the city states of Greece had the same goal: democracy as means to achieve equality, justice and prosperity, what is termed as good life. The classical liberals such as J.S Mill, G.H Green and others have supported democracy as means to preserve liberty; the utilitarian too subscribed to this view.

Lately democracy has been transformed into an end in itself. This has been reinforced rather immortalized by Wilson, who declared 'making the world safe for democracy.'[11] This has been picked by neo-classicals who have trampled the very basis of democracy—justice, liberty, freedom and prosperity—just to perpetuate democracy for their vested interests. The great powers and not so great powers have fought or are fighting national and international war, just to make 'world safe for democracy'. It does not matter whether in this process very basis of democracy is being undermined.

This transformation of democracy as an end in itself is as fascist an act as Fascism which glorifies the state or society as an end in itself. By making democracy as an end in itself, all types of anti-democratic practices and acts are being perpetrated in the name of democracy. The dictatorship, the hollow army rule, feudalism, barbarism, fundamentalism, and all sort of undemocratic means are being resorted to 'make world safe for democracy'. And for that if the democratic ideals are to be sacrificed or democratic institutions dismantled, or democratic states towed away or ignored questioning the very legitimacy of democracy, these are being done in the name of democracy.

This appears to be a classical case of 'phrase games' and this can be put to the test of 'differend' as propounded Lyotard, "In general, the plaintiff becomes a victim when no presentation is possible for the wrong .... suffered. Reciprocally, the 'perfect crime' does not consist in killing the victim or the witness (that adds new crimes to one and aggravates the difficulty of effacing everything.) but rather in obtaining the silence of witness, the deafness of judges and the inconsistency (insanity) of the testimony. You neutralize the addressor, the addressee and sense of the testimony, then everything is as if there were no referents (No damage)."[12]

If one analyzes democracy and puts it to the litmus test of 'differend', one would not miss how ideals and prospects have been grounded to mere 'phrase games'. The civil society or associations who accuse the high jacking of democracy (addressor and addressee) has been neutralized (by argument that world or situation is being created for making democracy safe), so has been the fate of the sense of testimony (democracy is being sacrificed at the altar of vested interests). So there is not an iota of doubt that there has been any wrong or 'referent' or any distortion of democratic ideals or 'the Iron law of Oligarchy' is spreading its arms over democracy. World is being made safe for democracy, in that process if the very foundation of democracy is thrown into winds, it does not matter because the safety of democracy is more important than democracy itself.

Thus, it appears that the postmodernism has resulted into confusing or waylaying the great march of ideas and the social institutions that democracy has embodied. There is right and left centric perspectives of postmodernism which only add to the confusion. "Postmodernism is born of the marriage of Left politics and skeptical epistemology. As socialist political thought was reaching a crisis in the 1950s, academic epistemology had, in Europe, come to take seriously Nietzsche and Heidegger and, in the Anglo-American world, it had seen the decline of Logical Positivism into Quine and Kuhn. The dominance of subjectivist and relativist epistemologies in academic philosophy thus provided the academic Left with a new tactic. ......Postmodernism is a response to the crisis in faith of the academic far Left. Its epistemology justifies the leap of faith necessary to continue believing in socialism, and the same epistemology justifies using language not as a vehicle for seeking truth but as rhetorical weapon in the continuing battle against capitalism."[13]

On the other hand, there is another group of thinkers, philosophers and political scientists who discard the rightist approach to postmodernism. Frederic Jameson, philosopher and literary critic describes postmodernism as the "dominant cultural logic of late capitalism"; that is as the cultural practices that are originally bound to postmodernism's historical correspondent (late capitalism is referred as globalization, financial capitalism, postindustrialism, consumer capitalism).[14] However, despite the concern for marginalized, oppressed, exploited and minority groups such linguistic, religious, women, cultural, Blacks, lower castes, etc, it has been unable to put forward tangible plans for the grounding of democracy.

As Bertens has observed while quoting McGowan: "Postmodernism finds itself between a rock and a hard place, unable to ground democracy by appeal to external, nonhuman principles, but unwilling to accept humanly generated principles as legitimate norms rather than further instances of arrangements imposed by power."[15] Despite all sensibility and feelings, and faith that postmodernism vows to repose in democracy, it has been unable to 'ground democracy'. This contradiction emanates from the postmodernist position that there is no universal truth, only partial or subjective truth. The death of 'grand narrative' or 'meta narrative' has only added to the confusion as what democracy is. Taking this logic to extreme, even aristocracy, Oligarchy, dictatorship or semi-dictatorship is being presented as democracy. Even, the anti-democratic tendency is termed as democratic. It is for this reason that war and aggression, very anti-thesis of democracy, is being resorted to in the name of saving or serving democracy.

Instead of grounding democracy, the postmodernism has been high jacked by liberal democratic messianism which appears as the worst possible fundamentalism.[16] Even Francis Fakuyama, the rightwing postmodernist who gave the clarion call of 'end of the history', seems to be peeved at this downside of the postmodernism vis-à-vis democracy, when he says: "The end of the history will be very sad time. The struggle for recognition, willingness to risk one's life for the purely abstract goal, the worldwide ideological struggle which called forth daring courage, imagination and idealism, will be replaced by economic calculation, the endless solving of technical problems, environmental concern and the satisfaction of sophisticated consumer demands. In the post historical period, there will be neither art nor philosophy, just the perpetual caretaking of the museum of human history."[17]

The main problem with postmodernism vis-a-vis democracy is that it 'precludes philosophical justification for democracy, undermining the role of philosophy of education and leaving us with weaker reason for educational democracy than is needed. If the 'postmodern challenge' is as Wilfred Carr conceives it, Jugen Habermas (his idea of public sphere, reconstructive Science, Theory of Communicative Action) meets that challenge.... Habermas can accept and explain that consciousness is historically and socially situated in discourse, yet still argue to the possibility of emancipation.'[18]

In his path breaking work, 'Theory of Communicative Action', Habermas criticized the one-sided process of modernization led by the forces of economic and administrative rationalization. He traces the growing intervention of formal systems in our everyday lives as parallel to the development of the welfare state, corporate capitalism and the culture of mass consumption. These reinforcing trends rationalize widening areas of public life, submitting them to a generalizing logic of efficiency and control. As routinized political parties and interest groups substitute for participatory democracy, society is increasingly administered at a level remote from input of citizens (1981).

Consequently, 'boundaries between public and private, the individual and society, the system and life world are deteriorating. Democratic public life only thrives where institutions enable citizens to debate matters of public importance. He describes an ideal type of "ideal speech situation", where actors are equally endowed with the capacities of discourse; recognize each other's basic social equality and speech is undistorted by ideology or misrecognition. In this version of consensus theory of truth Habermas maintains that truth is what would be agreed upon in an ideal speech situation. (*ibid*)

Habermas has expressed optimism about the possibility of the revival of the public sphere for grounding of democracy that has been high jacked by the "Iron Law of Oligarchy". He discerns a hope in the new era of political community that transcends the nation-state based on ethnic and cultural likeness for one based on the equal rights and obligations of legally vested citizens. This deliberative theory of democracy requires a political community which can collectively define its political will and implement it as a policy at the level of the legislative system. This political system requires an activist public sphere, where matters of common interest and political issue can be discussed, and the force of public opinion can influence the decision-making process.[19]

However, public sphere has been criticized for excluding minorities and marginalized groups such as Feminists, Black, subjugated, oppressed, etc. The feminists have criticized it for exclusion of gender specific questions, while leftists have taken them to task for omitting workers, marginalized from this public sphere. Nonetheless, this can be rectified by making it more broad based and all inclusive. This can be supplemented by 'discursive democracy' based on theory of dialogue as developed by Fox and Miller (1996) which envisions a pro-active role for public administration as well as for the people at large. Unlike 'loop theory of democracy' wherein the citizens express demands at the bottom, public administrators respond with the services from the top, loop theory implies passive role for administrators and active role for the people.[20]

Nevertheless, the most remarkable effect of postmodernism on democracy has been weakening or almost vanishing act of representative democracy. Rosenau believes that postmodernism repudiated the meaningfulness of representative democracy.[21] It discarded the representative democracy as effective model for development and growth. As representative democracy does not recognize a conflict of interests between the citizens participating, those affected or victimized by the process being undertaken, and the group-entity that organizes the decision, it is unable to involve an extensive outreach effort to include marginalized, isolated, ignored groups in decision and to extensively document dissent, grounds for dissent, and future predictions of consequences of actions.

As the postmodernism has rendered representative democracy meaningless, the discursive democracy has taken its place. Discursive democracy gives recognition to the symbolic nature of politics, seeking to establish a genuine and authentic public dialogue. It implies a pro-active role for administrators and policy makers which are in stark contrast of 'loop theory of democracy'.

In loop theory of democracy which is currently dominant, the citizens express demands at the bottom, the policy makers and administrators respond from top. It gives rise to unending new iteration, which makes democracy responsive to all and sundry. Whereas the discursive or deliberative allows or recognizes a conflict of interests between the citizen participating, those affected or victimized by the process being undertaken, and the group entity which organizes the decision. Thus, it generally implies an extensive outreach effort to include marginalized, isolated, ignored groups in decisions, and to extensively document dissent, grounds for dissent, and future predictions of consequences of action.[22]

However, in this process the role of representatives elected though popular election has been curtailed, making representative democracy hollow and meaningless. Nevertheless, it has given rise to the social and cultural movements which has taken hitherto marginalized sections in its fold. These movement range from New Age Movement, New Social Movement to the Islamic Fundamentalism, terrorism, etc. The common thread running through these seemingly diverse movements is the cultural opposition to the rational-scientific modernism (Rosenau, *op. cit.*)

In fact, Fukuyama, while propounding the "end of history theory", has mentioned that the terrorism and Islamic Fundamentalism would compete with liberal democracy and neo-classics as the dominant theme of present and future history. But he slighted them as minor aberrations in the uninterrupted march of liberal democracy and capitalism in all forms (Fukuyama, *op. cit*).

These are, however, not minor as understood, it seems to be grand game of undeclared war with having all trappings and maneuverings of asymmetrical game threatening the very foundation of democracy—freedom, liberty and rights. Any move by any party results into loss for democracy in forms of curtailed liberties and freedoms apart from payload of loss to democracy. The public space instead of being occupied by debates and discussion on the issues of common interests and concerns is being haunted by fear or memory of terrorist acts or possibility of such acts.

II

Democracy: Existential Problem

Democracy has crisscrossed many centuries and continents across matrix of the time and space, starting from village republic in ancient India and finding its roots in Athens in 5th century BC. It has also undergone see-saw like situation so far its existence across the world and during different periods is concerned. '..... Democracy has been tried and then rejected on many occasions in human history. Athenian democracy of the 5th century BC did not establish a viable form of governance. The two and a half millennia that followed were dominated by other political regimes. In fact, a visiting Martian might well conclude that the most popular regime in Planet Earth was hereditary monarchy and not democracy, which has been the exception rather than the rule.'[23]

During the past century, the advance of democracy has followed a see-saw pattern. For instance, Latin American countries have swung between democracy and totalitarianism almost with great regularity. Argentina established male suffrage in 1912, but lost it to a coup in 1930. Democracy was restored in 1946, overthrown in 1955, re-introduced in 1973, subverted in 1976 and renewed in 1983. Asia, the Middle East and nations of the former Soviet block, including Russia, have been following an approach-avoidance vis-à-vis government by the people. China, the world's most populated country, is not a democracy in the western sense. Iran in 2006 had democratic institutions but their modus operandi subjected to the supreme authority. However, in recent years, the tide of democracy both at the national and the global level has been, at least nominally, on the rise, which is very encouraging. There are very few nations on this earth, which openly reject the notion of democracy. Most of the countries espouse it, or at least offer it lip service. (Valaskakis, *ibid*)

According to a survey by Freedom House, the non-partisan organization that monitors political rights and civil liberties around the world, electoral democracies now represent 120 of the 192 existing countries and constitutes 62 per cent of the world's population. By 1950, the defeat of Nazi totalitarianism, the post-war momentum toward de-colonization, and the post-war reconstruction of Europe and Japan resulted in an increase in the number of democratic states. At mid-century, there were 22 democracies accounting for 31 percent of the world population and a further 21 states with restricted democratic practices, accounting for 11.9 percent of the globe's population.

Nonetheless, in its glorious history of more than 2,500 years[24], democracy in general and liberal democracy in particular has never faced such existential problem as it is facing now. Not even during black days of Inter War period (the period between First World War and Second World War) when the combined onslaught of Hitler and Mussolini were threatening the very existence of democracy world over. Then, the enemies of democracy were visible, now enemies are invisible. The globalization has globalized the arc of enemies of democracy and liberalization and has cemented their mutual bonds. Moreover, the situation has become so confusing that it is difficult to decide which one is strengthening democracy and which one is preparing its burial ground.

The free market economy has further exacerbated the situation for democracy. The amalgamation of democracy and free market economy has moved all motivations towards profit. Such "predatory capitalism" stands behind the strengthening of neo-liberalism that cohabits with government that remains ever incorrigible in collaborating with economic giants for short-term gain.[25] "Could it be that democracy, the sacred answer to our hopes and prayers, the protector of our individual freedom and number of our avaricious dreams will be the endgame for human race?"[26] Though this may be discarded as 'note of exasperation and anger at the dismal evolution of Indian democracy', yet it has raised very pertinent question regarding democracy. The way democracy has evolved world over in general and in India particularly, there is no doubt that future of democracy is pregnant with foreboding, if things continue to go southward.

Democracy and liberal democracy has suffered many distortion and manipulations over the years. As the only beacon amidst the whirlwind of breathtaking changes and upheavals, whereby national and world politics are shedding earlier concern for teeming masses of the world and acquiring penchant for amassing wealth and riches and power in few nations and few hands; there has been all-round assault on liberal democracy, covertly most time while overtly some time, from the forces unleashed by globalization and privatization. "When the Berlin Wall fell in 1989, the assumption was that free markets and free societies would work in perfect harmony. Instead, people in all countries found a way to disengage from the political process while seeking greater comfort."[27]

In this context India, being microcosm of world, both metaphorically and literally, is a suitable case study for the state of world democracy and direction that it is charting across the world. India, with its sub-continental dimension, its potpourri of different races, religions, languages, cultures, with its historical and civilization stretching unto antiquity of unknowable dimension, its assimilative culture preceding well before this term was coined, its umbrella like social and political structure, its different time zones, and what not, is nothing but a mini-world. If its historical spatial expansion, stretching well beyond the far east and unto Persia in West, and cultural outreach taking China, Mongolia, Japan in its fold is taken into account, it is a prototype of world.

Likewise Indian democracy can be taken as microcosm of world democracy as existing in different countries, including that of Europe and America. Not only because it is the largest democracy, but there are also many similarities and commonalities, if not in historical and cultural experience, (though there is some substantial and procedural reservation in this regard) then in many respects such as democratic structure, institution and system, norm, convention, etc. that have been borrowed from Europe and America. Moreover, there are many distortions, abnormalities, perversions and undemocratic tendencies that have crept into Indian democracy which are quite common in democracies of the developed countries.

For developing, least developed and the most backward countries that are tossing between democracy, civil war, dictatorship, army rule, forcible seizure of power by feuding warlords, theocracies and tribalism, Indian democracy is like a torch bearer, a flicker of hope amidst the darkness of no governance, no civil and political right, freedom and liberty trampled under the feet of dictators and feuding lords; and hunger and poverty prevalent like reigning deities of tribal folks.

There is another similarity which can get us some brownie points of insight so far as study of state of democracy in India and that of world are concerned as democracy is reigning theory, way of life, organizing and conducting the governments in the world. With number of poor in India around 80 crore (as per Arjun Das Gupta Committee Report, which is based on consumption and 78 per cent Indian eking their existence on income less than Rs 20 daily (2009) and number of poor world over being 3.6 billion (as per UNDP report, 2010, who are living on less than $2 per day), democracy has to bear the burden of such vast and mind-boggling number of poor. This is the official figure; there might be many more suffering from hidden poverty.

Democracy as political theory and capitalism as economic theory has been, is and will be only hope for the teeming billions of the world who are suffering the daily agony and pain of the poverty, hunger, inequality and exploitation, particularly, after the demise of communism masquerading as socialism. As Fukuyama, the early 19th century thesis of Hegel also maintained that there are two powerful forces at work in human history: he calls them 'the logic of modern science' and the 'struggle for recognition'. His thesis is based on the premise that historical process finally culminates in universal capitalist and democratic order. He believes that at 'the end of history' social engineering would not be enough to achieve further improvement. What he means that there is no full stop and history does not end here. One as individual, group, society and nation has to persistently strive to achieve for that. It is not the end of the history.[28]

But the most painful and agonizing question is what has happened to these two of the new millennia? Would these two enable the mankind the emancipation from such sordid state of things or life would be wiped out if the brinkmanship, shortsightedness and hypocrisies that the political actors across the world are showing vis-a-vis myriad of problems such as terrorism, Global warming, poverty, inequality, etc. are continued? However, 'the broader picture is troubling: the extent to which the aspirations and behaviours of citizens in the so-called democracies and authoritarian regimes have converged over the past 20 years of globalization. From Mumbai to Shanghai to Dubai via London and New York, we have witnessed the erosion of the liberties in our seemingly insatiable quest for wealth and our urge for illusory security. ....Barrington's Moore's theories of "no bourgeoisie, no democracy" have been disavowed by these two decades of uber materialism.'[29]

In spite of providing leadership and force multiplier in emancipating 3.6 billion of people world over from the hunger and poverty, including those of 80 crore (800 million) hapless Indians, democracy and capitalism or liberal democracy has been sucked into 'Iron law of Oligarchy', 'Predatory Capitalism', 'Erstraz Capitalism', in active and rather toxic collaboration with democratic institutions, leaders and values and norms. It may be argued that Gandhi accepted the presence of history, and yet he refused the determinism implicit in history: the belief that certain impersonal forces of the history, certain institutions, like the market or democracy could by themselves liberate human beings.

Pluralism, identity politics, assimilation, inclusive principal, communitarinism and other minority principals have been given short shrift; the world's wealth, resources and power are being appropriated by few nations, groups, class and individuals. Instead of chipping in to help poor, marginalized and excluded people and nations and societies, the liberal democracy, in very active but inhuman and shameful collaboration with its political economy – capitalism, is further pushing this vast humanity down to precipice. Terrorism, insurgency, civil war, ethnic strife and life threatening global warming are natural fallout of failure of this binary.

After the demise of communism, the globalized and liberalized world has provided capitalism and liberal democracy tremendous opportunity, scope and power to realize, at least, the hunger and poverty-free world, if not one world, one people with one international government with satellites of government of nation states in toe. At least it was expected that the least developed, under-developed and developing societies and economies would be integrated and brought forth into the mainstream, heralding a harmonious and friction-free world. 'With its principal ideological opponent effectively defeated, democracy exultantly proclaimed itself the political form of the future. It has now become the preponderant idea of the modern world and has done so by vanishing its only substantial opponent. Communism is dead! Long Live Democracy!'[30]

It may well be that this mood of triumphalism will be jolted in the years ahead which cannot but pose huge social, economic, and political problems for the fledgling democracies that are striving to emerge. Virulent nationalism already threatens to usurp democracy by imposing a new intolerance. Ethnic and religious animosities, buried for the past seventy years, have already erupted with vengeance and have found fertile ground in the economic austerity, unemployment and dislocation that mark almost all ex-communist regimes......... There can be no guarantee that in the post-Communist world democracy will always be a benign, humanitarian, and tolerant structure of ideas or institutions.' (*ibid*, p37)

The history of our own century (Twentieth century and even the twenty first century may be included) is cautionary note enough to the fragility of democracy when it demonstratably fails to attend to acute social and economic dislocation or fails to answer the frustrated aspirations of national group.

As communism has already foundered largely because of its evident failure to resolve such problems, we would do well to remember that Marxism – Leninism first rose to prominence in the world precisely through the force of its critique of democracy's incapacity to satisfy the minimum expectations of ordinary people (*ibid*, p186).

There is, in short, a sort of dramatic flux in the turbulent relationship between democracy and Marxism-Leninism. Marxism-Leninism presented itself to the world as both a critique and an alternative to the theory and the practice of Western democracy that proved attractive in the acute crisis of the First World War. It was to rise to renewed prominence and power only during the crises of Second World War and its aftermath. Only when it, in turn, displayed its incapacity to realize the economic (national) aspirations of its people did Communism itself become vulnerable to the democratic critique. The question now is whether democracy (and its implicit twin, the market economy) can succeed where Marxism-Leninism has obviously failed and discredited itself.' (*ibid*, Para 2)

The scenario seems to be not positive when one considers the fact that liberal democracy and its political economy—capitalism—has ushered in a world where there is great imbalances, the power, wealth and resources are being concentrated into few and fewer hands at macro and micro level (in few nations and within nations few groups, individuals and families). The vast section of nations and within nations like India (where 78 per cent of the population are eking their existence on bare minimum amount of less than Rs. 20 a day[31] more than half of populations (in the world 3.6 billion are living with less than $2 per day[32]) living life that is not worth living, with hunger, poverty and injustice taking toll of their physical and mental well-beings.

The queer play of money, power and muscles in cahoots with dynastic, monopolistic (or cartelization) tendency, 'Iron law of oligarchy' taking nations and within nations every section or field of activities in its nefarious fold, the obnoxious nexus of 'Crony Capitalism', 'Erstraz Capitalism and phony liberal democracy and its pliant and pliable agencies has rendered world and every nations, be it India or USA or Mauritius a paper tiger 'of the people, by the people and for the people'.

The identity politics has been given short shrift and reduced to single identity such as Christians, Muslims, Jews, Hindus and Buddhists. Even the enlightened citizens, even if free from bottomless pit of fundamentalism and sectarianism, seem to be limited to the nationalist identity. The wind of xenophobia, sectarianism, fundamentalism and ethnic strife are sweeping across the world taking 'liberated Europe', 'freedom and liberty obsessed America' and *et la* into their poisonous and fragmented fold. The poor, weak, Blacks, women, minorities, Dalits, backward castes and classes, labour, both blue and white collared, farmers, tribals, aborigines, the middle class, old and children have been further marginalized and become handy tools of power play

The liberal democratic theory and other theories in general and its political economy – capitalism as economic theory or system (even in postmodernist way accepting there is no grand or meta theory) appear to have failed to deal effectively the host of issues such as terrorism, increasing socio-economic imbalances, growing number of poor and hungry, cyclical glut and recession hitting the world economies below the belt, political, social and economic marginalization of the masses, the dislocation of the tribal and aborigine people world over in the name of development, which just bypasses them while benefiting only those who are already sitting pretty on their riches and resources. The lawless Africa with civil war, ethnic and social tension, political disorientation and collateral effects of hunger, poverty, malnutrition and other such maladies is just a case in point where nothing seems to be working.

The liberal democracy and capitalism as its fundamental economic theory has not delivered the good and general well-being as it should have been. The question is not what the combo has done; on record there are volumes after volumes coming out to just enlist its achievements and feat of success. There is not objection in respect of what these two have delivered, but the point is the way these two have evolved, particularly after the demise of communism has given rise to more problems than it has solved.

The debate of Welfare State vs. Minimal state and the underlying principal requires to be given fresh lease of life. It will have to be reopened to infuse some sort of balance and sanity in world rendered unbalanced, unequal, unjust, exploitative, xenophobic and insane by rather unbridled and immoral free play of liberal democracy and market economy (or democracy plus capitalism be it classical, neoclassical or crony or Erstraz Capitalism.) Some sort of balances, correction or rather course corrections or regulation or regulator must be put into place to check such maladies affecting our world.

Intense debate and discussions about putting some sort of checks and balances in the form of Regulatory body in post recession world, is being considered as panacea for all ills affecting capitalism. This has been the regular feature after each and every economic or financial crisis that has been hitting the world. Once things become normal, everything is forgotten afterwards until the next crisis hits. However, the million dollar question is: Who will regulate the regulator? The same system and institutions or the same person bound by the same norms and ethos or different person with same guiding principles?

The proposed regulator would function in the same system of liberal democracy (democracy plus capitalism) with minimal state looking aside nonchalantly, while some section of the system in cahoots with whole system or its significant part will be using it for their vested interest, wrecking the whole system with cascading effects. The crony capitalism in cahoots with Erstraz capitalism or socialism and liberal democracy would use the loopholes or gap holes (which are purportedly left) or the weakest links in the chain, to fill up their coffers at the expense of general good.

Some sort of State Welfarism, with adequate mechanism to prevent it from sliding into state authoritarianism or Maximal state, will have to be put in place to infuse some sort of correction, sanity, balance and equality in the liberal democracy. The libertarian principal, which gained its ground in 60s and got further integrated into liberal democracy, will have to set aside for state Welfarism. Even Adam Smith warned that 'Competition is good but it requires political control.'

The type of Welfarism that would be resorted to would be decided in due course of time. However, there should not be any doubt that some sort of state Welfarism and effective control by people whether direct or indirect must be put in place. There must be some control—a real, incorruptible, insulated from systemic and vested interests' pulls and pressures. The political scientists along with economists and other generalists and specialists must ponder over as to why the benefit of the development and breathtaking growth has not percolated down to more than two third of the nations and within the nations more than three-fourth of the population despite all developments, double digit growth, booming GDP, globalization, liberalization, shrinking of time and space, crumbling of all barriers?

The globalization has remained limited to the economic field that is the argument which has been going around in the wake of global crisis and recession. It is being debated that had the world been globalized in true sense and all respects, there would not have such problem. Can we imagine one world, one people with such baggage of economic, political and social contradictions where more than 60 per cent people and nations of the world are reeling under poverty, hunger, disease, malnutrition, civil war, ethnic war, terrorism and what not?

The world, far from being globalized, seems to be becoming more and more xenophobic, cloistered and closed, if we do not consider the economic aspect of globalization. Even in respect of the economic and financial matters, there are many hidden and obscure barriers in the form of tariffs and other restrictions couched in the alibi of various interests. The wind of xenophobia in the form of tightening of migration laws, community profiling in the name of checking terrorism and other sort of nationalist check posts, regional barriers, intra and inter regional are creating new barriers for world.

There is increasing religious fundamentalism, not of one religion as is generally understood and it should not be overlooked that so called 'jihadi terrorism' has, among other things, been risen in direct response to 'real and perceived' injustices, cultural and political domination by major powers. However, the slaughter of innocent people cannot be justified on any ground, whatsoever are the grievances. Terrorism seems to be cause and effect of this 'hidden xenophobia', and unless every actor involved in this asymmetrical tug of war accepts their respective hidden agenda and its futility and possibility of unprecedented collateral damage it can cause, there is no scope of its being subdued for the time being.

Even in respect of world peace, disarmament and non-proliferation of weapons of mass destruction, there has been such 'hidden agenda' which has been given various names and alibis. The proliferation of nuclear weapons and other weapons of mass destruction has been going and still going with tacit support from those who are regulator or self-proclaimed watch-dog of international relations. The veto-wielding powers, which are another manifestation of imbalance in international relations, have been indulging in brinkmanship so far as non-proliferation is concerned. They have been directly or indirectly assisting some of the known proliferators in South Asia, Far East and West Asia. Same sort of hypocrisy and one-upmanship is being played in respect of global warming.

These all are the cause and effect of lack of transparency and democracy in the conduct of foreign policy. Lately, the conduct of foreign policy has become secretive and away from public domain. In the name of back channel diplomacy and national interest, many undemocratic tendencies have crept into the conduct of foreign policies of almost all democratic countries. If such is the position of the democratic countries, one can imagine the predicament of non-democratic countries. The recent revelation of WikiLeaks, which has made public secret documents in the form of cables exchanged between policy makers and foreign emissaries validate this point.

Periodically it seemed democracy could be its own worst enemy. Presently, democracy appears to be passing from this phase. Over the course of last century (19th century) there has been another cross-current to the progress of mass democracy—less violent, more persuasive, and well suited for an age of technological advance. To many of its critics, by 1900 democracy appeared irrelevant and harmful. Democracy sought to build itself around knowledge. This 'technocratic' approach to government envisaged government by expert or institutional engineer. Much of the thinking permeated British Fabian Socialism, giving it the flavour of a more elitist crypto-socialism. It also characterized urban elites of the United States who distrusted the new immigrant electorate, feared urban patronage and corruption and longed for government by professional managerial class. These innovations were not seen as hostile to mass aspirations; they embodied the higher wisdom that properly enlightened citizens must also want, assuming that they wished to maximize social peace and economic well-being.[33]

This technocratic management could be paired with some sort of belief in such new democratic institution as referendum and direct election or political auditing. This could be used to "undercut machine politics and legislative corruption". Real democracy in short has to be rescued from masses not yet mature or informed enough to govern themselves. Disinterested expertise was required in large, modern societies, but it was always by "demagogic tendencies" (Maier, *ibid*), and this could be filtered by democratized and institutionalized political auditing. As Walter Lippmann has rightly commented in 'Public Opinion' (1922) that it was no longer possible to believe in the 'original dogma of democracy: that the knowledge needed for the management of human affairs comes up spontaneously enough from the human heart' (Steel, 1980).

Walter Lippmann has envisioned a mass based society which could be guided and controlled only from above, whereas John Dewey emphasized the prospect from below where rational belief rules over the dogma. He was confident of the local community in grounding democracy and it could thrive on unabated experiments that would be free from any dogma, and a modern and progressive education. However, the technocratic dogma that pragmatic government must be protected from the demagogy of the "mass electorate" still holds the forte more in practice than in theory (Riccio, 1994).

Another assault on democracy and welfares came from the proponents of "Overloaded theory' at the fag end of the twentieth century. It was based on the application of crisis theory to the modern state. It implied that Modern states have more demands made upon them than they can meet. They are, by analogy with machines, overloaded and break down, or inefficiency results. It was another manifestation of "democratic pessimism" which was denounced by the Left as failure of capitalism and the Right viewed it as breakdown of welfare socialism.[34]

Political economists and so-called public-choice theorists likewise claimed that in democracy special interests would extract concentrated benefits whose costs would be charged almost imperceptibly to taxpayers as a whole. Democracy would thus continually tend to generate more claims than it could finance. By the end of the 1970s this democratic pessimism enjoyed widespread resonance among European and American elites. But the fact that opponents of welfare tendencies managed to win crucial elections in the early 1980s at least temporarily eclipsed the appeal of such generalized democratic disillusion. Democratic majorities, it seemed, were not so wedded to the short-sighted welfare state dismantling of capitalism as had been feared.[35] Ironically, the opposite has happened: capitalism seems to haves dismantled the welfare state, if not in theory then in practice.

However, situation has not reached the point of no return, and democracy and capitalism are still relevant and capable of dealing with myriad of problems facing the mankind. What is required are a sort of course corrections and reinstating the control of the people or the masses that has not been able to put effective check. This type of smugness and elitist, and anti-people thinking seems to have got ingrained with overconfidence and invincibility resulting from the collapse of Marxist Leninist bloc. It further got the boost from the inevitability of 'the end of the history" project that would have to be revisited for the sake of saving democracy from becoming a failed project of the human history.

The masses and people that have been sidelined, neutralized and marginalized would have to be restored and rehabilitated to the center of democracy and its political economy. Habermas' public sphere would have to be revived with participation from all segments of society, particularly marginalized, unorganized economic and social sectors, and the public sphere, grabbed by media houses in cahoots with political-industrial-financial oligarchy which are claiming to be functioning as Fourth State of democracy, would have to be restored to people and masses. This can be done by broadening the scope of representative democracy, through mitigating the limitations inherent in first-past-the-post ballot or electoral system that most of the democracies across the world follow, with institutionalization of democratized Political Auditing.

III

Democracy and Capitalism

The civil society over the years has grown weaker than the institutions, system and sub-systems, various organizations and groups that are meant, particularly in democracy, to serve the majority of people. The people power through voting and other democratic means have been reduced to minimal level. Whatever interventions or movement pertaining to political or social agenda that the civil society initiated has been sporadic, issue specific and limited to some parts of the country. Moreover, it has been unsustainable in the sense that it petered down after some time or subverted by the political interest.[36]

This is not good for democracy. Participation whether direct or indirect or at personal or at least ideational level is essential for vibrant and healthy democracy. People and their forums have been rendered weak and useless, and even a petty official or peon or a shopkeeper can intimidate the people. The people are finding themselves weak and helpless even before minnow that are meant to serve them. Behind these are corruption and dilution of democratic values and ethos. "The past few years have seen a steady dilution of citizens' powers vis-à-vis the official establishment.... It is colonial reflex to believe that the government knows better than the citizens how to best improve his life..... Laws are as good as those implementing them, and even the most conformist statist would hesitate to call governance in India transparent and clean."[37]

The type of relationship that exists or will be existing in future between democracy (liberal or neo-liberal) and capitalism (classical or neo classical) will decide the fate of both these two pillars of modern civilization. Whether there is 'end of history' or 'end of the end of history', on it hangs the future course of humanity. The crony capitalism and Erstraz capitalism as propounded by the neo-liberals where profits are privatized and losses are socialized are certainly going to prepare the burial ground for these two if such type of misuse is not checked. But the question is who will do this? It is like the proverbial belling of the cat.

The collapse of neoliberal economic order or globalization, as underlined by recent financial breakdown and collaterals in the form of the poverty, unemployment and hardships faced by the people and government has highlighted the importance of a just world order. In quest for rapid globalization and liberalization, the just world order has been given short shrift. The UN General Assembly, in its sixth Special session on May 1, 1974, adopted the Declaration on the Establishment of a New International Order, giving special emphasis on the sovereign equality of the states. The declaration, emphasizing the basic principles of a just economic order, demanded "Full and effective participation on the basis of equality of all countries in the solving of world economic problems in the common interest of all countries." The member-states also emphasized that 'full permanent sovereignty of every state over its natural resources and all economic activities.'[38]

The International Progress Organization, in a conference held on the challenges of globalization at the University of Munich in 1999 had warned of the threat to global instability resulting from unregulated markets, operated on the basis of a misunderstood notion of individual freedom. Regrettably, in the three decades after the UN initiative for a new international economic order, the global economy developed in the opposite direction. The General Assembly's vision was effectively denounced by the industrialized countries at the summit of 22 world leaders in Cancun, Mexico in October 1981. The US delegation under President Ronald Reagan played a leading role as far as the rejection of the demands of the developing countries was concerned. Thus, the notion of a new international economic order was indeed buried at that time.[39]

Since then the Neoliberal project of globalization has been going on with ever-increasing ideological zeal, in spite of warnings and protests by many leaders from the developing world. As far as the ideology of globalization is concerned, since the beginning of the 1970s, the world has witnessed an almost "crazy" belief in a kind of financial perpetuum mobile, or the assumption that wealth could be created by means of financial transactions, or instruments, alone. The belief was obvious in certain attitudes and practices, which included, for instance, policies according to which regulatory mechanisms were deliberately weakened, or completely given up, in the name of economic liberalization, defying Adam Smith's dictum of 'political control.... of competition'. However, instead of a new world order, a state of global disorder was brought as a result of the abdication of the state's sovereignty over economic and financial policies. (Koechler, p16)

The state gradually gave way to powerful, but unaccountable vested interests at the transnational level. Under the slogan of globalization, the "cycle of greed" in which the economy got entangled, brought about a systemic crisis not only of the methods of international economic exchange, but of international relations in general. In spite of the magnitude of the problem, the advocates of Neoliberal ideology still insist on addressing the crisis by way of dealing only with its symptoms and engage in a rather stubborn denial of reality when it comes to the identification of the real cause for the collapse of globalization—namely, its exclusion, not only of geographical but of all moral boundaries that govern economic activity (*ibid*).

The exclusion of moral boundaries has done more damage than anything else, leading to the current imbalances and crises that have plagued the world. The loosening of moral ground has acted as force multiplier in neutralizing or mitigating the equality, justice and freedom. The unchecked profit motive with no moral string has in fact let loose the forces of greed and plunder of the resources. The moral and social obligation is openly mocked at and it is said that crass sentimentalism has no practical values. The rest has been done by the neoliberal ideology for treating symptoms of any problem or malaise facing any situation or anything rather than handling the root cause. The management of things, not the solution of things has become credo of the neo-liberal ideology. Apart from it, the way and manner that relationship between democracy and capitalism has evolved has also contributed to the many problems.

The relationship between Constitutional representative democracy and capitalism is both intimate and deeply untransparent. The historical services which each has rendered to the other over the last two centuries have been profound. But neither, in the end, can be wholly at ease with the other: completely confident of its ultimate fidelity. The source of this ultimate disharmony is not obscure. Each, clearly understood, is in essence a system of free individual choice..... Political choice governs the content and enforcement of public law. Its imaginative aim, however, fitfully attained, is the collective good of the set of human beings directly concerned. (Dunn, *op.cit*)

This is one of the major problems in the complex relations between democracy and its political economy – capitalism, that it is intimate and deeply untransparent. While intimacy fosters relations based on a mutual basis of give and take, and has been the major factor in making it most versatile and highly adjustable system, the entrenched untransparent nature has led it to be dominated by the 'iron law of Oligarchy'. The untransparent and propaganda in veil of public relation exercises-based relationship has provided fertile ground for the tightening of the grip by all sorts of oligarchies and cartels. This has subverted the very goal of democracy and capitalism—liberty, equality and justice, and development of free market system where demand and supply decide everything.

Moreover, the uneasiness and a sort of suspicion that characterize the relations between democracy and capitalism has been one of the major factors in divergence of their respective goals or agenda, if not overtly then covertly. This has been so because both democracy and its political economy—capitalism is based on free individual choice. As the individual choice of democracy is political and that of the capitalism is economic, there is bound to arise some sort of disharmony and disconnect. The free choice in political arena may lead to choice of wrong or unintelligent leaders, free choice in that of economic would certainly result into free for all and infinite exploitation of finite resources leading to all sorts of imbalances and maladies. Hence, there arises the need of political control and some sort of the check and balance. Even Adam Smith has endorsed some type of "political control" and check and balance.

Economic choice in a capitalist economy takes the form (however unobviously) of individual decisions to sell and buy; and virtually everything may well turn out to be for sale. Some goods of the greatest importance, of course, are irretrievable, as Adam Smith clearly recognized. They will only be supplied if they are bought collectively (paid for out of taxes imposed and enforced by public). But no account of why a capitalist economy can be trusted to work spontaneously for the long-term overall advantage of its participants has ever succeeded in explaining why any system of public-decision-making can be trusted to identify and secure the public goods required to enable it to work effectively. Nor has any such account explained why the political defenders of that economy can be relied upon not to pursue other apparent human goods which may (may not) impede its effective working quite dramatically (*ibid*).

The neo-liberals have taken the view of Adam Smith and Hume as their basis for their scant regard for economic and social equality. 'Smith himself emphasized brusquely that the main task of the government was the defense of rich against the poor (a task necessarily less dependably performed where it is the poor who choose who is to govern, let alone where the poor themselves, as in Athens, in large simply are the government.) [*ibid*] What if the number of the poor became unmanageable or ninety per cent populace becomes poor; will the government be able to defend the rich against the onslaught of the hungry majority? Will not government itself or that matter democracy itself be challenged?

Hume explained with meticulous care that the structure of the property rights on which a market economy fundamentally rests will inevitably and systematically clash with natural workings of human sympathy, relentlessly allocating scarce good to those palpably neither deserve nor need them, and at the expense of those who emphatically do so. Both Hume and Smith stressed imperturbably that the system of private property must be protected in its entirety and as a system, since its collective benefits over the time required it to operate as such; and any distribution of these benefits at a particular time under the impress of concern for suffering and deprivation, short of real famine, would inevitably sooner or later threaten its capacity to generate those collective benefits, and so disrupt the natural progress of opulence (*ibid*).

Nevertheless, the heady mixture of Erstraz and crony capitalism using democracy, democratic institutions, system and spineless and shortsighted leaders, who are ever ready to comply for short-term gain, are furthering the interest of plunder and loot putting both these system on precipice. As the aim of capitalism, in view of Adam Smith, to save rich from poor by the state has been realized, the other aspect of the Smithnian coin that it is the rich's responsibility to reduce the number of poor so that there could not be threat to its free market environment has been given short shrift. The number of poor has increased not only in India but also all over the world. Moreover, the political control that Adam Smith talks about in respect of competition and free market has been thrown to winds as it has been loosening in favour of globalization and in the name of liberalization.

As many political commentators pointed out, by the 1950s no great differences of principal divided social democrats from Christian Democrats. What, then, did social democrats stand for? Their programmes generally had two major thrusts: One involved control, the other welfare. Socialist programmes envisaged placing leading economic sectors (banks, transportation, and key industries) under democratic political control, whether through outright nationalization or extensive regulation. The Western German SPD could never push through early 'planning' concepts, though the labour union federation did win the right of labour delegates to sit on corporate boards. But electoral defeats throughout the 1950s tempered the collectivist impulse in Britain and Germany. By the 1960s the 'welfare' agenda largely superseded the objectives of democratic control. It seemed more crucial to guarantee continuing high employment and the progressive expansion of public services – health and education—for all citizens.[40]

Advocates for the welfare state expressed the modern agenda of social democracy most eloquently when Richard Titmuss pleaded for a responsible society. Particularly, T.H. Marshall explained the historical emergence of the three dimensions of citizenship: first liberal rights, later political participation and most recently economic entitlement. He analyzed the development of citizenship as a development of civil, political, and then social rights, emanating from social struggles of the eighteenth, nineteenth and twentieth centuries respectively. The concept of social rights as awarded not on the basis of class or need, but rather on the status of citizenship made the foundation of democracy strong by integrating the credo of social democracy (Marshall, 1950). The latter, in fact, witnesses the zenith of the social democratic movement in 1960s. The conservative political coalition of the 1950 gave way to more reformist politics.

The conflicts associated with 1968 ushered in two major developments. One involved the realm of values, the other economic dogma. The clashes of 1968 did not bring victory to the Left; but they did establish that political contention might revolve around such issues as cultural lifestyles, family structure, minority entitlements, and the Cold War stasis. The concept of democracy grew more encompassing in its cultural and social implications.[41]

On the other hand, the concept of democracy grew more restrictive as a basis for economic policy. By the end of 1960s Western political economies entered a long decade of inflation. After a decade of largely ineffectual corporatist bargaining for wage restraint, voters returned more confrontational conservatives, Margaret Thatcher and Ronald Reagan. Where Socialists still governed, they reversed their traditional priority to extensive welfare and full employment. .... Democracy became more modest in its economic aspirations: social democrats claimed to be more efficient, no more reformist......... a crypto-antidemocratic discourse emerged around the management of the economy. (Maier, *op. cit*,1992)

By 1980s, the market economy became well-accepted "reservoir of non-democratic traditions" where "even in the democracies, masses are persuaded to ask from elites only what elites wish to give them." Thus real choices and competition became limited and any development of alternative choices or even any serious discussion and consideration of them were discouraged (Lindblom, 1977). By the beginning of 21st century or new millennium, it became clear that market system is not very efficient at assigning non-economic values and distributing social or economic justice, despite being "the best mechanism yet devised for creating wealth and innovations". (*ibid*, 2001).

"In any case the rapprochement between capitalism and democracy found no equivalent in issues outside the economic sphere. Issues of cultural conflict, migration, urban security and the control of public space remained intensely charged. .... Just as the 'First World' earlier reinforced economic stratification in the 'Third World', so now the Third World recreated its deep social divisions in the First.....".[42]

Even that rapprochement in the economic sphere has been torn apart by the highjacking of neo-liberals who gave free play to rampant globalization and liberalization, throwing political control to winds and rampant profiteering masqueraded as competition and free market was let loose. The result is before the whole world: global imbalances, financial crisis, inequality, unemployment and poverty stalking across the continents, concentration of wealth in a few hands. The homogenization and uniformity and hegemony which is 'cultural logic of late capitalism' masqueraded as predatory capitalism has given rise to all sorts of sectarian and fundamentalist and terrorism or to be precise, Islamic fundamentalism.

Capitalism, masquerading as 'Corporate Welfarism', 'Erstraz Capitalism', and 'Crony Capitalism' piggy riding on democracy (Classical liberalism or liberalism or neo-liberalism) has led the world where there is frequent cycle of boom and bust, resulting into job loss, hunger, poverty and dislocation of people and families. While the sufferers of this colossus – taxpayers, middle class, lower class and general people – are left to fend for themselves, those who perpetrate this cyclical boom and bust are rewarded : when there is boom, the bumper profit is reward, while the system compensates them with 'Stimulus package' or whatever be the terms, in bust as happened in latest one (2008-09).

As regard Capitalism and its mantra of free market, the serious doubt is being raised regarding its basic paradigm that the society is always best served when individuals are left to pursue their self-interest in free markets. It seems to be "utopian economics'. From the very shaky starts in 1776 when Adam Smith's butchers, brewers and bakers who supplied their wares as if guided by unseen hand to the Friedrich von Hayek's idea of market prices as signals of which goods were scarce and which were in plenty, and his idea of free market as machine for processing and transmitting information was 'one of the great insight of 20th century'. Then capitalism found its new moorings 'General Equilibrium theory' which gave it stamps of scientific approval to unfettered markets. From it came the purist market views of likes of Alan Greenspan.[43]

Rest is the history. Individual self interest does not always benefit society and draws on deep pool of research of 'reality-based economic'. Markets fall if the prices send the wrong signals. Markets also tumble when information is hidden –either seller or buyers know more than each other, and when the prices that individuals paid do not reflect social such as environmental degradation. Such failures were evident before many crises including recent one. Policy makers should have intervened but they dithered due to free-market ideology and 'free-market idolatry'. Hence there is a need for better balance between individual freedom and state intervention.[44]

It is not accident that the most devastating blow to the twentieth century socialist hopes of protecting the poor against the would–be rich came from the open failure of the state to elicit, grasp, and act upon the endless deluge of accurate information which it needed to master to be able to provide that protection........ Whig confidence that rich is, in a subtle way, a sort of public good: that protecting them against the anger and resentment of the poor might be as much as in the latter's interests as protecting the poor against the direct oppression of the rich has always been so evidently.[45]

This rather misplaced "Whig Confidence" seems to have percolated down to the post-liberalized and post-globalized world, but only as half-truths as state seems to be fending only for rich while poor has been left in lurch. Recently in the wake of economic crisis hitting the world, the states and the political actors vied for each other in providing 'stimulus package' and "tax incentives and other benefits" to those whose greed and unchecked "profit motive" led to the glut and recession in economies across the world. While the poor, the ordinary citizens and people have been left to fend for themselves. Or at the best they are being fed on the propaganda and lies that 'price rise and inflation' are the price one has to pay for the development and prosperity.

However, it should not be concluded that market economy or capitalism has lost its relevance, and it should be replaced by some other system As the noted Nobel Prize winner Amartya Sen has commented: 'To be generically against the markets would be almost as odd as being generically against the conversation between people." This seems to be pertinent if one considers the fact that market is a form of human exchange. As any conversation between people should not breach some limitations and values mutually agreed to maintain socio-economic equilibrium and social security. So there must be some limitation, some restraints and some sort of control and regulation to check the market from breaching the limitations of profit making. Just as unrestrained and uncontrolled conversation can wreak havoc on our social relations; the unfettered market forces may put into jeopardy the very existence of the markets and capitalism or liberal capitalism

The responsibility to rein in market and market forces must not and should not be put on government only, but also on markets to understand their pivotal function. Moreover, the 'the nonmarket and nongovernmental institutions' must also realize that they also have constructive role intended to bring about a balance of responsibility. There is an urgent need to reinvent the economic policies in backdrop of crisis management and a sincere concern with the ramifications of the crisis. Expediency has to be replaced by imaginative programmes to eradicate the wide gap between the rich and poor. There is urgent need for strong, transparent institutions to address overriding economic issues. There is the possibility of bringing to a halt the recent economic collapse with the tightening of fiscal controls on bank, and by shaping policies to make growth balanced and sustainable globally.[46]

Even conceding the Smithnian prescription that the main role of the government in a capitalist system is to let the free market manage its affair and allow infinite profit motive to plunder the finite resources, and protect rich from the poor, the problem does not end here. But again it is the same Adam Smith who vouch for political control over the competitive forces let loose for profit, lest it stooped to a level where it jeopardizes the very foundation of capitalist economy. In fact, it is the beginning of all problems plaguing the free market and conjoined twins—liberal democracy. If free market is free and should be so, then why it comes begging for public money when crisis hits below its belt. Whether be it recent crisis of 2008 or Great Depression of 1930s, the sail of free market is downed to allow the public fund to grease their palm dried by crass profiteering. These votaries of Erstraz capitalism who privatize the profit and socialize the losses take shelter back into their phony cocoon of no governmental interference, no claptrap of distributive justice or public charity after they avail the public money.

This doublespeak and hollowness of capitalism or Neoliberal again takes a centrestage when it comes to rich vs. poor. If main duty of the government, in a capitalist or free market economy or liberal democracy is to defend rich against the poor on strength of the taxes and money paid by former as well as latter to the government, there are many implications arising out of this plank. The first and foremost one is that if it is responsibility of the government to defend the rich against the poor (it means not only physical but includes every interests of the rich), then it is also the duty of the government and rich as well that number of poor does not swell to unmanageable limit. Then why the votaries of free market and liberal democracy led by libertarians and neo-liberals make hue and cries when there is any hint of redistribution of the distributive justice.

Can any government or the state worth its salt defend the rich and their interest when the number of poor keeps on rising by leap and bound or their lives become too miserable to bear the dictate of the government? This hollowness and doublespeak of capitalism has led to rise of the fascism, communism, all sort of dictatorships in the past, and still pushing many societies to the civil war, genocide and mayhem at micro level. The recent crisis has opened the old debate of governmental interference vs. free market for time being and is likely to lose its intensity and sheen once economies have started to recover. This has been the standard practice going on in the aftermath of every economic crisis that has been hitting the world so far.

The evolution of democracy and capitalism, particularly after the collapse of Marxist-Leninist system, if put in the matrix of game theory perspective, Zero sum game and asymmetrical game, would show how capitalism as political economy of liberal democracy has used it as milch cow, rendering it hollow and on life support. However, there must be some institutional mechanism, backed by popular mandate to check the vested interests overshadowing democracy and its political economy – capitalism.

Even Keynes, in the wake of Great Depression had abandoned the belief in self-correcting markets as 'he started placing less emphasis on efficiency and more on duty.' One can infer that without government intervention, relief to unemployed would not be possible. The Keynesian economics is an explanation of business cycles as waves of optimism succeeded by waves of pessimism in investment market, real as well as financial. As per General theory 'our knowledge of the factors which will govern the yield of an investment some years hence is usually very slight and negligible', it is difficult to predict the course that market would take. Moreover, due to the divergence between an investor's expectations and the 'conventional wisdom' of stockbrokers, there is generally a gap between the expectations of the individual investors and the evaluation of the market which causes the waves in business cycles. Booms and burst or depressions are caused, according to Keynes, when there is divergence between individual expectations and general belief in the market. This has been the reason for cyclical booms and bursts witnessed frequently, including current one (Skidelsky, 2009).

Basing their assumptions on 'rational expectations' many advisers to investment banks develop projections of future trends of asset prices which fail to materialize and causes governments and central banks to come to banks' rescue. They fail to allow for maladjustments between 'wisdom of crowd' and expectations of individuals. The neo-Keynesian recognizes this possibility of divergence between the two and hence supports the interventions of the governments in the short term to adjust aggregate demand as well as assist banks in trouble. More importantly, the economic policies will remain subject to the uncertainty due to interrelationships between economics, politics, social psychology and institutional changes. Therefore, the Keynesian analysis of business cycles as due to waves of optimism and pessimism would prevail, and the adjustment in money supply to deal with booms and recessions would not lead to any secular inflation (*ibid*).

There is an urgent need to infuse Keynesian political philosophy in the political economy at both macro and micro level. The basic premise on which Keynesian political philosophy is based is that 'to make the world ethically better was (is) the only justifiable purpose of economic strivings'. Keynes was more interested in 'good life' than earning and accumulating riches. He approved the making of money and riches to the extent that these are means of improving living standards of common populace; beyond it accumulation is not good for the health of the society. His political philosophy may be summed up as 'politics should be so arranged as not to distract people unduly, and certainly not continuously, from the cultivation of good states of mind.'(*ibid*, p153) The good states of mind cover everything that makes people life comfortable, and certainly inclusive and equitable growth do so.

In the wake of recent crisis gripping the globalized world, there has been variegated and multi-layered discourse on reviving Keynesianism. Particularly, the Neo-Keynesian has been putting forward global Keynesianism as alternative to Neo-liberal global world order. It is being argued that Keynesianism would do away the imbalances and inequalities that have crept in the neo-liberal global order. Through demand management and state intervention it would do the required course correction.

Challenging these positions, Araghi (2010) argues that neoliberalism is neither opposite of Keynesianism, nor is global Keynesianism a possible alternative to global neoliberalism as a moment within Keynesianism and being anti-thesis to it, neoliberalism was the Keynesian response to its own contradictions. Reacting to wage inflation and stagflation at home and unruly developmentism abroad, (Araghi, 1994; McMichael, 2008) it used the state (supra state) intervention to shift the basis of demand management from wage contracts and 'development compromise' to micro and macro credit and debt-based globalization. (Araghi, 2009) It was this strategic shift from 'positive' to 'negative' means of managing effective demand, rather than abandoning the Keynesian system altogether that was a core element of the 'neoliberal innovation' (Araghi, 2010).

If it is not possible to replace the neoliberal global order with that of neo-Keynesian one, then efforts must be made to conjoin socialism and democracy by positing socialism as fundamentally a democratic project as it conjoins the political with economic democracy. (Basu, 2008) If one takes into account the political and economic philosophy of Gandhi, Tagore and Neogi (who through his creative politics in Chhattisgarh bridged the gap between the policy-making bodies and the people) who tried to formulate a political project based on local communitarian ethic as against the individualized based one, it becomes clear that capitalist-based industrialization does not simply produce structural transformation, but institutes in parallel a subjectivity transformation from the communitarian to the individualized. (Chakarbarty, 2010)

Gandhi, Tagore and Neogi start from premise that any alternative structure to the global must consciously involve an alternative production of subjectivity – an alternative to capitalism must telescope a different worldview to capitalism. Departing from outright oppositional politics to a social constructivist and creative language, it implies a paradigm shift in the arena of politics. Consequently, the very meaning and objective of politics is transformed as political focus is shifted from state and its institutions to society and societal transformation. It is not that they do way with State or demote it or make it subordinate to communitarian goal; only the state centric political philosophy is transcended for ensuring the social transformation. (Basu, *op.cit*)

Whether it is Gandhi through his concept of Satyagrahi (Truth seeker) and Tagore through Prajapati (leader of the community) stumbles upon the concept of democracy, even it is direct democracy. These two along with Neogi, who takes Marxist model of political organization away from vanguardist model and basing them on self-rule and self-governance, are important link in conjoining democracy with socialism by positing socialism as fundamentally a democratic project. The most important aspect of this approach is that it conjoins political democracy with economic one (*ibid*). That is what is required at this moment of history of liberalism, as this conjoinment would provide much needed course correction.

IV

'Equal Irrelevance' and 'Equi-distance'

The thesis of 'equal irrelevance and 'Equi-distance' propounded by Dr. Ram Manohar Lohia in context of capitalism and communism for world in general and non-western societies in particular (Lohia, 1963) has been proved right in the wake of collapse of neo-global world order led by capitalism that has been having field day after the eclipse of communism in 1990s and ebbing of Cold war. The historical process at the fag end of the Twentieth century and beginning of new millennia that 21st century has testified to the fact both capitalism and communism has been unable to solve the basic problem of mankind and politics as how to conduct the temporal affairs of human society, so that it leads to happiness and prosperity to all and sundry.

The collapse of communist system in Russia, Central Asia and East Europe in the early 1990s led to the sudden upsurge of the market economy and capitalist system at the global level. Communist China also embraced the policy of private ownership and market economy. Now, the perpetual story of the capitalist crisis has surfaced in a more unmanageable form. There are inherent contradictions in the capitalist and the communist systems. In these circumstances, Lohia's thesis of 'equal irrelevance' and 'equi-distance' from capitalism and communism has been vindicated. (Dubey, 2009)

Politics is the prime and real moving force in Lohia's framework of social-economic transformation. His concept of politics combines theory and practice, struggle and constructive work, democracy and civil disobedience. Like Marx he put emphasis on struggle but disapproved use of violence as the basis for struggle. He made innovative efforts to improve and refine the Gandhian techniques of non-violence and Satyagrah which is more often than not based on fast and individual actions. Though he accepted non-violent methods of struggle, he added to it the mass based civil disobedience against injustice and exploitation. (*ibid*, 2009)

Lohia differed from the Marxist theses of forces of production, surplus values and imperialism as the last stage of capitalism. He is of view that the techniques of production such as huge machines, mass production and heavy technology remain the same in the capitalist and communist system. Only difference between these two systems of political and economic organization is, apart from some jargons, in respect of forces of the production and ownership of the means of production. The private ownership of the means of the production is replaced by the state ownership in the communist system. However, labour which is the major force of production is denied the benefit of surplus value. Like the capitalism, the labour remains alienated in communist system and has no scope for becoming master of production. (Lohia, 1963)

Lohia, to correct this anomaly, puts emphasis on production system based on small tools and units, and ownership under the control of cooperatives and communities. He also disapproves and disagrees with Marxian position of imperialism as the last stage of capitalism. On the contrary he maintains that imperialism as practised by England and other European countries has played significant role in giving rise to the capitalism in Europe and he supports this argument by citing the concrete examples from the economic history of India, Africa, Western Europe and England. The rise of the first phase of capitalism in Britain resulted form unabated loot and capital flow from East India (Bengal). After the British occupation of whole India and rampant economic exploitation, the colonial force managed to capture and colonize Africa and South-East Asia with booty and fortune looted form India. This, in turn, led to the strengthening of capitalist system in Europe. The same occupation and exploitation patterns were followed by Spain, France and Holland 'where the growth of capitalism largely depended on the imperialist expansion and the exploitation of resources of their colonies' (*ibid*).

With the collapse of communism in Soviet Russia, East Europe, rejection of it by China and the recent global economic crisis generated by capitalism based on market economy, the relevance of his theory of 'equi-distance' and 'equal irrelevance' has to be factored in for rescuing world from the crisis at macro and micro level. Related with this is the fate of democracy in India as well as world over. He propounded that Indian and Non-western socialism of Asia (as well as Africa and Latin America) should be different from the European Marxist thought process of socialism, because historical, material and social conditions are different in the two continents. At the ideological level, the path of socialism must be distinct and at equal relevance from the paths of capitalism and communism. These two systems are equally irrelevant in assuring freedom, equality and prosperity to mankind. In the era of military blocs of cold war days, his thrust was that countries of Asia, Africa, Latin America in general and India in particular should be at equal-distance from the Atlantic and Warsaw pacts. In the place of toothless idea of non-alignment, his stress was on the creation of vibrant positive third bloc. Similarly, in the domestic Indian politics, socialists should be at equal-distance from the Congress and the communist parties. (Dubey, *op. cit*)

Coming to Lohia thesis of non-sustainability and non-feasibility of capitalism for non-western countries as there are no colonies to sustain capitalism (Lohia, 1963), the series of crisis in capitalism and liberal democracy should be seen in this perspective. Lohia tries to understand the capitalism by questioning the Marxist theory regarding the origins of capitalism. His focal point of criticism of Marxism was that it provides explanation of the rise of capitalism only in reference to the developments specific to the western societies. He puts forward the argument that right from its beginning capitalism has been dependent on external resources. These external sources were provided by the colonies which they established after occupying the land and subjugating the people. Marx was not off the mark in maintaining that capitalism is based on the exploitation of workers by the capital. However, he was unable to notice that both of these are based on more fundamental exploitation of the colonies. In this sense the capitalism and colonialism had the same origin. This is the main angle of Lohia's theory of 'twin origin of capitalism and colonialism' (Lohia, 1964).

Lohia is not only skeptical about the viability of capitalism in India and other non-western countries but also the future of this system in America and Europe. The dismantling of colonialism consequent upon freedom struggles in the colonies and the fallouts of Second World War has posed a serious challenge for the existence of this system. According to him, neither capitalism and nor communism could escape the crisis of modern civilization, as technology has reached the dead-end. It is not to be missed that the breakthrough in technology and vast virgin resources of colonies—both manpower and raw materials—has reached dead end and these could not sustain the systems for good. As this civilization could not invent a revolutionary technology any more and resources are fast depleting or already exhausted, it could not spread any further in geographical terms and loose its pre-eminence in the world. According to him, the crisis in modern civilization can be traced to the moral and spiritual decline in these societies, and reduction of individual as mere cog in the machine. (Lohia, 1963)

If one analyzes the current crisis facing these two systems in the backdrop of this thesis, many things would become clear. At least, the recent crisis and crisis like situations that have engulfed the neoliberal global order both at macro and micro level can be put in proper perspective. That capitalism is unsustainable in the absence of colonies has been proved beyond doubt in the wake of recent crisis and slow and steady decline of western countries in the post-colonial period which started after Second World War. The failure of capitalist model of development as followed by Argentina, Brazil and other Latin American countries recently and that of Asian Tigers not recently has proved Lohia thesis that capitalism is not sustainable and appropriate for non-Western countries. Another thesis that capitalism based as it is on colonies for its growth and very survival would be unsustainable and untenable in the post Second World War era when most of the colonies have become free and independent nations merits some attention and consideration.

The current crisis should be seen in this perspective and it would add some credence to Marxist critique which sees globalization, liberalization and privatization as disguised arms of neo-imperialism. Whatever be the basis of their criticism, it is clear that globalization and liberalization has been desperate to find market and avenues for parking of the capital in non-western countries and getting resources to sustain it. The despotic attitude and winners-take-it-all approach that western countries have shown during various multilateral talks related to world trade or global warming betrays some concern in this regard.

The Marxist critique sees globalization, liberalization and privatization as disguised neo-imperialism and survival strategy to be in reckoning in the affairs of the world. Without going into merit of the discourse, the possibility of markets acting as colonies in its new avatar cannot be denied. The urgency and alacrity bordering on war-like frenzy that old as well as new politico-economic powers are showing or have shown in case of acquiring foothold in the virgin markets of Africa, Latin America and Asia is a case in point in this regard.

The transformation or the development of capitalism in guise of neo-imperialism or predatory capitalism or Erstraz capitalism, particularly the Marxists who view globalization and liberalization as the disguised form of neo-imperialism should be analyzed in the light of what Lohia has said about the non-viability of capitalism in western and non-western world (Lohia, 1963). The desperate attempt to find alternatives to colonies can be discerned in putting in place neo-liberal global order wherein goods, capital, finances and ideas can run amok without showing its true nature. The neo-liberal global world order has collapsed and its rumblings are for everybody to see as how it is gasping for life support. The whole of western world including USA has been plunged in crisis. The economies are in shamble, the growth rate has plummeted and unemployment and poverty is increasing.

Moreover, the operation of market economy at micro level also vindicates Lohia thesis of non-viability of capitalism in absence of colonies. To overcome this shortcoming (of colonies), market economy or neoliberal has tried to reduce one part or region or class into colony to get succour for its development. This fact can be further substantiated with rise of haphazard, unbalanced and lopsided growth and development within a country, region and continents. This has been true particularly in case of non-western countries such as India, China, Brazil and other countries. For example, one region has developed at the cost of another, even if it has not been done intentionally. If the poverty, squalor and backwardness of the tribal and mineral rich parts of Eastern and Central region of India which is also Naxalites (left wing extremism as called in the official language) affected and insurgency infested areas, and developed regions of North and West is juxtaposed, this would be validated. Same is the case in China where two continents of contrast—developed Europe and underdeveloped Africa—exist metaphorically as well otherwise.

Apart from difficulties faced by western countries in sustaining market economy or capitalism or neo-liberalism in the absence of the colonies, non-western countries that went for it faced unprecedented economic hardship and difficulties. The failure of Soviet style bureaucratic central planning, a virtual U-turn by officially socialist China and Vietnam in embracing capitalism based policies undermined the confidence in the old fashioned socialist ideas. Economic success stories of countries like South Korea, Singapore, Taiwan, Malaysia and Hong Kong pointed to attractive possibilities. Nevertheless, in the orchestrated celebration of the market economy, one tends to forget that this is one-sided saga. It must be kept in mind, though it may be inconvenient to accept for the pro-market economists, that most countries of sub-Sahara Africa, of Latin America, of Central Asia underwent dramatic economic stagnation or decline for several years by embracing the same principle of market-based liberalization (Madison, 2001).

Theoretically speaking, the very logic of market economy as self-regulating and equilibrium inducing mechanism is flawed, as it has origin in the idea of perfect competition as the prototype market form. Under highly unrealistic assumptions, which rules out all forms of uncertainties and banishes the unknown future from the analysis, some results are obtained. The prices in equilibrium correspond to an efficient arrangement in the sense that production of no commodity can be increased further without decreasing the production of some other. No participant in the market can do better either as a producer or consumer, without someone else becoming worse off. The powerful ideological metaphor is that of invisible hand of the self-regulating market leading the society of selfish individuals to an optimum. This is indeed a most spectacular case of self-organization where neither intervention of the state nor any concern for the collective expressed in social norms like trust and fellow feeling is needed to reach the optimum economic state (Bhaduri, 2009).

Moreover, there is contradiction between market economy and democracy vis-a-vis accountability. While in democracy accountability is the foundational concept on which the whole idea of democracy pivots, in market economy there is no accountability within specified time frame. In democracy, the political actors are accountable to the people in the sense that they have to face electorates. There is no such thing in market economy as accountability; only accountability, if any is in 'the largely make-believe ideology of self-regulation.' Apart from it, there is a deeper logical flaw: the stability of the equilibrium in a competitive market is not guaranteed without imposing further stringent conditions, and it remains unspecified how long it would take to converge to it (*ibid*).

In addition, market economy or neo-liberalism, to keep our conscience comfortable, claims that market can substitute for social ethics by deciding what is profitable to produce, and who should be in charge of production. So we can no longer question without extensive public opinion and state intervention in favour of poor, in this country of overwhelming poverty the logic of political democracy of one-adult-one-vote cannot be compatible with the logic of market dictated by the rich with many more votes with their higher purchasing power than poor. These are almost the subversive question: and yet, the ability to pose them is the first step to liberate ourselves from the ruling system of conventional wisdom that has failed us so badly despite the big show of producing precise technocratic economic knowledge.... (*ibid*)

It is for this reason that Adam Smith later in his life talked about some sort of 'political control' or Keynes vouched for putting conditions of 'good life' on market forces. In the nutshell, the primacy of politics should be restored which has been taken away by the economics or finance. It is because of this that much of the problems that world is facing has cropped up. Eminent political philosopher Bernard Crick cautioned about this danger way back in 1960s, when he argued vigorously for "primacy of politics" (Crick, 1962). The democratized political auditing and its institutionalization would restore the primacy of politics by making it more accountable and transparent.

Endnotes

1 Lyotard, Jean-Francois, *La Condition Postmoderne: Rapport sur le savoir. Les Editions de Minuit*, pp7. 1979. (translated version)

2 Lyotard, Jean-Francoise, *ibid*, pp8

3 Richard K. Ashley and R. B. J Walker, *Introduction: Speaking the Language of Exile: Dissident Thought in International Studies*, International Studies Quarterly, Vol. 34 No. 3 (Sp, 1990, pp 259-268

4 http://faculty.chass.ncsu.edu/garson/PA765/postmod.htm, 4/29/2010

5 Joel F. Handler, *Postmodernism, Protest and the New Social Movements*, Law and Society Review, Vol. 26, No 4 (1992), pp 697-732 http://www.jstor.org/pss/30538115/24/2010

6 Bertens, H, *The Idea of Postmodern*, Routledge: London, 1995

7 Nandy, Ashish, *Indian Persuasions: 50 Years of Seminar*, Edited by Rudrangshu Mukherjee, Roli Books, New Delhi, 2009.

8 http://en.wikipedia.org/wiki/criticism_of_postmodernism4/28/2010

9 *ibid*

10 Handler, Joel F., *Postmodernism, protest and the New Social Movements*, Law and Society Review, Vol 26, No 4 (1992), pp697-733).

11 http://the-eclectic-rambler.blogpost.com/2008/06/postmodernism-and-democracy.html4/29/2010

12 Lyotard, Jeans Francois, *The Differend: Phrases in Dispute*, 1988, University of Minnesota Press.

13 Hicks, Prof. Stephen R. C, *Deconstructing Postmodernism, Liberty*. 2005. http://evans-experimentalism.freewebspace.com/jason.htm4/29/2010

14 Jameson, Fredric, *Postmodern or the Cultural logic of later Capitalism*, Durham, NC: Duke University Press, 1991.

15 Bertens, H, *The Idea of the Postmodern*. Routledge: London. 1995

16 Karunarathne. Dr. Vickramabahu, *Postmodernism, Liberal Democracy and the War in Iraq*,

http://www.adelinotorres.com/filosofia/postmodernism,%20Liberal%20Democracy%20 an.... 4/29/2010

17 Fukuyama, Francis, *The End of the History and the Last Man*, 1992

18 Blake, Nigel, *Democracy We Need: Situation, Post-Foundationalism and Enlightenment*, http://www3.interscience.wiley.com/journal/119215890/abstract?CRETRY=1andSRETRY =04/29/2010

19 http://en.wikipedia.org/wiki/j%BCrgen_Habermas 7/14/2010

20 Fox, Charles J and Hugh T. Miller, '*Postmodern Public Administration: Toward Discourse*, Thousands Oaks, CA: Sage Publications, 1994.

21 Rosenau, Pauline, '*Postmodernism and the Social Sciences*'. Princeton, NJ: Princeton

22 http://en.wikipedia.org/wiki/Deliberative_democracy7/14/2010

23 Valaskakis, Kimon, President of Global Group. http://heinonline.org/HOL/ ViewImageLocal?handle=hein.journals/wlsj13&div=18&collec.... 4/29/2010

24 Dunn, John, Democracy: *The Unfinished Journey 508 BC To AD 1993*, (Ed) Oxford University Press, 1992

25 Walia, Shelley, '*Acts of Resistance*', Tribune, 06.09.09

26 Roy, Arundhati, "*Listening to Grasshoppers: Field Notes on Democracy*", Harrish Hamilton, 2009

27 Kampfner, John, Freedom, '*For Sale: How We Made Money And Lost Our Liberty*, Penguin: London 2009

28 Fukuyama, *op. cit*, pp15

29 Khilnani, Sunil, '*Indian Persuasions: 50 Years of Seminar*' (Ed.) Rudrangshu Mukherjee, Roli Books, New Delhi, 2009.

30 Harding, Neil, '*The Marxist- Leninist Detour*', in John Dunn (Ed) *Democracy: The Unfinished Journey—508 BC to AD 1993*, Oxford University Press,1992.

31 National Commission on Enterprises in the Unorganized Report, 2009 as quoted in *Economic Times*, 01. 01.2010

32 Rural Development Institute website

33 Maier, Charles S, "*Democracy Since the French Revolution*" in John Dunn (ed.) *Democracy: The Unfinished Journey—508 BC to AD 1993*. Oxford University Press: 1992

34 Geoffrey Roberts and Alistair Edwards, *A New Dictionary of Political Analysis*, London:1991

35 Maier, *op. cit*. p141

36 Tandon, Rajesh and Mohanty Ranjita, '*Civil Society and Governance*', PRIA, New Delhi, 2005

37 Nalpat, M.D. '*Civil Society Awakes*', The Times of India, dated 16.02. 10.

38 http://www.undocuments.net 03.09.10

39 Koechler, Hans, '*The Collapse of Neoliberal Globalization and the Quest for a Just World Order*', World Affairs summer, 2010, (April-June) Vol14 no 2.

40 Maier, Charles S , '*The Marshall Plan and Germany*' edited volume, Berg Press (1991)

41 Maier, Charles S. '*In Search of Stability: Explorations in Historical and Political Economy*', Cambridge University Press ,1987

42 Maier, *op. cit* p141 1992

43 Cassidy, John, '*How Markets Fail: The Logic of Economic Calamities*,' Farrar, Straus and Giroux. 2009.

44 *ibid*

45 Maier, Charles S "*Consigning the Twentieth Century to History: Alternative Narratives for the Modern Era*" in American Historical Review , June 2000

46 Stilgitz, Joseph, '*Freefall: Free Markets and the Sinking of the Global Economy*', Allen Lane, London, 2010.

References

Araghi, Farshad (2009): *The Invisible Hand and Visible Foot: Peasants, Dispossession and Globalization*, in A Haroon, Akram Lodhi and Cristobel Kay (Ed.) Peasants and *Globalization: Political Economy, Rural Transformation and the Agrarian Question*: Routledge: New York.

------------------(2010) *The End of 'cheap Ecology* and the crisis of *Long Keynesianism* Economic and Political Weekly, Vol. XLV No.4, Jan 23

Araghi, Giovaum (1994): *The long twentieth Century: Money, Power and the Origins of Our Times*, Verso: London.

Aronowitz, Stanley (1987) *Postmodernism and Politics*, Duke University Press, http://www.jstor.org/pss/488695 (5/24/2010)

Basu, Pranab Kanti (2008): *Globalization An Anti-text: A Local View*, Akar Publications, New Delhi

Bhaduri, Amit (2009): *A Failed World View*, Economic and Political Weekly, Vol XLIV No4, January 31

Chakarbarty, Anjan (2010): *Local Space in Global Map*, Economic and Political Weekly, Vol. XLV, No. 9 February 27

Crick, Bernard (1962): *In Defense of Politics*, Oxford: London

Dubey, Satya Mitra: (2009) www.drlohiacentenary.org/index_more.html4/28/2010

Jameson, Fredric (1991) *Postmodernism or the Cultural Logic of Late Capitalism Verso*

Lohia, Ram Manohar (1963) *Marx, Gandhi and Socialism*, Navhind Publisher, New Delhi, originally from the University of California Press

--------------------- – (1963) *Wheel of History*, Navhind Prakashan, New Delhi, originally from the University of Michigan Press

---------------------- – (1962) *Caste System*, Navhind Prakashan, New Delhi

----------------------- – (1965) *Interval during Politics*, University of Michigan Press

--------------------- – (1964) *Economics after Marx* Essay, published by Navhind Prakashan, Delhi.

Madison, Angus (2001) *The World economy: A Millennial Perspective*, Paris

McMichael, Philip (2008): *Development and Social Change: A Global Perspective*, Pine Forge Press: Thousand Oaks

Riccio, Barry D. (1994). *Walter Lippmann – Odyssey of a liberal*. Transaction Publishers.

Skidelsky, Robert (2009): *Keynes: The Return of the Master*, Public Affairs: London

Steel, Ronald (1980) *Walter Lippmann and the American century*, Little, Brown and Company.

General References

Atkinson, A. B. (1995). *Incomes and the Welfare State*, Cambridge University Press.

Barzilai, Gad (2003) *Communities and Law: Politics and Cultures of Legal Identities*. Ann Arbor: University of Michigan Press.

Buechler, S, M. (1995) '*New Social Movement Theories*' in The Sociological Quarterly, 36 (3): 441-64

------. (1999) *Social Movements in Advanced Capitalism*, Oxford University Press,

Castells, M. (2004) *The Power of Identity* London: Blackwell

Charles, N. (2002) *Feminism, the State and Social Policy* London: Macmillan

Chomsky, Noam, Carlos Peregrin, Otero (2004) *Language and Politics*, AK Press. p.739

Connolly, William E (1995) *The Ethos of Pluralization*. University of Minnesota Press.

Connor, Walker (1969) *Ethnology and the Peace of South Asia*, World Politics, Vol. 22, No. 1 (October), pp. 51–86

Diana Kendall. (2005) Sociology *In Our Times*, Thomson Wadsworth.

Ghai, Yash, (2003) *Public Participation and Minorities*, London: Minority Rights, Group International Hamlin, A. and Pettit, P (ed.) [1989], *The Good Polity*, Oxford: Blackwell

Hanisch, Carol (2003) *The Personal is Political*, in Shulamith Firestone, *The Dialectic of Sex*. New York: Farrar, Straus and Giroux, (first pub. 1970). ISBN 978-0641711688

Hobsbawm, Eric (1994) *The Age of Extremes: A History of the World, 1914–1991*. New York: Pantheon Books,.

Jenkins, Richard, (2008) *Social Identity*. London: Routledge

Long, Roderick T (1998). *Towards A Libertarian Theory of Class*, Social Philosophy and Policy 15 (2): 303-349: PP 304-308

Malesevic, Sinisa (2006) *Identity as Ideology*, New York: Palgrave

Marshall, T.H. (1950), *Citizenship and Social Class*, Cambridge

McAllister, Ted V. (1996). *Revolt against modernity: Leo Strauss*, Eric Voegelin and the search for postliberal order. Lawrence, Kansas, University Press of Kansas; pp. 58-68.

Meyer, David S Meyer and Lindsey Lupo (2009) *Assessing the Politics of Protest: Political Science and the study of Social Movement* in Klandermans, Bert, and Conny Roggerrband. *Handbook of Social Movements Across Discipline: Handbooks of Sociology and Social Research*. New York: Springer. P. 130

Ostegaard, Geoffrey (1991) *Anarchism: A Dictionary of Marxist Thought*. Blackwell Publishing P.21

Paul, Ellen F (2007) *Liberalism: Old and New*, Cambridge University Press, p. 187

Pichardo, Nelson A. (1997) *New Social Movements: A Critical Review*, Annual Review of Sociology, Vol. 23: pp. 411-430

Polsby, Nelson W. (1960) *How to Study Community Power: The Pluralist Alternative*, The Journal of Politics, (22)3, 474-484 Rose, N (1999), *Powers of Freedom: Reforming Political Thoughts*, Cambridge University Press

Sapon, Vladimir, Robino, Sam (2010). *Right and Left wings in Libertarianism*, Social Science 5(6).

Schattschneider, E.E. (1960) *The Semi-Sovereign People*. New York: Holt.

Rinehart and Winston Scott, A. (1990) *Ideology and the New Social Movements*, London: Unwin Hyman Simons, (1996) *A Community of Freedoms*. Austrian Quarterly 68(1):31-42 Talisse.

Robert (2004), *Democracy after Liberalism*, Routledge Toft, Monica Duffy (2003) *The Geography of Ethnic Violence: Identity, Interests, and the Indivisibility of Territory* (Princeton NJ: Princeton University Press). *Towards a New Sovereignty*, Presented by Carl Bildt., Woodrow Wilson School of Public and International Affairs, Princeton University, 18 November 2004.

www.princeton.edu/lisd/events/talks/Bildt_Text.pdf

Section Three

Indian Democracy: An Overview

Before going into nature and evolution of democracy in general and Indian democracy in particular, it would be pertinent to mention Robert A Dahl's Two Principles of Democracy. While discussing democracy, Robert Dahl has presented two Principles of democracy: The Principle of inclusion and the Principle of inequality (Dahl, 1971). His Principle is veritable and scientific touchstone for measuring up democracy in general. Even Pareto's cyclical theory seems to endorse the inclusion Principle, despite the fact that Pareto has been the staunch critic of democracy. He has observed that democratic regimes tend to operate cyclically. This is necessary as it keeps democracy vibrant and vigorous by including those hitherto left out of political and cultural and political entitlement (Pareto, 1971).

Even Robert Michels, through his theory of 'Iron Law of Oligarchy' has stated that it is just opposite of democratic Principle of inclusion and equality. While studying political parties, he came to conclusion that the problem lay in the very nature of organizations. Modern democracy allowed the formation of organizations such as political parties, but as such organizations grew in complexity, they became less and less democratic.

Michels formulated the 'Iron Law of Oligarchy': "Who says organization, say oligarchy." Any large organization, Michels pointed out, is faced with problems of coordination that can be solved only by creating bureaucracy. A bureaucracy, by design, is hierarchically organized to achieve efficiency—many decisions have to be made daily that cannot efficiently be made by large numbers of people. The effective functioning of an organization therefore requires the concentration of much power in the hands of few. Those few, in turn—the oligarchy—will use all means necessary to preserve and further increase their power (Nye, 1977). Even though both Pareto and Robert Michaels are considered as anti-democratic, they have provided important criteria for measuring democracy.

I

Democracy World Over

According to Freedom House, nine democratic countries experienced rollback of democracy in 2005. In its report in 2009, it registered declines in '40 countries in Africa, Latin America, the Middle East, and the former Soviet Union.' It was found that number of electoral democracies had fallen back to 116, its lowest number since 1995. As to why this happened, it is understood that early leaders of the young democracies that emerged in the 1990s failed to recognize that free societies require strong institutions, a loyal opposition to the ruling party, and willingness to compromise. Instead they saw democracy as just semi-regular votes; after they won, they then used all tools of power to dominate their countries and to hand out benefits to their allies or tribe. This narrow interpretation of democracy not only distorted the true meaning of the word (democracy) but also alienated the public in many countries, who became disgusted that these democracies seemed no more committed to the common good than their authoritarian predecessor.[1]

Western countries, which after 9/11 refocused their attention from democratization of the 1990s to the war on terror, paid little attention as democracy world over went down the drain. Sometimes, the West simply no longer had the time to stand up for democrats abroad. Other times, as in the case of Malaysia and Pakistan, authoritarian rule suddenly benefited the West, since the US could rely on autocrats to help detain terror suspects indefinitely. Meanwhile, the Bush administration's linkage of the war in Iraq to democracy promotion tainted democratization in the minds of many, particularly in the Middle East. The global economic crisis has also damaged democracy's appeal. To many middle-class men and women in the developing world, the spread of democracy was linked to the spread of capitalism since many of these countries opened their economies at the same time as they embraced political freedom. (Kurlantzick, *ibid*, Para 4 and 5)

The result is that on nearly every continent, democracy is sputtering out.... Disappointed with these elected autocrats and frustrated with the graft of young democracies, many middle-class activists in developing nations are even longing for the old days of authoritarian rule. In Africa, recent coups in Mauritania and Niger were welcomed by the urban middle class, while data from the Asian Barometer surveys, regular polls that examine Asian attitudes toward democracy, show that many respondents have become dissatisfied with the democratic system. (*ibid*, page 33 Para 3) This is not an encouraging trend as it is adversely affecting the credibility of democracy. The situation is not good even in the developed and other countries where democracy has taken roots, with well established institutions and norms.

Coming to the Principle of equality and inclusion, it may be said that inequality world over has increased as is clear from the many reports, surveys and comments. The democracies world over have not fared well so far the Principle of inclusion is concerned. The biggest culprit in this regard seems to be the elites and leaders of democratic countries. '..They (leaders and elites) saw democracy as just semi-regular votes; after they won, they then used all tools of power to dominate their countries and hand out benefits to their allies or tribe. This narrow interpretation of democracy not only distorted the true meaning of the word but also alienated the public in many countries,…. (*ibid*, p 30 para 3).

There is growing trend of elitism in Europe and America as reflected from the constitution of parliaments and Senates, apart that of in Asia and Africa. So far as African continent is concerned, 'political freedoms declined in 10 countries on the continent in 2009, while they improved in just four. … In others, the refusal to challenge autocratic regimes has been driven by security—Ugandan, Burundian and Ethiopian troops have functioned as de facto Western proxies in battling radical Somali Islamists in Mogadishu.[2]

Many studies, public opinion polls and market research conducted in respect of the state of democracies world over have underlined the growing elitism and 'Iron Law of Oligarchy' getting firm footholds in the democratic institutions and agencies of government. Even in UK, the mother of democracy, there is widely held viewpoint that 'Westminster Village' is a gathering of the elite, and out of touch with the working class or outlying regions of UK. … 'Parliament as a whole remains very much a social elite. In a separate study comparing new entrants in the Class of 2010 with the previous Parliament, Manado Partnership, a business communication has found that there is unusually high count of MPs educated at private schools, almost 90 per cent with university degree, of which almost 35 per cent are from Oxbridge[3]. This is the situation in almost all the democracies world over. Moreover, the participation of people in the election or referendum or other movement such as protest on some common issues have been falling down, threatening the very basis of democracy.

If one analyzes the dynamics of working of democracy at macro and micro level, one would not fail to discern the two undercurrents (termed differently as 'to save democracy' 'to make world safe for democracy' 'Strategic and other vested interests to undermine democracy by supporting autocratic at macro level, and 'to respect the mandate of people (read benefiting their own tribe or class or caste or race at micro level,) undermining democracy world over. While some democratic countries are trampling the democratic rights and norms of other countries in the name of 'making world safe for democracy', some other is supporting the autocratic regimes or dictatorship for their vested or strategic interests.

At micro level or national level, democracy has been highjacked by the 'Iron Law of Oligarchy' or in the name of the 'mandate of the people' whether it is America or Asia or Europe or Africa. The world has been flattened by these maverick oligarchs, who are monopolizing all democratic spaces and crowding all the democratic institutions or using them like invisible puppeteer, pulling all the strings. This has led to galloping poverty and inequality across the world.

However, the most disturbing trend across the democracies that has been observed is the viewing of democracy as 'semi-regular votes' which is behind the decline of democracy across the continents. This rather narrow interpretation of democracy has invoked feelings of frustration and anger among masses particularly those who have left out from the ambit of development and basket of benefits, forcing them to take to the street. Such type of narrow democracy has led to violent demonstrations and change of the regimes in the countries like Thailand, Philippines and other countries.

However, what is the most disturbing rather alarming trend being witnessed across the young, not so young and old democracies is that this narrow interpretation of democracy has resulted into class or caste cleavages, which threaten the very basis of democracy—dialogue, peaceful and amicable settlement of disputes social harmony and holding of regular elections and smooth transition of power. Disappointed with these elected autocrats and frustrated with the graft of young democracies, many middle-class activists in developing nations are even now longing for the old days of authoritarian rule. In Africa, recent coups in Mauritania and Niger were welcome by the urban middle class, while data from the Asian Barometer surveys, regular polls that examine Asian attitudes toward democracy, show that many respondents have become dissatisfied with their democratic system. (McClure, *op. cit*)

The middle class's push back against democracy, by way of coups and other antidemocratic means, has disenfranchised the poor, sparking still more protests. In Thailand, crowds of protestors, most of them poor, have launched their own violent demonstrations that target the middle classes who tried to push (the leader of poor) Thaksin out of office. Similarly in Bolivia, the middle-class anti-Morales protesters now have been met with angry Pro-Morales protesters mostly drawn from the ranks of the poor. In Philippines, poor men and women furious that their hero Estrada had been forced out by the middle class launched their own counter-protests...... These counter protests have led to a class divides that could take generations to reconcile. (Kurlantzick, *op.cit*)

This rather disturbing trend is perceptible across the full-fledged, semi, partially and sham democracies of the world. While in some it has come into open, in others it is undercurrent or simmering within the hearts and minds of the people. The ruling elite or class is monopolizing the power and perks, and in the name of people filling up their coffers, while benefiting and propping the middle class only. Everything is being done for the middle class as the leaders and important functionaries come from middle class and their vote bank mostly constitute it, while the poor or lower class is being left out. Even the programmes, schemes, developmental activities and other benefits meant for poor are being cornered by the middle class, leading to social and economic imbalances. In some countries such as Thailand and Philippines, this has come into open with toppling of middle class or lower class leaders by their rival supporters.

Another thing that makes or mars the operation of democracy in real sense of the term is the presence or absence of decentralized institutions and values that is very vital for its fruition. It is surprising that it has not been given real importance and weightage, despite the fact that decentralization has found required space and priority so far as the discourse on democracy is concerned. The very fact that democracy is sputtering out across the world both qualitatively and quantitatively testifies to the fact that decentralized and grassroot level democracy should be utmost priority, if it is to be saved from iron law of oligarchy and centralization. The unrest in democratic world and simmering tension perceptible from a fledgling democracy of Iraq to the well established democracies of Europe and America emanates from the lack of decentralized and grassroot institutions. Consequently, the people are feeling that democracy is just bypassing them and has become a tool for rich and dominant to subjugate them.

It is not that decentralization and grassroot democracy has not been given attention as tool to make democracy effective. There has been no dearth of such discourse and efforts to make decentralized and grassroot democracy effective. However, these efforts have not fructified in the evolution of any effective institutions which can give shape to decentralized and grassroot democracy. In this respect, Indian village democracy that has been existing well before the very term democracy was invented can act as model. Though this decentralized institution has been tried to be resurrected through enactment of 73rd and 74th Amendment to the Constitution of India, yet its real ideals and purpose has been lost to the power politics, corruption and centralized structure of governance in general as prevalent in Indian democracy, yet it can act as model for the revival of grassroot democracy.

The village democracy – age old institutions, though badly bruised and corroded by feudalism and colonial rules, and western model of democracy borrowed from European and American democracies – acted as bulwark against corrosiveness of ant-democratic forces operating across the democracies of the world. It is for this reason that democracy, despite being borrowed wholesale from western countries, has survived in India, in spite of all odds staked against it. If people across the democracies of the world are feeling let down by it, as it is crystal clear from the news of discontentment and tension pouring down from the fourcorners of the world, it has, to a larger extent, do with lack of such grassroot institutions such as village democracy as has been existing in India. Even Indian democracy is facing such problem because the village democracies destroyed by colonial rulers and feudalism has not been resurrected, despite the lip service paid and constitutional intervention mentioned in this regard.

II

Indian Saga

Democracy survived in India not as many western analysts and political scientists believe, because of the structures, institutions, rules, regulations and political culture seeded by the colonial rulers. Democracy in India survived because long and deep-rooted tradition of village republic in the form of Village Panchayat, caste Panchayat and above all republican democracies like Lichchavi and Vaishali existing long before the concept of democracy dawned in Western hemisphere. Though there are no substantial facts and source to confirm this, as India unlike the western civilization had oral tradition of history which has erroneously been termed by the western scholars as so-called 'lack of history and tradition', in literature and religious texts there are plenty of references indicating the deep-rooted tradition of democracy. However, it is not gainsaying that these concepts, diction and terms had their origin in the western countries.

"…. Indian democracy is one of the longer living and older democracies in the world. The first Indian republic has lasted longer than any of the five French republics, except the Third; longer than the inter-war German Weimer and Austrian republics or the Spanish republic that was destroyed in the civil war. It has done this while preserving India's territorial integrity with only one episode of a (Constitutionally sanctioned) suspension of the basic freedoms. The key to survival has been its inclusiveness. The revolutionary decision of the Constituent Assembly to adopt universal adult franchise has helped Indian society to unleash the demands for inclusion from lower and backward castes and Dalits and from marginalized groups everywhere in the country. …"[4]

However, this achievement has been bought at a price. It is arguable that while the slow growth in per capita income in the first thirty years after Independence was probably a result of well-meant but misguided economic policies, in the last twenty five years India has been held by as the price of political fragmentation. The Governments have had to maintain fragile coalitions and pacify competing vote banks by extending uneconomic, often regressive, subsidies, which lead to persistent budget deficits and growth rate slower than what could otherwise be achieved (Desai, *ibid*).

Democracy in India, particularly procedural one, has fared well: Regular elections, smooth transfer of power, a semblance of rule of law reigning, a vibrant Parliamentary system, free and independent judiciary and press has made democracy a success. Moreover, the very survival of democracy in India has added to its credibility and viability, despite the doubt and cynicism shown by democratic fraternity across the world.

Except for brief interregnum during period of 26 June, 1975 to March, 1977s, democracy in India has been functioning with modicum of success. The elections are being held regularly; 15 General Elections have been held so far. There has been smooth and frictionless transfer of power, a semblance of rule of law reigning over country; parliamentary practices and norms being followed without fail, debate and discussion going on continuously, citizen enjoying the rights and privileges enjoined by the Constitution and an independent judiciary safeguarding their rights from the power and quirks of executive and legislature. The participatory democracy has taken roots in the wake of Panchyati Raj Institutions at grassroot level (which became effective after 73rd and 74th Amendment in the Constitution). These all have added to the credentials of Indian democracy.

This is not to forget that '…In India, democracy was constructed against the grain, both of a society founded upon the inequality of the caste order, and of an imperial and authoritarian state. If the initial conditions were unlikely, democracy has had to exist in circumstances that conventional political theories identify as being equally unpropitious: amidst a poor, illiterate and staggeringly diverse citizenry. Not only has it survived, it has succeeded in energizing Indian society in unprecedented ways. Introduced initially by a mincingly legalistic nationalist elite as a form of government, democracy has been extended and deepened to become a principal of society, transforming the possibilities available to Indians.'[5]

If democracy has survived, not only survived but prospered defying conventional political theories, it has more to do with our society which had long tradition of democracy, of course not in western sense and perspective, in the form of village republic, Panchyats and tradition of dialogues and arguments. Otherwise everything from the beginning was stacked against it; "society founded upon the inequality of caste order and of an imperial and authoritarian state" was the main basis on which democracy in western liberal tradition was supplanted with political economy based on capital intensive industry with mixed mode of development or the mixed economy. Yet democracy has been institutionalized and a modicum of democratic culture has developed.

All institutions of democratic governance—Parliament, executive and judiciary – have been working in the best tradition of procedural democracy. Indian judiciary with Supreme Court at apex with High Courts at State level has ensured smooth functioning of all wings of systems—Executive and Legislature. It has religiously guarded citizen's rights and liberty against any executive and legislative transgression, upholding constitutional provisions and reinforcing rule of law. Above and overall these positivities, an independent and free press and media has performed satisfactorily as fourth State of democracy, acting as watchdog.

The religious and linguistic minorities have been enjoying freedom and rights without any discrimination. The Human Rights Commission of India and its counterparts in states have censored any transgressions by the State and its agencies undermining the rights and freedom of minorities. The Party System has evolved with national, regional, sectional, communal and linguistic underpinnings and perspective, aiding and abetting democratic values and norms, making the foundations of democracy in India stronger. From one party system to two party systems to multiparty—the Indian democracy has been, to some extent, aided and reinforced by the political parties.

The most remarkable and distinguishing aspect of Indian democracy is that it has outpaced its counterparts in western hemisphere in some respects, and may act as a model some time in future. While multiculturalism and minority views in democracies of Europe and American continents, mother and cradle of democracy respectively, are on descent, in Indian democracy it is on ascent as these are getting well-ingrained in the system. While Europe is getting increasingly xenophobic and suspicious about its minorities, tightening immigration rules and America going overboard in tightening the laws at the cost of some fundamental rights, the Indian democracy is providing a role model as how to respect minorities' views where they are enjoying more rights and preference as compared to other countries. Moreover, its ingrained value of village republic can act as truly decentralized institutional bulwark against the corrosive forces of democracy.

However, if one analyzes ground realities of Indian polity, one would not fail to notice, 'the fragmentation of polity in post Nerhuvian India has been coeval with the loss of faith in certainty of scientific objectivity. It is no longer possible to argue 'scientifically or rationally as it once was possible in the high modern era: the grounds of discourse have undergone tectonic shift, the very parameters of debate have changed, and the emotional needs of marginal have become as important as the so-called rational demand of central planning.[6] This has further cemented the bond of democracy by deepening its roots. The emotional needs of the marginalized have given Indian democracy much needed succour and support, grounding it to the hopes and aspirations of the common people, apart from that of elite and privileged.

Indian democracy, however, seems to be stuck up between the cliffs of centralized system, callous, insensitive and corrupt politico-bureaucratic set up grooved in colonial mindset, and the deep water of growing inequality, with 'Iron Law of Oligarchy' tightening its grip over every part of the system, and diminishing participation and representation. And this predicament in which Indian democracy finds itself wallowing for last two or three decades has become more precarious after chance globalization and liberalization in 1990 when balance of payment forced Indian political economy to go for privatization and liberalization, without any guidelines or plans.

This has resulted into, to put into what a former minister and Member of Parliament has to say, 'is it then surprising that we now face a huge contradiction between accelerating growth and inclusive growth? GDP measures the acceleration for few; the Gini coefficient measures the exclusion of more than three-quarters of our people from the acceleration. This is at the roots of conflicts…income and wealth inequalities are growing so alarmingly in our society that instead of being obsessed with the wholly misleading impression of progress indicated by the statistics of GDP growth (and per capita income derived from that figure) we need to recognize the more profound truth cached behind Oxford's Multi-Dimensional Poverty Index and the UN Human Development Index…'[7]

This is not the lonely voice of a frustrated politician or a socialist minister trapped in an environment becoming more capitalist, being further raided by predatory capitalism and growing arch of 'Iron Law of Oligarchy'. He has summed up the maladies having afflicted not only Indian democracy but that of general state of democracy as existing across the world. The inequality is growing across the world as is clear from various indicators, reports and shrinking standard of living, and growing number of poor and hungry. Despite the democracies across the world churning reams of paper singing GDP growth story and all round development registered thereby, the state of affairs is not that rosy as painted by the state and its agencies.

The Indian state after Independence inherited the same colonial structure of governance and administration, in the form of the Constitution, drafted by politico-legal coterie that colonial rulers put into place to serve their imperial interests. Whatever reforms and representation that colonial rulers conceded was mere cosmetic in nature, conceding only consultative power, and was primarily aimed at pacifying the nationalists who were demanding nothing sort of Independence. Whether it is Government of India Act 1935 or 1919 Act, it was in reference to pacifying their urge for 'Swaraj' or participation in executive or legislative body of colonial administration.

The document (Constitution) was set squarely in the best Western liberal tradition: no real trace of Gandhi's view could be found, and little was done to dismantle the centralizing and authoritarian powers of the state (the emergency provisions inserted by the British remained in place, conveniently available for future draconian use.[8] As one mortified member of the Constituent Assembly that was drafting the Indian Constitution put it, 'we wanted music of Veena and Sitar, but here we have the music of an English band' (Austin, 1966, 2009)

Pt. Nehru being idealist and influenced with western liberal tradition tried to neutralize the colonial and repressive state apparatus by superimposing some socialistic ideals. He mocked those for whom 'Swaraj (Self-government) means that everything continues as before, only with a darker shade.'[9] The Socialistic pattern of society that the Indian Constitution seeks to establish was included to counterpoise the draconian and colonial state apparatus. It gave some sort of semblance of the legitimacy to the indigenous rule as it seeks to chart a course of balanced development and growth, different from colonial rule. The insertion of Directive Principle of State Policies and Fundamental Rights were commendable step in this direction, matched with political economy or mixed economy with major role of public sector.

III

Political Economy of Indian Democracy

The socialist pattern of economy with maximum participation of public sector and limited share of private sector, which was adopted as panacea for all the ills of social and economic disparity, inequality, poverty and overall backwardness of the country failed miserably; and was scrapped altogether in 1991, when liberalization and privatization was resorted to blindly, just to tide over the temporary crisis of foreign exchange and beat the 'Hindu rate of growth'. When there was crisis in political economy in 1991 with growth rate hovering around, what is called 'Hindu growth rate' of 1.5 to 2 per cent , the contradiction came to fore. And foreign exchange kitty was not enough to sustain even one month of import bill.

There was no option but to forego the socialist economy and with that gone was dream of just and equalitarian society. It is one of the basic structures of our Constitution, but none dared or dares to raise their voice. One Public Interest Litigation (PIL) was filed at the fag end of 2009, but it was buried in the 'insensitive and mechanical state apparatus' and final burial ground was provided by the Supreme Court, which is final authority and interpreter of the Constitution. It was buck passing of all three pillars of Indian democracy which led to its demise. Undoubtedly, Indian state had no option other than dismantling the socialistic pattern of economic development as slow growth rate, precarious state of balance of payment, tardy industrial growth and stagnation that has set in the sector of economy has foreclosed any other option.

However, there would have been at least some clause or some check and balance which would have restricted unbridled growth of 'Predatory Capitalism' resulting into concentration of wealth and resources of the nation in a few hands of 54 billionaire and one million big and medium investors and entrepreneurs in cahoots with corrupt, myopic and shortsighted 'politicians-bureaucrats' nexus for short term ends. Had the policy makers given to some introspection and catharsis as to why the mixed economy based on socialistic pattern of development failed, they would have certainly found the common spoilers—centralized structure of power, corruption, lack of proper institutional and attitudinal support, predatory capitalists, oligarchy, cartelization, inefficient and corrupt bureaucracy, colonial mindset, petty politicking, crony capitalism – and would have perhaps saved the Indian democracy from present state of hollowness and loss of credibility.

After the demise of Soviet Union and communism, the term socialism was tagged with communism just to pre-empt any threat of socialism that it might pose. While the communist tried their best to hide their centralized and freedom denying system in the attractive jargon of socialism, and to gain respectability among gullible masses, the capitalism had field day. The way and the manner democracy has evolved since then has led to a system which has, and still is weakening democracy and democratic institutions by accentuating the inequality, monopolistic tendencies and imbalanced growth.

The tension in Indian society and systemic imbalance that has resulted from state apparatus working with colonial structures, rules and regulations, and above all the colonial mindset has weakened the case of democracy. The growing number of poor, hungry stomach, has intensified unrest in tribal land with Naxalism finding fertile ground for their clutch over hapless and exploited tribals who have been left out from all the 'economic boom and high GDP growth'. Ironically the state apparatus is going after Naxal, instead of trying to bring these tribal brethren within the fold of development and growth and mainstream. This is another manifestation of colonial mindset which sees Naxal problem as purely a law and order one.

There has been thinking among the members of the civil society that anti-Naxal operation has coincided with the move of some big business and industry houses in a bid to establish mining and other profit making ventures in these areas. Nevertheless, the socialistic pattern of economy and society envisioned on that was bound to fail, as colonial state apparatus, colonial structures and mindset remained intact [Khilnani, *op.cit*,125]. So may be the fate of new economic regime based on privatization, liberalization and globalization as the same colonial mindset, structures and rules and regulations have not only continued but has been further reinforced.

There is no doubt that the bad state of economy in general and that of balance of payment (with foreign exchange as meager as not able to foot the bill of one month of import) in particular in 1991 warranted a change or rather a sort of paradigm shift in Indian economy. Before going for privatization, liberalization and globalization lock, stock and barrel, there should have been some mechanism as to how high GDP growth would percolate to not only upper 20 per cent of Indian population but down to 80 per cent as well. But there was no such planning and thinking, the crisis of foreign exchange forced the government of the day to go for wholesale privatization and liberalization reportedly at the behest of the World Bank and International Monetary Fund.

Above all, the socialistic pattern of society, that our Constitution envisions, which is also one of the basic structures of the Constitution, should have at least been guiding principle for wholesale and reckless liberalization and privatization. Or some of its tenets such as minimal equalitarian or balanced growth or poverty removal in real sense of the term, not only on the paper should have been retained or acted as guiding principle. Had these been there, the cartelization, monopolistic and Erstraz capitalism would not have taken our political economy in its vicious grip. Even in the high temple of capitalistic and privatized economy, whose reigning deity is USA, there are many socialistic features such as public sector, social security system, and medical care, a sensitive and pro-people state apparatus.

Just contrast it with how post-1991 political economy in our country has evolved: the high GDP growth, which was slated to be panacea of problems such as poverty, unemployment, balanced growth, and touted to 'be one-shot dose for all evils of our economy and collateral damage that these give to our society and polity' has benefited only the upper 20 per cent of our population (including the middle class, the blue boy of national and international capitalists) in general and 54 billionaires and 1 million investor-cum-entrepreneur-middlemen-cum-corporate politicians. The 'trickle-down effect' has dried up while percolating downwards and meanwhile it has been diverted to tax haven banks of Switzerland where it has been transformed into 'ocean of corruption'.[10] Despite the fact that India has emerged as one of the key economy of the world and as on today it has become world's largest economy on PPP basis,[11] has also the highest number of poor, hungry and disparity in income and imbalanced growth.[12]

If one analyzes the political economy of Indian democracy, one would not fail to notice that first strand of economic development, which was patterned on major share of public sector and minor one for private or what was called mixed economy was based on 'trickle down approach'. It was thought that the development would trickle down to lower segment, but it did not happen as only upper and middle class were benefited. The vast masses were left out from it. It was thought that it was so because of the slow rate of growth, what was derogatorily called as 'Hindu rate of growth'. This was borrowed from western model of development prevalent in many European countries.

This imitative strategy of West (development) failed to contribute to the development and well-being of the deprived and disadvantageous sections of the rural people and to improve the quality of life of rural poor in India. While western style of economic progress was not forthcoming, the gap between the rich and poor particularly in the rural sector was widening in both relative and absolute terms. There were widespread economic disparities between regions and social groups, urban conglomeration marked by absence of minimum conditions of civic life, environmental degradation, rapid growth of unemployment, and erosion of traditional support system and an atomized society without providing alternative values of communal life.[13]

When the second strand of political economy was being mooted in 70s, there was again this oversight. Our policy makers did not learn their lesson from the first phase when the 'trickle down approach' failed to trickle down the lower segment of the society. When the third phase of political economy was being mooted, same approach was adopted whether inadvertently or advertently. It was thought that the GDP growth, financial speculation and booming share market and stock exchange would do way the poverty, inequality and other related problems. But it did not happen.

It was bound not to happen as the exploitative, corrupt and commission (an euphemism for bribe) based senior and middle level state and central machinery in rather obnoxious collaboration with businesses and political actors, aggrandized the benefits and help meant for the rural poor and masses. The famous quotation of one political actor, from the dynastic scion of Gandhi Family who has been ruling for the most of the Independent India be it directly or through proxy, that one Rupee meant for various schemes and development got reduced to 25 percent of the amount by the time it reached to the target still holds the stark reality. The observation was made in the context of the 'licence-permit Raj'. It is another matter that he did not do anything in this regard or was unable to do so due to the hold that his party satrap had or still have over this corrupt and insensitive state and non-state actors. In post-liberalized era, it is still holding the fort, only colour and complexion has changed.[14 15]

However, before jumping to any conclusion, it is pertinent to mention what Rudolphs[16] have to say in this regard. They have grounded the development of politics and political economy in India during the post-Independent period in the history of culture and economy. Firstly they question the projection of universality of European nation states with 'the loosely structured, sequentary, power sharing, multinational imperial form characteristic of Indian state formation.' What they want to put across is that the historical reality, which has been rejected by scholars and political scientists of all streams as jingoistic or narrow view of the state formation, has played vital role in state formation and political economy and growth of democracy.

The centrist form of Indian polity and political economy is a continuation of historical state formation and political economy from ancient time of (*sic* Krishna), Chandragupta-Chanakya, and Asoka, which was followed by Mughal, particularly Akbar in establishing an Empire *a la* Asoka the Great in mediaeval period to British Imperialism in modern period. According to them, Indian politics and political economy would remain centrist—middle of the road politically and economically as it has been in the past. Centrism has evolved as typical sub-continental phenomenon where state or central authority has upper hand in deciding the course of the history. In political economy, centrism means the state's role as powerful third actor balancing the antagonistic relationship between capital and labour. Apart from it, there are some other factors that warrant centrism: Fragmentation of politics, fracture in consensual politics, grabbing of the central power and constraints of federal structure arising out of social pluralism and cultural diversity. (Rudolphs, 2008)

According to Rudolphs, Indian state is strong and weak at the same time. The strong aspect emanates from remarkable industrial growth, and management of social and economic frictions. It is weak because it has failed in inclusive growth and development; vast section of rural population and depressed classes has been left out from the ambit of development and growth. Despite it, the state in India has remained autonomous due to lack of class politics. Its unique centrism in politics and political economy has remained untangled from fractious class politics due to social pluralism and cultural diversity making it inhospitable for class politics (*ibid*).

However, it is wellknown that Congress government in 1991 altered the development strategy and policy initiative to restructure the basis of economy leadıng to a major ideological shift from state-regulated economy to market-centred one. Some scholars believe that the foundation of this tectonic shift in Indian political economy was laid during the rule of Indira Gandhi and later during Rajiv Gandhi's regime. There were many indicators which pointed towards growing influence of private capital and big business group. Consequently, privatization and liberalization led to a change in balance of forces among public, private and foreign capital leading to greater role of capitalist sector. This endangered 'social contract' on which modern state is based (Hasan, 2009).

The shift in the class underpinnings of state in favour of an openly pro-capitalist state with neo-liberal ideology involved a switch from one set of policies to another. It entailed a shift from 'neutral' state standing above classes and mediating them to one that began to act prominently in the interest of the upper echelons of society and increasingly integrated in the global economy. Active state intervention can mitigate social and economic inequalities but the state has backed away from its role in providing welfare benefits to the vulnerable population (*ibid*).

This rather U-turn of the Indian political economy has left its Welfarism in limbo *a la* neoliberal credo. While corporate capital is dispossessing millions through primitive accumulation, the dispossessed are neither getting absorbed in to industry nor getting socially transformed as they were supposed to be, through proletriatization. This floating mass of labour, an enormous but shifting population of potential workers has instead become a constituent of what is called 'Political Society', as opposed to civil society, other important constituents of political society are small and marginal peasants, artisans, vendors and petty producers (Chatterjee, 2008).

The talk of ameliorative state intervention put forward by many scholars across the world is flawed. One of the defining characteristics of state under neoliberalism is its gradual retreat from the provision of public goods and social services, especially those services that might benefit the poor and the dispossessed. How Indian state under the influence of neoliberalism is withdrawing from welfare and ameliorative activities, there are many examples. During the last two or three decades of neoliberalism, the universal public distribution system (PDS) meant for the poor, marginalized and general public, has been systematically dismantled (Basu and Das, 2009).

Priority sector lending, expenditure on health, education and other areas of social sector has been blunted, if not dismantled altogether. The priority sector lending which was devised by Nehru to help farming, agriculture and related activities has been given debilitating blow steadily under the aegis of Indian neoliberal state. During the last 15 years, 4,750 rural banks branches have been closed down at the rate of one rural bank branch each day. During the year 2006 alone, one branch was shut down every six hours (Sainath, 2008).

Social sector expenditure has plummeted to the lowest possible limit during the past few years. In 1996, rural development expenditure as a proportion of net domestic product was 2.6 per cent, whereas the corresponding figure during the pre-liberalization Seventh Plan (1985 to 1989) was almost double at 4 per cent. From the mid-1980s to the fiscal of 2000, public development expenditure as a percentage of the gross domestic product (GDP) fell from 16 per cent to 6 per cent. Consequently, the growth rate of all crops fell from 3.8 per cent in the 1980s to 1.8 per cent in 1990s, while total agriculture investment expenditure as percentage of GDP fell from 1.6 per cent to 1.3 per cent. Using a constant calorie norm of 2000 calories, headcount poverty has risen from 56.4 to 69.5 per cent (Basu and Das, *op. cit*).

So far as various poverty alleviation programmes which are being touted as ameliorative face of the neoliberal state are aimed at keeping poor just alive. That is why the nomenclature of these programmes is mostly alleviation, not removal. 'Do we want to eliminate poverty, or just alleviate it? Can one legislate the poor should only have ailments that cost no more than Rs 30,000 a year? Are there diseases of the rich and those of the poor. .....Had (the ameliorative programmes such as) RSBY (Rashtriya Swasthya Bima Yojana) made the rich and poor indistinguishable at least in the field of health, that would have amounted to a policy breakthrough. In the same vein, the right to education should eliminate the distinction, at least egregious ones, between school facilities for the rich and the poor. Can we look that far ahead (Gupta, 2010)?

IV

Substantial Democracy

Nevertheless, only alternative to democracy and its political economy – capitalism – is democracy and capitalism itself, because democracy in its all forms, variations in general and representative democracy in particular has done yeomen service to the state, society and humanity in many respects.

"Representative democracy is democracy made safe for the modern state: democracy converted from unruly and incoherent master to docile and dependable servant. The second major political service which modern representative has furnished to its citizens is a modest measure of governmental responsibility to the governed...... In the face of sheer domestic power of the modern state, its ability to intrude into and devastate the lives of all its citizens, this is very considerable service indeed. It cannot ensure that prosperity or popular contentment. But what it can guarantee, for as long as the immediate civil and military servants of the State sustain and protect its constitutional order, is a collective security against a notably disagreeable common risk, the risk of permanent subjection to a keenly resented apparatus of rule."[17]

But this second form of protection against the risk of governmental harm has been one of the major goals of political action across the world in twentieth century—the main ideological premises of the collapse of the alien rule in the great European Empires, Eastern Europe and the Soviet Union itself and a permanent basis for the challenge to the existing territorial integrity of most of even the advanced states in the world. Another contribution of representative democracy, which may be counted as third contribution, has been making it safe for the modern state. Though it may appear a less significant one, yet it has some value in the sense that it has acted in tandem with modern state and modern capitalist economy. (Dunn, *ibid*)

However, this aspect of making democracy safe for the modern capitalist economy seems to have done more harm to democracy than anything else. Whatever distortions, inequality, injustices and imbalances that have set in have been because of the uninterrupted efforts to make democracy safe for the capitalist economy. The ideal situation should have been mutual give and take in making democracy safe for the capitalist economy as well as making latter safe for democracy. But this has been uni-directional: democracy and its foundational principles such as justice, equality and liberty have been compromised for the sake of the making it safe for market economy. Now this has slide to the free for all where 'making world safe for democracy' has led to the unravelling of democracy in many countries.

Herein lies the zero sum game matrix for democracy when every move or initiative taken in making democracy safe for capitalist economy resulted into loss for democracy, in the form of concentration of wealth and power in few hands, 'Iron Law of Oligarchy' making equality, justice and liberty hollow. The globalization and liberalization can be seen as suitable passage or pathway for this process of making democracy safe for capitalist economy. It is another matter that in that process democracy has become more hollowed. Now this has been reduced to the rhetoric of making democracy safe by neo-liberals and in that process it has inflicted irreparable damage to democracy and its loss of credibility. Had the things evolved other way round, making capitalist economy safe for democracy, it would have strengthened both and situation has not reached to precipice and vacuum that is at this historical moment.

While coming to substantial democracy as existing in India, one must consider as to what Dr. BR Ambedkar has to say in this regard: "In politics we will be recognizing the principle of one man, one vote and one vote one value. In our social and economic life, we shall, by reason of our social and economic structure, continue to deny the principle of one man one value. How long shall we continue to live this life of contradiction?"[18] Juxtaposed it with what Pt. Nehru has to say in this regard: 'In Pt. Nehru's picture of Indian politics, democracy would in time enable the disadvantaged to pursue their own interests. Social conflict would center on a struggle between rich and poor, as the poor came to organize for themselves and press for better terms.'[19]

While Nehru's vision has been realized to some extent, Dr. Ambedkar observation is still ringing and haunting the working of democracy. Though politically one man, one vote and one vote one value has been realized to some extent, in our social and economic life, this principle of one man one value continues to be denied to the vast majority of people due to our unjust, archaic, regimental and exploitative social and economic order. Ironically, that social and economic life that Dr Ambedkar mentioned during the framing of Indian Constitution still remains intact, denying social and economic equality to the vast majority of the people. "Even today, despite laws and policies against caste discrimination, more than 165 million of Dalits (Downtrodden, lower caste, Scheduled Castes and Scheduled Tribes and exploited ones) are condemned to a life time abuse simply because of their caste."[20]

Despite elaborate provisions in the Constitution and other laws, it is an unfortunate reality that there is social injustice and exploitation of Scheduled Cates and Scheduled Tribes and other weaker sections.[21] Over one-sixth of India's population, some 170 million people lives a precaricus existence, shunned by much of Indian society because of their rank as 'Untouchable' or Scheduled Castes at the bottom of society.[22] The system of such social inequality is still intact despite the opposite stand taken by political and social elites and official record. What is worse that this vast section of the populace is also suffering from economic inequality which makes their lives inhuman and barbaric.

Hence, so far as substantial democracy is concerned, India has fared very miserably. This has been primarily because the state apparatus that colonial rulers have resurrected to maintain its oppressive and exploitative rule have remained intact. While during first Plan, the priority was given to agriculture, the priority and emphasis was shifted to industry in second plan. Since then, agriculture and rural development has never found priority among the policy makers and decision making bodies whether from Left or the Right or Right of the Center or Left of the Centre. Whether be it in pre-liberalization era or the post-liberalization era of political economy, the root of the problem was never attended to. The collaborators and beneficiaries of 'licence-permit' Raj has changed their colours like chameleon over the years and become the champions of liberalization, and globalization to loot the public money and chiffon them to the secret accounts of foreign banks, in the name of doing business.

There may be some merit in opinion held by some scholars that the "mismatch between people's expectation and inability of the system to deliver the good" has been because Indian democracy was 'choice by elite' which has not been earned through "popular pressure". The Constituent Assembly that drafted the Constitution of India was "unrepresentative", the election for this was held on 'limited franchise' and 300 additional members from the princely states were just added, and it was 'baroque legal promissory note, with 'ambitious political design'(Khilnani, *ibid*). However, this ambitious political design has failed to materialize and has been unable to ground democracy.

Setting aside the debate of Constitution, which is a visionary document seeking to establish an egalitarian society based on justice and equality[23], it is the political actors who have failed miserably to deliver the promise granted by the Constitution. It may appear to be 'baroque legal promissory note', but those who are its custodian have to share major blame for this chaos. For example, the socialistic pattern of society that the Constitution seeks to establish has been implemented half-heartedly and even that has been discarded for what has been termed as 'predatory capitalism' without any disquiet on any front, without any protest. This was taken as a stamp of consensus for the dumping of socialistic pattern of society, without any hullabaloo. Moreover, scant regard has been given to the Directive Principle of State Policy which is a visionary and the most revolutionary part containing Gandhian dreams and values, apart from other lofty ideals.

Meanwhile, the lopsided, imbalanced and haphazard growth and development has led to disquiet, simmering tension, which has manifested in different forms of insurgency, Naxalism, secessionist and sub-national movements, demand for autonomy, sectional and sectarian violence and other problems. The tribals, the Dalits (Scheduled Castes, Scheduled Tribes, lower and backward classes) who constitute almost 70-80 per cent of the population has been left out from the development and growth story; in fact their plight has been aggravated by the insensitive state apparatus, which has moved farther away from their reach, hopes and aspirations. Our democracy has made the people enjoy freedom. But it has not made the people to lead a healthy and creative life. Our democracy faces challenges in managing economic growth and development. Our governance and administration faces challenges in managing poor.[24]

This is not good for the future of democracy in India as it would lead to its virtual withering and then 'end of the end of the history project' would not be far away. However, it can be saved by the awakened civil society which has been in deep slumber for over the years. Though civil society has been acting on some local issues such as acquiring of agricultural land for private business, for SEZ (Special Economic Zone) or some environmental issues, yet there has been no organized mass movement for the broader issue of governance or economic or social right as has been witnessed preceding, during and after Emergency when political movement under the leadership of Jayaprakash Narayan or the social movements such as civil liberty, ecology, women and Dalits.

There has been no dearth of political and social movements in the past, but in post-liberalization era these have been missing in political or social sphere. This has emboldened the state and government to ride roughshod in implementing neo-liberal agenda undermining the social, economic and political equality, and the rights of people. '…. (These) have not contributed much to the overall social transformation, primarily because the efforts in most instances are sporadic and short term and civil society assertions have by and large remained isolated, and have failed to link up with similar assertions in other part of the country. This has hampered the overall social (*sic* political) transformational agenda. A well-organized alliance within civil society has been lacking.'[25]

These lacuna needs to be attended to so that civil society and various organizations can play their transformational agenda on more broad based level. Hence hitherto left out segment such as traditional groups need to be included. Moreover, there is a need to instuitionalise this transformative agenda of the civil society through democratized political auditing and its institutionalization.

Endnotes

1 Joshua Kurlantzick, *How democracy dies: A global decline in political freedom is partly the fault of the Middle Class,* Newsweek, March 22, 2010

2 McClure, Jason, *'Africa: Why Democracy is not Working'*, Newsweek, June 28 and July 5, 2010.

3 Sutton Trust has warned that UK's parliament has become more elitist and 'does not reflect society at large'. Sudeshna Sen, 'Oxbridge MPs Britain bane! Observers Dub Parliament Gathering of Elite & Out of Touch With Working Classes', *The Economic Times*, dated 11.05.2010.

4 Desai, Meghnad, "Why is India a Democracy?" in David Page (ed.) *Divided by Democracy*, Lotus Collection\Roli Books : New Delhi, 2005. p56

5 Khilnani, *ibid*

6 Banerjee, Milinda, 'An Intellectual History of Independent India', *The Sunday Statesman*, 27.12. 2009

7 Aiyar, Mani Shankar, 'India is prospering, Indians are not', *The Hindustan Times*, dated 15th August, 2010.

8 Khilnani,, '*op. cit.* pp 89

9 Nehru, Jawaharlal, *Autobiography*, 1936, London

10 'There are other guesstimates that black money in India is equal to the legitimate of the GNP of the country. Black money in India is estimated at between Rs. 80,000 to 150,000 crore. And it is growing in size and its menacing. 'Public money is like holy water; everybody dips his hand into it.' 'Ghotala (Shady dealings), scam, scandals and fraud—these terms represent the essentials of the dominant discourses from the market place to the secluded and walled bastions of power. One of the main causes of this pervasive black money is the grabbing by corrupt leaders, officials and contractors, of a big chunk of funds meant for construction and development. They collect this money as it was accruing from their 'private tax'. Ahmad Shamshad and Nafees Ahmad Ansari, 'Corruption, Criminalization of politics and Development', *Indian Journal of Public Administration*, vol. LIV, No. 4, October-December, 2008, p.868

11 World Bank, http://siteresources.worldbank.org/datastatitics/ Resources/gdp.ppp

12 UNDP Human Development Report, 2010.

13 Ghosh, Maya, 'Institutionalizing Democracy at the Grassroots for People's participation in Development Planning – An Experiment in West Bengal', *The Indian Journal of Public Adminisrtation*, Vol. LV, no2 , pn. 209, 2009.

14 '....The government machinery remains colonial in its functioning because it is not constituted to be accountable and responsible to the rights of citizens as citizens. Acquiring a foothold in the government machinery brings with it enormous clout and opportunities for upward mobility through means fair and foul. People perforce have to mobilize themselves as communities in order to gain a measure of protection and privilege. Those who cannot pull through their caste and family ties feel vulnerable and thwarted. ...The resultant vicious tussles over gaining a foothold in offices of power have made virtually every group feel aggrieved and insecure. Therefore, it does not take much effort to mobilize new groups to demand their share of the pie. ... The faults of our representative institutions and colonial-minded governance cannot really be corrected through the quota mechanism. Other more radical remedies are required involving far-reaching electoral and administrative reforms. Kishwar, Madhu Purnima, *op. cit.*56

15 'Indian democracy is in danger of subversion by a self confident, aggressive, articulate, patriotic and well meaning force, the oligarchy of successful.... Danger lies in the

fact that this creamy layer of 20 per cent at the top has no interest in involving the froth of 80 per cent in decision-making. This emerging constituency, perhaps a maximum of 300 million, is keen to outsource its future to an oligarchy because it has sniffed the latter's success. It is strong enough to shift general elections towards one political or other, but it is not strong enough to sustain governance. That leaves 800 million on goodwill.' Akbar, M. J, 'Danger from the New Brahmins', *The Times of India*, dated 07.02.2010

16 See Rudolphs

17 Dunn, John, (Ed), *Democracy: The Unfinished Journey—508Bc to Ad 1993*, Oxford University Press, London 1992.

18 Dr. Ambedkar, B.R, 1948, Discussion during Constituent Assembly, AIR

19 Khilnani, S, *The Idea of India*, p 39, Hamish Hamilton, London, 1997.

20 National Human Rights Commission Report, 2002.

21 NHRC, 2004

22 Darshan Singh, *Atrocities against Scheduled caste: Highlights the role of Police.* Indian Police Journal, Vol.LVII, No1, New Delhi

23 See the Constitution of India: Fundamental Rights and Directive Principle of State Policy

24 Gupta, Naresh, *Democracy and Human Development in India*, Publication Division, New Delhi, 2008.

25 Tandon, Rajesh and Mohanty Ranjita, *Civil Society and Governance*, PRIA, New Delhi, 2005

References

Ambedkar, B. R. (1950) Speech in the Constituent Assembly, 25th November 1949, *Constituent Assembly Debates*, Vol 12. New Delhi

Austin, Granville (1966) *The Indian Constitution: Cornerstone of Nation*, Oxford University Press

---------------- – (2009) *Working a Democratic Constitution: The Indian Experience*, Vedam Books: Delhi/Chennai

Basu, Deepankar, Das, Debarishi (2009): "Political Economy of Contemporary India: Some Comments" *The Economic and Political Economy*, Vol XLIV, no 22, May 30

Chatterjee, Partha (2008): "Democracy and Economic Transformation in India", *Economic and Political Weekly*, volume 43, No 16, 19-25 April.

Dahl, Robert A, (1971) *Polarchy*, New Heaven: Connecticut

Dumenil, G and D Levvy (2004): *Resurgent Capital: The Roots of the Neoliberal Revolution*, Cambridge, MA: Harvard University Press.

Drez, Jean (2008): "Employment Guarantee: Beyond Propaganda', *The Hindu*, 11 January

Gupta, Dipankar (2010) 'Keeping the Poor Alive' *The Times of India,* April 2, 2010

Hasan, Zoya, "The Enduring Challenge of Building a Just Society", *The Economic and Political Weekly*, Vol XLIV No. 22, May 30, 2009, p 24

Kohli, Atul, Ed. (1988) *India's Democracy*, Princeton

Pareto, Vilfredo, (1971) *Manual of Political Economy*. Augustus M. Kelley, (translation of French edition from 1927).

Patnaik, Utsa (2008) "Neoliberal Roots", *Frontline*, Vol 25, Issue 06, 15-28 March.

Lindblom Charles E. (1977), *Politics and Markets: The World's Political-Economic Systems*, New York: Basic

---------------------- (2001) *The Market System: What It Is, How It Works, and What to Make of It*, Yale University Press

Nye, Robert A. (1977) *The Anti-democratic Sources of Elite Theory : Pareto, Mosca, Michels*, Sage Publications:

Rudolph, Lloyd and Rudolph, Susanne Hoeber (2008): *Explaining Indian Democracy: A Fifty Year Perspective*, 1956-2006, Oxford: Delhi

---------------------- *'The Sub-continental Empire and Regional Kingdom in Indian State Formation' in their book, Explaining Indian Democracy: A Fifty Year Perspective*, 1956-2006, Oxford: Delhi. 2008

Saad-Filho, A and D Johnston (2005): *Neoliberalism: A Critical Reader* (ed) London: Pluto Press

Sanyal, Kalyan (2007): *Rethinking Capitalist Development: Primitive Accumulation, Governmentality and Post-Colonial Capitalism*, New Delhi: Pluto Press.

Sainath, P (2008): "4,750 Rural Bank Branches Closed Down in 15 years". *The Hindu*, 28 March

Vasudev, Uma (1974) *Indira Gandhi: Revolution in Restraint.*

SECTION FOUR

ENEMIES OF DEMOCRACY

Democracy has been subjected to all round onslaught from all possible fronts- and there is every possibility that there would be 'end of end of history' project, if urgent corrective measures are not taken at macro and micro level. There are many forces and factors that may seem to be strengthening or aiding democracy but in fact are preparing the burial ground for democracy. For example, the latest in-thing in the jargon of democracy is making world safe for democracy and it is being championed by neo-liberal hawks. How the world has been made safe for democracy is being witnessed in the instability and unending violence in Iraq, Indonesia, Afghanistan, Sudan, Libya, Somalia and other countries where efforts are being made to make it safe for democracy.

Borrowing terms from Karl Popper's works,[1] one can easily trace as to which one is a friend or foe of democracy. The enemy-friend distinction is just an effort to illustrate as to which factor is aiding democracy and which is not. It is just an attempt to examine whether the factor that is supposed to strengthen democracy is doing so or otherwise.

Before going into the discussion of as to which one is the friend or foe of democracy, it is pertinent to clear the web of haze and ambiguity, created advertently or inadvertently, regarding the role of tradition and traditional institutions vis-a-vis. It is believed that tradition and traditional institutions such as caste, tribal council, creed, race or very structure of the traditional societies is holding back the democracies across the continents of Asia, Africa and Latin America. Tradition and traditional institutions have been blamed for the failure of democracy grounding in these countries, ranging from India to Sudan, from West Asia to Bolivia. Even Western thinkers and scholars cannot absolve themselves from reinforcing this myth of tradition vs. modernity so far as the grounding of democracy is concerned.

This myth has been discarded by many scholars, ranging from Sunil Khilnani[2] to Lloyd Rudolph and Susanne Hoeber Rudolph.[3] While Khilnani has categorically said that it is wrong to blame traditional institutions such as caste and clan or tribalism for the backwardness of India and its inability to ground democracy, contrary to general belief it has given momentum and more succinct ground to give a new direction to Indian politics. The marginalized and downtrodden groups have used these institutions to rally around to have their share in power and privileges, giving inclusiveness touch to Indian democracy (Khilnani, 2005).

After analyzing the Indian situation in matrix of modernity vs. traditional, Rudolphs have found them as supplementary of modernity contrary to popular or general prevalent view that castes have held back India's development. Casteism has provided rather much needed impetus to Indian democracy by providing an important link between electorate and leadership. This challenges the prevalent notion of culture and caste as fixed system and views these as dynamic system instead. Contrary to it as an anachronistic role, caste and caste-based groups and organizations have helped in political mobilization through participation in the formal and informal political process.

Discarding the binary of modernity and tradition, Rudolphs have discovered that traditional form of social organizations such as caste have grounded and strengthened democracy, facilitating political integration into modern politics. Thus, contrary to belief that caste is an archaic institution, it is a medium of political integration and development. The dismantling and penetration of traditional system of power and hierarchy by lower and backward castes through social and political association and mobilization proves this point (Rudolphs, 2008).

Despite the criticism that such identity politics as caste, creed, etc has resulted into fragmentation of Indian polity and virtual breakdown of party system, it has done yeoman service to Indian democracy by giving voice to marginalized and depressed classes of Indian society. But even within the realm of identity politics it is open to criticism that it neglects the politics of more disadvantaged group or the politics from below (Hasan, 2009). However, recent churnings in Indian politics, particularly in some North Indian states have proved that even this 'more disadvantaged groups' could not be ignored any more.

I

Poor Governance and Selfish and Short-sighted Elites (Leaders)

In recent discourses on democracy and development, governance or lack of governance has found wide acceptance. It is being emphasized as an important factor in the development and the grounding of democracy. The credit for this rather paradigm shift goes to World Bank which brought forth the concept of 'good governance' in the discourse on development.[4] The shift from government to 'governance' has taken more than four to five decades after the Second World War when reconstruction of war ravaged world and the nation building of countries newly freed from colonial rule was launched on war footing. However, the governments across the world failed to respond effectively to the diverse need of the populace. It resulted in the increasing marginalization of poor, downtrodden and even common people.

"With increasing gap in the policies of the governments and their practical elaboration, with growing distance with the alienation of the poor and marginalized from the elite-dominated institutions of government with continuous persistence of problems of poverty, exclusion and marginalization in many countries of the world, and with growing importance of national and transnational private business interest, the concept of the government has given way to governance. In its basic meaning, the governance is however equated with functioning of the state and consequently, the good governance is equated with the efficient functioning of the state and institutions and promotion of equity and social justice."[5]

The World Bank defines governance as the manner in which power is exercised in the management of economic and social resources of a country (World Bank, 2009). The Department for International Development programme (DFID) sees governance as how the rules and systems of the state or different branches of the government—the executive, legislative and judiciary—operate at central and local levels and how the state relates to individual citizens, civil society and private sector (DFID Papers, 2008).

According to United Nations Development Programme (UNDP), the governance is an exercise of economic, political, and the administrative authority to manage a country's affairs at all levels. It comprises mechanisms, processes and institutions through which citizens and groups articulate their interests, exercise their legal rights, meet their obligations and mediate their differences. (UNDP, 2008) Whereas the Organization for Economic Cooperation and Development (OECD) views governance as the use of political authority and exercise of control in a society in relation to the management of its resources for social and economic development, encompassing the role of public authorities in establishing the environment in which economic operators function and in determining the distribution of benefits as well as the nature of the relationship between the ruler and ruled (OECD, 2009).

However, before going deep in discussing as to how bad governance and selfish leadership is enemy of democracy, it is pertinent to quote an anecdote concerning Kautilya or Chanakya and a Chinese ambassador. When a Chinese ambassador visited the then Prime Minister of Great Patliputra Empire and saw his residence as merely built of mud and thatch, he commented: 'Oh! How come the Prime Minister of a great country resides in hut'? Chanakya replied: 'Where the prime minister resides in a hut, the people of that country have grand palaces and beautiful houses. Whereas if the prime minister of a country has grand palaces, the people have to live in huts.[6]

'If King (Ruler) is good and benevolent, then the people will be good and benevolent, and if the Ruler is evil-hearted and negligent, the people or subject or ruled will be the same. The people follow their King or ruler. The people or the subject is just like their rulers.'[7] These two sum up the role of leadership in governance and transformation of a society or a nation. The leaders and their leadership qualities such as foresightedness, long term and short term plans, vision and love and dedication decide the fate and future of nation, society and the people. However, recently in a discourse on leadership and the type of the people or political culture, it is otherwise: People are being blamed for the type of leaders who are elected in democratic countries across the world. It seems to be just an alibi for the ruling elites to hide their shortsightedness and selfishness.

The type of governance that a country like India and other developing countries are being subjected to is best reflected in their poverty alleviation programmes. The very nomenclature of 'alleviation' itself denotes the ad hoc approach having streaks of populism. The suffix 'eradication' missing from the various programmes related to poverty, employment and rural development itself speaks for the type of governance that is being given to the people. 'Poverty attracts two kinds of policy interventions. The first hopes to eradicate it and the second wants to keep the poor alive. In India, our prime effort has always been, right from the days of *antodaya* (upliftment of people living on margins), to somehow keep the poor ticking, even at the lowest level of subsistence. The National Rural Employment Guarantee Act (NREGA) saves the impoverished from starvation on a six-monthly basis. We see the same mindset at work in the way national health insurance policy, the Rashtriya Swasthya Bima Yojana (RSBY) has been devised. Here again the target group is below poverty line (BPL) families and the relief given is inadequate.'[8]

'India is a natural superpower kept under leash by colonial control through native leaders….. The ugliest phase of capitalism is continuing in India for the benefit of the elite, in violation of even the inappropriate Indian Constitution.' (Mukhopadhya, *ibid*, Para 2) Even the violation of one of the basic structures of Constitution, which is mentioned in the Preamble of Constitution as establishment of 'socialistic pattern of society…' has been given short-shrift. How these elites have demolished colonies and shop of poor and marginalized to open Mall, how these elites are being dictated by foreign powers in economic and foreign policies[9] are some of the few examples that illustrate the type of political actors we have. They are trying to keep us limited to our region through proxies of Pakistan and China, but our bigoted and selfish leaders are parroting the stand as dictated by neo-liberal hawks swooping down across the Atlantic.

"It is perplexing how the world's most populous democracy is so flawed. How can a country whose elections are cited as an example of people-power, produce governments that serve their people so badly."[10] They do not serve the people but rules over them. This is the crux of the problem. This ethos has been born and mixed in the blood of politicians and bureaucrats that have been borrowed from colonial rulers. It is the sub-culture of the culture of colonial rules, system and apparatus that we have supplanted after Independence.

Economic growth, rather than being a force for democratic involvement, reinforced the confidence of business elites. These neo-liberal advocates became consumed by their own intellectual overshoot, redefining democracy and liberty through notions such as privatization, profit maximization, disdain for the needs of civil society and social justice. What matters, particularly for the middle class, are 'private freedoms'—the right to own property; to run businesses according to contract law; the right to travel unimpeded and right to determine one's own personal life. The pre-eminent freedom is financial—the right to earn money and consume it unimpeded. Public freedom such as free speech, free association, and participatory politics become dispensable.[11]

This is the type of growth and development that has been ushered into by the governance based on GDP and share market. Democracy and liberty has come to mean freedom to loot the resources for the benefits of the few. To justify their loot, democracy and liberty is being cleverly rather cunningly reinterpreted in the context of privatization, profit maximization and utter disdain for the social justice and the welfare of civil society. The very concept of freedom and liberty has changed from political and social to financial one. For middle class freedom has become privatized divested from social context and becoming a mere licence to wallow in luxuries, while the masses are fighting their battle with hunger and poverty.

The main problem is that India lacks a "clearly defined ruling class", having the capacity to enforce their vision. In most of the cases they don't have a vision at all as personality cult and personal or class or caste interests that he or she may belong to dominate their dealings. Right from the beginning, this has been the feature and it is continued till date. And this generally entices the "social groups and classes to form alliances" for successfull 'recapture' of the state. It transforms the identity of political actors from an agent of change and development to a "selective disburser of public resources."[12]

Such selfish elites in general and political leaders in particular are the one of the main enemies of Indian democracy. 'Those in power, and those hungering for power, play the religious/ethnic card for collective action without responsibility.... The power-wielders are clearly callous to the needs of the public that elect them, and contrary to being servants of the people, they soon make people servants. ... We truly do not deserve the leaders we get. The phoenix (metaphor for India) is trapped in the conjoint effect of status differentials, extreme scarcity at the lower levels, and inaccessibility to institutions of democratic governance.'[13]

Governance, for these bigoted and myopic leaders, is just façade to follow their own narrow, personal and pecuniary interests. At best, they can throw the largesse of attractive contracts, coveted posts and unlimited scope for ill-gotten money at public expense to their kinsmen or caste or class interests. To win elections and put stay in power, they may dump their own very plank on which they have been elected and openly flout religious and ethnic interests, undermining the collective interest. These leaders are the typical examples of enjoying power without any responsibility. No wonder that these self-proclaimed leaders soon dump the very public which voted them to the power, and make them virtual servant who wait incessantly with folded hands for their glimpse. And the wait more often than not gets stretched to weeks and months until and unless they give in.

The accessibility to the institutions of democratic governance has become so restricted and privileged that a class of touts, middlemen and *Dalal*, who like vultures feed on the helplessness and weaknesses of the people, have come into scene to facilitate this. For getting the basic necessities or what are fundamental rights, people have to grease the palms of the greedy state authorities and government functionaries. In such a scenario, how can the masses feel associated with such callous system that keep them waiting and where there are hierarchies of restrictions? This is what is being given in the name of governance, democratic institutions and by the democratically elected leaders and bureaucracy functioning under democracy!

Same is the case with world leaders whose selfish and myopic view is taking world to precipice, the leaders world over are advertently or inadvertently presiding over 'end of the end of history' project. Those who are ruling over the world are putting our civilization to the risk of devastation and destruction due to their selfishness and disillusion. The world leaders think that they can face the challenges of 21st century through renaissance ethos and values of 18th century. The main problem of these leaders irrespective of the countries and continents is that they are self-centred and myopic in their view. They are so selfish that they cannot think beyond their own interest, forgetting that every ripple that is generated in a lake touches or affects the whole.

The whole world, more so in a globalized era, is interlinked. But they are unable to see beyond their boundaries in a time when borders are crumbling and distances are shrinking. They want to develop their countries at the expense of others. The result is for everyone to see: Global warming, depletion of resources, world sitting on the ticking bomb of weapon of mass destruction and terrorism, civil war, food riots, etc. The only hope for people of the world is to come forward, organize themselves and realize the ideal of a global village.[14]

Governance vs. Opportunism

The governance is being given short-shrift by the leaders as they are more concerned in maintaining their hold on power and perks. There is vast mismatch between the promises and actual delivery. As one member of Planning Commission has commented that government declaration is high on rhetoric but low on actual delivery. The government promised that it would allocate six per cent of Gross Domestic Product (GDP) to education, but only 3.02 per cent was allocated during 2006-07. This is less than even that of least developed countries like Ethiopia. Even health is given a paltry amount as during 2005-06 it was allocated 0.27 per cent of GDP, in 2006-07 it was 0.28 per cent and in 2007-08 0.37 per cent of GDP. Under 11th Five Year Plan, only 3.08 per cent of GDP was allocated for depressed classes (SC and ST) and backward classes constituting 22.5 per cent and 52 per cent of the population respectively.[15]

The government of the day has been making much noise and self-patting in case of employment guarantee schemes. The irony is that majority of the people are not aware of the scheme. This scheme like other plethora schemes is just benefiting the intermediary and agents who are cornering the money and showing result on paper. Even the so-called audit of the scheme is the more publicity and propaganda stunt than real concern for the upliftment of the poor. The surprising fact is that despite implementation of many plans and schemes and spending billion of rupees on these, the number of landless have increased from 22 per cent in 1990s to 35 per cent at the end of first decade of new millennium.[16]

Almost 65 per cent of the Indian population is dependent upon agriculture, but it is proving to be loss making venture. As most of the farmers are landless, they cannot avail the benefits of the schemes and various subsidies doled out by the government which is being cornered by the rural rich, big and intermediate farmers. ... While farmers are committing suicide, the government is unable to put any agriculture policy and scheme for them. One of the downside of the removal of 'Licence–permit Raj' or in another word the liberalization and privatization is that while earlier the rural women and artisan used to earn their livelihood by selling homemade items such as spices, and other consumables, now they have been replaced by the big national and foreign companies. The big business houses like Tatas and Ambanis have started selling grounded flour, salt, pickles, vegetables and consequently millions have been rendered jobless and hungry as their professions have been gobbled up by these giants of Indian industries. The big companies have snatched the livelihood of the millions connected with small and cottage industries.[17]

As Pankaj Mishra points out in order to fulfill their ambition in a country of such poverty, inequality and misrule, the Indian elites have had to create a parallel universe.[18] A universe where even the aroma of poverty and inequality did not filter and they have everything at their disposal: money stacked in stock market, real estate, businesses, and black money in tax heavens of foreign banks. They are oblivious of the ground reality. Once they are elected, they are least bothered about their people, their country and society. They have their private jet and ready money (that of poor Indians) to cool their heels in cooler climes of Europe and America, and like their counterparts in dictatorship or authoritarian countries a mansion to flee the heat and the dirt of the country, if the exigencies demand. This is the rule rather than the exception to be found in almost all countries whether it is democracy or dictatorship.

It is interesting to note the way the Indian and Chinese systems fare in the delivery of good governance and liberty. In China, most of the wealthy (political or as otherwise) elites find the small pro-democracy movement as encumbrance. These political activists are disturbing the pact that ensures one-party hegemony in return for social stability, continual economic growth and respect for 'private' freedoms. In return, individuals do not meddle with the state. As Pallavi Aiyar, a China based journalist has commented, 'while in China the Communist party derived its legitimacy from delivering growth' in India the government derived its legitimacy simply from having been voted in. The legitimacy of democracy in many ways absolved Indian governments from the necessity of performing. The Chinese Communist party could afford no such luxury (Kamfner; *op. cit.*).

The problem in India, particularly since economic liberalization in 1991, is not wealth creation; nor is it democratic institutions. It is the governance, the inability to deliver freedoms (economic, social and other related) for the vast majority of its people. Politics and business have worked together to use power as a means of enrichment. The comfortable classes could have been active in the public realm. Unlike in authoritarian states, they would not have been punished for causing trouble. They chose not to. The level of complicity is, therefore, surely higher.[19]

Governance vs. Vested interests

The governance has degenerated into proxy rule by capitalist and big business. During the election, they do untransparent funding and sponsoring. Once government is saddled into power, they extricate the prices which are usually ten times more than what they contributed to. The rulers obliged by trading their legitimacy for gaining short term petty interest of financial security, abdicating their morality in favour of hyperbole and rhetoric. It has become standard practice that after every election, there is steep rise in the prices of essential and non-essential commodities across the board.[20]

It is just other way to extricate or recover the huge cash and kinds that big, intermediate and even small industrial and business houses generously splurge during election. The government that comes to power oblige them by looking other way while the prices are being jacked up. The opposition makes some noises, but do not go overboard lest it upset the system of election as they also get some share of this booty depending upon their chance of winning. Many attempts in past to streamline the election funding by making it state-funded and transparent have been bulldozed by collective might of ruling and opposition parties

After much haggling and protracted struggle between the political parties, Election Commission, judiciary, Non-governmental organizations (NGOs) working in the field of clean public life and civil society, the only progress has been the partial ceding of ground in this regard. The limit of per candidate that he or she can spend has been set and there is provision of filing election expenditure before Election Commission. A candidate is not free to spend as much as he likes on his election. The law prescribes that the total election expenditure shall not exceed the maximum limit prescribed under Rule 90 of the Conduct of Election Rules, 1961. It would also amount to a corrupt practice under Sec 123 (6) of RP Act, 1951. The limit for election expenditure is revised from time to time. At present the limit of expenditure for a parliamentary constituency in bigger states like UP, Bihar, Andhra Pradesh, Madhya Pradesh is Rs. 25 lakhs. The limit of election expenditure for an assembly constituency in the bigger states is Rs. 10 lakhs.[21]

It is very easy for political parties to hoodwink the watchdog by filing underinvoiced election expenditure. This is a very convenient arrangement where there is win-win situation for all involved in this untransparent, unaccountable and undemocratic practice. The only looser is governance and people or masses or civil society.

However, sometimes situation goes out of control, particularly in case of price rise of essential commodities, hoarding, speculation, etc. When faced with such situation, the skeletons form cupboard of government of the day starts tumbling, exposing complicity of all stakeholders in this undemocratic practice. Started by Mrs. Indira Gandhi in 1967s when she broke the backbone of the 'Syndicate' and 'regional satraps' by splitting the Congress into two, this culture has got well ingrained in the system known by many nomenclatures such 'Suitcase Culture' or 'Personal meeting between the leader of parties and Industrialist or businessman', etc. (Khilnani, *op. cit.*). More often than not it comes in open as in case of price rise when there is free for all, exposing chinks in the collective armour of ruling parties at centre, state and opposition respectively.

Usually, there is free for all; charges and counter charges fly from all directions. There starts a game wherein all are winners, only looser is democracy and its principles of transparency, accountability and ultimately the governance. While opposition party or parties blame the ruling party or the government of the day, the government at the centre does the most convenient thing of passing the buck to the governments in states ruled by different parties from that of at centre. '.....the government (at centre) working under the influence of capitalists and its policies were helping "balckmarketeers and hoarders". ... 'It is clear that centre is working under the influence and pressure of capitalists'. ... 'The center's 'faulty' economic, import and export policies and its "tendency to benefit capitalist and big business". ... Instead of framing capitalist-oriented policies, the centre should frame policies keeping in mind the common people"..... for this (price rise) states are responsible.[22]

The governance and its commitment are best reflected through resource allocation to various social sectors. The resource allocations to the education, health, etc are cause and effect of balanced development, and it also reflects the commitment of the government towards general populace. The 134th ranking of India on the Human Development Index out of 182 countries itself is a tell-tale sign of the type of governance existing in the country. The budgetary allocation to various social sectors also reflects the state of governance. The total budget outlay on education has increased marginally from 3.88 per cent in 2009-10 to 4.5 per cent in 2010-11(Economic Survey, 2010). It is much below the minimum 6 per cent which was recommended 44 years ago by Kothari Commission.

The state of health sector seems to be far worse than the education. While the health expenditure accounts for less than one per cent of GDP, private sector has monopoly over healthcare services. There has been marginal increase of 0.2 per cent from 2.1 per cent of GDP in 2009-10 to 2.3 per cent in 2010-11. As far as proportion of GDP, the total expenditure of Centre and states increased from approximately 1.02 per cent in 2008-09 to 1.06 per cent in 2009-10.[23]

What is deplorable is that even this paltry sum allocated for important social sectors such as health remains unspent. Many cases of unspent sum allocated for health has come to notice of the competent authority. It has been found in the review of National Rural Health Mission that a huge amount was not spent in the balances of the many states. Many flaws and irregularities have also been found and these range from centralized planning, poor fund management and non-achievement of targets.[24]

The continuation of reservation policy is another commentary on the state of governance in India. 'In a multi-ethnic, multilingual, multi-religious, multi-caste society with wide disparities, there are bound to be ever newer claimants for reservations, especially considering the poor state of governance in India, the lack of basic security, especially for women, and widespread nepotism.'[25]

The state of general administration and policing is intrinsically related to governance and is a succinct barometer to measure the type of leadership being provided. It is more relevant in a country like India where these two come under the direct control of political actors. The general administration and policing is based on the same structures and superstructures that colonial rulers resurrected to prolong their rule and administer their colony. Even the very wordings have been borrowed from the imperial legal code. The police and general administration to a large extent in South Asia, modelled on Irish colonial-militaristic which British colonial masters imported in their erstwhile colonial empire, mostly operated as an 'oppressive instrument of state power rather than as protectors of citizen's rights. It has resulted into large scale human rights violations and denial of justice. "Even the absolute and non-decodable right against the use of torture is abused by the police throughout South Asia."[26]

The problems with policing in the region are that it is oppressive, unfair and inefficient; there is a culture of impunity for wrongful acts perpetrated by the police; there is very little effective oversight or review of police conduct; there is a serious lack of resources for policing; there is illegitimate political interference in all aspects of police administration and finally 'the conditions and conditioning' of the lower rank are bad (Subramanian, 2009). The paramilitary structures of even the civilian police are colonial and oppressive which have led to most of its regressive political-organizational features (Subramanian, 2007; Baxi 1982; Arnold 1986).

Politicization of the police is the price we have to pay for the democratic functioning of our polity (Verma, 2005). There is a need for decentralization of the highly centralized police structure, which was suitable for the British Raj but is not relevant in a rapidly decentralizing governance system of a democratic country, evolving the three-tier system of Panchyats Raj Institutions, operating from the district level to the village (Subramanian, *op.cit*). Since the political actors use police and general administration as power without responsibility or accountability, and it gives them immense scope to fulfill their political agenda, any police reform has been torpedoed at worst and at the best it is snowballed.

II

Corruption

Corruption is the most versatile enemy of democracy as it makes the system, institution and leadership hollow, weak and spineless. Corruption is to democracy as termite is to wood, both making democracy and wood hollow, leading to slow and steady demise. Generally speaking, corruption is defined as the misuse of pubic power or office for private gain or profit. There is a close relation between corruption and power as underlined by Lord Acton.

'Power tends to corrupt and absolute power corrupts absolutely.' Corruption is very hideous and innovative in nature as its perpetrators keep on mastering new techniques and mode of corruption. It is like iceberg submerged in water, what is seen is much less than what is concealed underneath the water.

Corruption is defined as 'the use of the public power for private profit in a way that constitutes breach of law.... as dishonesty and illegal behaviour in position of authority and power.'[27] As per World Bank Report, corruption is the 'use of public office for private gain.'[28] As corruption has been growing in proportion and dimension, its definition and scope is also getting enlarged in that proportion. For example, Santhanam Committee, set up by the Government of India for prevention of corruption submitted its report in 1964 which is known as the Santhanam Committee on the Prevention of Corruption, enlarged the scope of corruption by adding failure to act for private gain, 'Any action or failure to take action in the performance of duty by a Government servant for some advantage is corruption.'[29]

However, Carl J. Friedrich sees corruption as deviation from the normal behaviour pattern or set rules and regulation or established pattern in a given context such as political or social. According to him, corruption is a deviant behaviour related with a specific motivation—private gain at the cost of public interest and it may be in various forms, not necessarily monetary as perceived by the people generally[30]. One thing very unique about corruption is that it transcends the barrier of time and space in the sense that it has been prevalent in all forms of government, societies and almost all periods of time. It seems to be constant, regular, and repetitive and an integral part of the organizational society and it is universal in its pervasiveness.[31]

Moreover, corruption and bureaucracy seem to be conjoined twins. Ralph Braibanti has aptly remarked that corruption is found in all forms of bureaucracies and governments in all periods of time.[32] Even, the great historian of Roman Empire, Edward Gibbon has attested to this universality of corruption, 'Corruption is the most infallible symptom of constitutional liberty.'[33] Thus, corruption seems to have become an endemic problem not only for democracy but the human society at large. It is 'harmful in three different ways: Corruption is anti-national, corruption is anti-poor and corruption is anti-economic development. The collapse of South East Asian economies in mid 1999 showed how even the so-called miraculously growing tiger economies of South Asia were not immune from the disastrous consequences of corruption and crony capitalism.'[34] Thus, corruption undercuts the very basis of democracy that is accountability, transparency, equality and development.

However, in India and other democracies across the world[35] corruption has become so entrenched in the system and psychic of people that there are some voices being raised that it should be legalized. These are the same players who have been filling up their coffers at the cost of public interest. 'In India, there are five major players on the corruption scene, interdependent, strengthening and supportive of this vicious circle. They are the corrupt politicians, corrupt bureaucrats, the corrupt businessmen, the corrupt NGOs, and the criminal of the underworld.[36]

The Central Vigilance Commission of India, a central body to keep tab on corruption, has identified more than 40 modes of corruption in India, which is not exhaustive. The list keeps on increasing every year (CVC web site or report).

Corruption has become so endemic that almost every institution and organization, with few exceptions, seems to have steeped in such malady. Even Panchyati Raj Institutions, poverty alleviation and rural development schemes are not immune from this all pervading clutches of corruption. Every office, whether be it Prime Minister, Chief Minister, Judiciary, elected representatives of Parliament, State Assemblies and Panchyati Raj Institutions are not immune from allegation or charges of corruption. There are even few former Prime Ministers and Chief Ministers who have been or being tried for corruption charges.

However, what is the most serious thing and it is certainly not good for the health and well-being of democracy is 'sanskritization of corruption'. The sanskritization is phenomenon that glorifies and glamorizes any custom or practice which people adopts it not for its inherent utility but because it is a badge of belonging to an elite class. It is in this sense that Gunner Myrdal talks about the 'folklore of corruption'.[37]

Moreover, 'Corruption in India has become a part of its socio-cultural ethos. There is a sizable numbers of "socially sanctioned corruption" which does not stir anyone's conscience or for that matter does not raise many eyebrows. In the culturally sanctioned corruption, there is no quid pro quo always. Indians (for that matter any democracy of the world) find it difficult to resist pressures from relatives and close friends. Even the most upright officers commit acts of indiscretion and favouritism against the better judgment, under pressures from family or friends. And then there are considerations of village, neighbourhood, ethnic groups and other extraneous loyalties that have a powerful bearing on the Indian psyche.'[38]

Lately, Gunner Myrdal in his Asian Drama has termed India as "Soft state". He termed India as soft state because of excessive leniency and complacency in the execution of laws in India and even in general administrative practices. Superior officers rarely exercise supervision over subordinates with effectiveness. There is too much of acceptance of the deviation and violation of laws and rules.[39] This, in turn, provides the fertile ground for the all pervading ground of corruption wherein even very mention of corrupt practices raises frowns across the officials and politicians. No wonder then the corrupt are ruling the roost, while honest are fighting for the very survival of their lives and conscience.

There used to be the notion that corruption is a by-product of the controlled economy and its "licence-permit Raj". But we find that corruption may have grown in scale and scope after controls were loosened. Is it because the individualism that gained strength in this period and is still growing was centred on an idea of the individual who grows at society's expense and who has little commitment to society? Importantly, the historical circumstances that helped the rise and growth of individualism elsewhere were not available in India.[40]

Speed Money and Black Money

To expedite the administrative decision or clearance, speed money is given to the concerned departments or the concerned authority. It has become a norm that if one wants clearance for any project or venture, without speed money there is no possibility of the clearance being granted by any other means. Now the situation has come to such a sorry state that even for minor things, such as issuance of birth or death certificate speed money is required. If one does not part with the money as solicited, then even small thing or petty matters may end in limbo with endless rounds to the concerned office.

Black money is the cause and effect of corruption rampant in our system. It is the barometer of the extent of corruption prevalent in our system. According to the study undertaken by the National Institute of Public Finance and Policy, the black money in proportion to the Gross National Income, even in as far as back in 1983-84 was 21 per cent. In 2000, it was estimated to be 40 per cent of the Indian economy.[41]

'There are other guesstimates that black money in India is equal to the legitimate of the GNP of the country. Black money in India is estimated at between Rs. 80,000 to 150,000 crore. And it is growing in size and its menacing. 'Public money is like holy water; everybody dips his hand into it. *Ghotala* (Shady dealings), scam, scandals and fraud—these terms represent the essentials of the dominant discourses from the market place to the secluded and walled bastions of power. One of the main causes of this pervasive black money is the grabbing by corrupt leaders, officials and contractors, of a big chunk of funds meant for construction and development. They collect this money as if it is accruing from their 'private tax'.[42]

Having seen the gravity of the situation, Baba Ramdev, the health guru of the world now trying to cleanse the body politic of India, has urged the civil society that capital punishment should be given to corrupt ones, and corruption should be declared as act of traitor. Even Dalai Lama seems to be concerned about the magnitude of the corruption when he mentioned about corruption in Judiciary (TOI, 2009). According to Admiral RH Tahilani, Chairman, Transparency International India, "Over the last decade, the nation's scam has gone global with the country's resources and taxpayer's money being parked in places hitherto unimagined. The stolen public funds make India a rich country with poor people. (This euphemism was used earlier for Bihar—one of the most backward state of India. Now, it is being used for the whole of India! What a progress we have made!) According to one estimate, Rs. 70 lakh crore (70,00,000) have been stolen through such scam" (*Asian Age*, 2009).

How much the government and whole system is concerned about corruption is best reflected by the fact that 'India has not signed or ratified the UN Convention against Corruption (UNCAC) as 'Fundamental Principle of Corruption'. The UNCAC is a very effective mechanism as it has got 141 signatories, having wider reach than the OECD, comprising 30 wealthy countries and the Council of Europe having 47 countries as its members. This powerful UN convention has very powerful clauses which not only deal with officials taking bribes but also has effective mechanism for recovering "ill-gotten gains stacked illegally in the tax haven banks of foreign countries."

Corruption has taken democratic dimension in as much as it prevails at all levels from the bottom and affects all parties (Tahilani, *ibid*). It is worth mentioning that how the political actors adopted dilly-dallying approach in asking for details from Swiss bank, despite the request forwarded by the bank. The information related to it was deliberately made public so that corrupt politicians, bureaucrats, businessmen, traders and balckmarketeers could chiffon the money to some other banks or to other countries. The opposition played the second fiddle by not pursuing the issue vigorously or making it an election issue for obvious reason.

One can guess the scale of corruption and unaccounted money when one comes across the fact that '$1.4 trillion which is equivalent to 70 lakh crore belonging to Indians have been parked in the safe heavens abroad, especially Swiss Banks. It is more than India's national income of around Rs. 50 lakh crore. As per the Global Financial Integrity Study, the average money taken away from India annually during 2002-2006 was $27.3 billion. Thus, during this five-year period, the amount stashed away comes to around $136.5 billion. As gleaned from the statistics available on the web site of the Union Finance Ministry on the country-wise approvals for direct investments in Joint Ventures and wholly-owned subsidiaries during 1996-2007, more than one-third of outflows out of the total of $31,000 million was to well-known tax heavens such as Channel Islands ($5,400 million) and Mauritius ($2,600 million)'.[43]

Corruption undermines democracy and good governance by flouting or even subverting formal processes. Corruption in elections and in legislative bodies reduces accountability and distorts representation in policymaking; corruption in the judiciary comprises the rule of law and its prevalence in public administration results in all types of unfairness in providing services. Moreover, corruption erodes the institutional capacity of government as procedures are disregarded, resources are plundered and the public offices are used for the personal or sectarian interests. Apart from these, it undermines the legitimacy of government and erodes the democratic values of trust and tolerance (Wikipedia, 2010).

Political elites and their cronies continue to take kickbacks at every available opportunity. Hands in glove with corrupt business houses and industrial tycoons, they are trapping whole nations in poverty and hampering sustainable development. Corruption is perceived to be dangerously high in poor parts of the world, but also in many countries whose firms invest in developing nations. Politicians increasingly pay lip-service to the fight against corruption but they fail to act on the clear message of TI's CPI; that they must clamp down on corruption to break the vicious circle of the poverty and graft.....Corrupt political elites in the developing world, working hand-in-hand with greedy business people and unscrupulous investors, are putting private gain before the welfare of citizens and the economic development of the countries.[44]

Corruption continues to deny the poor, the marginalized, and the least educated members of every society, the social, economic and political benefits that should accrue to them naturally. Thus, corruption denies the people their legitimate dues on the one hand, while on other it creates inequality and injustice in the system, attacking the very foundation of democracy.

III

Dynastic Politics

The dynastic politics is very anti-thesis of democracy and its principle of inclusion and diffusion of ideas and resources and leadership. If the leadership is rotated among the family, it would pursue the same interest or class or the caste or clan or vested interests despite being elected on wider plank or reportedly representing broader categories of the people. While the visionary and grassroot level leader never hopes to make it to the top, the system has perforce to settle with a leader carrying the tradition and old legacies, at the best with new label while content remains same. Such dynastic leader puts premium on loyalty and family tradition and he or she would prefer the person having such qualities over others. What is more dangerous that he or she would like to implant the person of known lineage or progenies of some or other families at the lower rungs of party or its organization.

This is such a vicious circle wherein more the dynastic politics it craves for more. If there is threat to its existence, it may transform into despotic leadership or the autocratic one overnight. And this dynastic trend in politics is replicated at every sub-system of the system—economic, societal, cultural and others. The net result is that the credibility of democracy suffers a heavy blow; people find it difficult to identify and associate with the system. Consequently democracy gets fossilized and waiting for a sleight of hand to collapse if not really then apparently or metaphorically. India or for that matter almost all democracies the world over are in the grip of this disgusting phenomenon which undercuts democracy in the same manner as does the woodpecker with silence and maintaining some sort of outer or outward normalcy while hallowing underneath.

As a party, the Congress has abandoned contested elections to its top posts and the chosen few at the top are the coteries of the Gandhi leadership. Indira Gandhi began this practice of personal rule over the party. It fell into disuse briefly after Rajiv Gandhi's assassination in 1992. Yet six years later, the party welcomed the leadership of Sonia Gandhi, his widow, with open arms. Dynastic politics is not unique to India. It is in Sri Lanka when Chandrika Kumaratunga succeeded as prime minister, her mother who erlier succeeded her father. Bhutto in Pakistan or Zia-ur-Rehman families in Bangladesh, Aung San Suu Kyi in Myanmar (Burma), and in Indonesia, there has been some sort of dynastic politics for one or two generation. 'Yet the longevity of Nehru-Gandhi dynasty is something unique and cannot be healthy for a democracy. The practice of the Congress party in institutionalizing personal rule has spread over to other political parties' (Desai, *op. cit*).

It is no wonder that dynastization of Indian politics has spread like wild fire gutting the values and principal of democracy to mere ashes. This dynastization has spread across economy, finances, bureaucracy, media, art and culture. 'India's politico scope is marked by steady surge in the trend of dynastic politics (*The Asian Age*, 2009). 'Across India, political families are entrenched at every level of government and politics. At least nine of the 32 members of Prime Minister Manmohan Singh's cabinet either descended from political families or have children seeking or holding office. Parliament is littered with political families; a recent study found that 31 of 58 women elected had a husband, brother, father or father-in-law in politics. The trend is even more glaring at the state level… .[45]

Thus, democracy is in imminent danger of being eclipsed by dynastic politics. The basis of democracy that is people as propounded by Abraham Lincoln 'democracy is government by the people, for the people and of the people' may turn into a government by, for and of the elite or dynastic scion. If this rather dangerous trend is not checked, the day is not far off when it would be very difficult to differentiate between democracy and monarchy, and that would seal the fate of democracy.

IV

Lopsided and Imbalanced Development

The lopsided and imbalanced development is another enemy of democracy which takes out the very basis of democracy – equality and justice – from its fold. It is for this reason that the UNESCO's position paper for the World Summit on Social Development maintains that "Social dimension is to be the starting point of development and should determine to a large extent the priorities of development policies."[46] It was realized at the outset that real indicators of development are such things as decrease in the rate of poverty, income inequality and unemployment. This gave birth to an alternative approach to development which was more pluralistic and encompassing not only growth but capacity, equity and empowerment as well.[47]

Development is intrinsically related with democracy as 'Development stems from the democratic principle that entails the right of people to govern them through participation in the decision that affects them (Ghosh, *ibid*). The lopsided and imbalanced growth and development nullifies this democratic principle as it implies that people have been denied the right to govern themselves through participation. This is what is happening as the development model of trickle down or tops-down does not leave much scope for people's participation in decision making or implementation of various development schemes and programmes.

There is no denying the fact that there has been commendable growth during the last two decades, particularly after the liberalization, privatization and globalization of the Indian economy. However, 'The remarkable growth rate is accompanied by poverty, by ethnic tension and identity politics. The miraculous growth of service sector conceals the miniscule proportion of country's vast number of educated unemployed. More than a quarter of the sector's FDI is attracted into its small-scale zone that it is making a quite killing by successfully exporting white-collar coolie work.' Moreover, the India's cotton textile industry which was an 'important index of the Indian economy' has been transformed into a fast growing small sector at the cost of traditional mills. The fact that the mill industry which was country's largest producer, employer and exporter was systematically stymied after Independence by the Congress which had contemptuous disliking for the organized private sector reflects the type of growth and development we are chartering. The last blow was delivered by the Congress controlled trade union which enforced a long strike. Thus the field was ready for informal small-scale sector to capture the cotton textile sector.[48]

The merchant producers profit by producing cheap and selling cheap. There is hardly any production area except the heavy industries which informal and unorganized sector has not penetrated. The lack of trade unions and any control that this sector is characterized has led to immense profiteering and exploitation by the entrepreneurs. This gives them the wherewithal not to give legal wages and other labour benefits. 'As a rule, contract workers get paid less than regular workers and are often unable to access their provident fund and retirement benefits.' It is here that migrant workers are employed who are at the mercy of employers. The sector continues to thrive on cheap labour and there is no incentive for improving their skill or any career progression. The export trade is dominated by this sector (Gupta, *ibid*, p10).

However, the situation in rural India is more pathetic as incessant migration and unabated suicide reflects the kind of developmental strategy that is being followed. The rural India is the hallowed village. What land reforms and land redistribution could not accomplish demography and subdivision of land holdings have done to land ownership. 'Emptying out of rural India, emotionally, economically and obviously is striking.' The uneconomic holdings of lands and its inability feed leads to migration to urban ghettoes and employment in 'urban sweetshops' among fast expanding small-scale informal industries. Among the farmers of all categories, uncertainty of agriculture future is prime reason for their migration to urban areas or to the foreign lands (*ibid*).

The ceaseless migration and exodus of rural population to urban areas is not on account of pure distress but rather because of a lack of hope for the future... The National Agriculture Policy as it stands today is largely a document full of good intentions but with no practical import. The cultivators want good floor price for their product, insurance cover for their standing crops, on the spot payment for their produce, reasonable input prices and supply of water and electricity. There are no such things to be found in the Agriculture policy (*ibid*). The rural sector in general and agriculture in particular has never found priority among the policy makers of India for some reason or other reason. When faced with humiliating situation in the wake of acute food shortage in 1960s, the technology based initiative was taken in a few states for intermediate and rich farmers, what is called as 'Green Revolution'. The land reform and rural development was botched down by the rural elites and satraps of the ruling party.

The Indian state was hardly unusual in setting itself colossal developmental ambitions; but it was virtually unique among new states in deciding to pursue these by democratic means. The relationship between the project of development and India's democratic politics tells no simple lesson: it has been complicated, shifting duet between the arguments and ideas of intellectuals, and the pressures and urgent claim of democratic politics. Unlike its giant northern neighbour, China, India did not dispense with democracy in order to make a brutal revolutionary leap into industrialization; nor did its leadership and intelligentsia intentionally veer to the market, as China's post-Mao leadership did. Liberalization and market-orientation did come to India in the 1990s, but their proponents were impelled to consider them by a self-created fiscal crisis which, in tandem with the arguments of intellectuals, pushed the Indian state towards reform. (*ibid*, p 64)

Despite this feat, it is not to forget that whatever development and growth has been achieved have been cornered by few influential and powerful section of the society both in the rural and urban India. 'Bullock Capitalist' a euphemism used by western and western-oriented Indian gentlemen or intelligentsia for underlining the clout of rural neo-rich have cornered all benefits of the programmes launched in post-Independent India. These sections, which constitute upper and upper middle class of rural areas, have successfully infiltrated the politics and businesses, preventing any land reform in almost all parts of India, barring few pockets.

'The heart of the problem,' Mahalanbois has said, in what was perhaps the most succinct statement of the way Nehru also saw the issue, 'is to make changes in all necessary directions at the same time, in a balanced way, so as to bring about structural transformation as quickly as possible. In the years of Nehru government, and during the Shastri interregnum, agriculture policy had moved from the earlier emphasis on institutional and structural reform of the property order towards technological solutions of the 'Green Revolution'. It directed investment heavily towards selected regions (especially Punjab and the north) and social groups (farmers from the intermediate castes with middle-sized landholdings). The results were impressive, and by the mid-1960s, these new 'bullock capitalists' began to form their own regional political parties (the beginning of a phenomenon that by the 1990s would transform national politics (Khilnani *op. cit.*).

These groups started asking for their pound of flesh in politics. The reverses that Congress got in the general election of 1967 forced Mrs. Gandhi to accommodate them through state subsidies. Later on she started wooing poor through attractive sloganeering of 'poverty alleviation'. 'Thus, 'India's fiscal sociology was altered, as the state made itself more sensitive to the demands of those successful enough to get themselves represented.' (*ibid*). Banks were nationalized and 'loan mela' was organized. In addition to free milk, saris, food and credit were offered by politicians as inducements to communities and groups in return for their block votes. Thus was started the 'sub-ordination economic to electoral exigencies, which, however, failed to provide 'immediate political legitimacy,' as high electoral support of 1971 gave way to loosing political ground and the 'Emergency' followed.

This 'fiscal sociology' led to economic crisis of 1991 which 'came in the midst of political difficulties. ... The most sweeping realignment of the state's relation to the economy was thus initiated by a minority Congress government, the weakest ever to rule.' The 'Indian socialism' – a doctrine to keep concentration of economic power out of private hands, to protect the small-scale sector such as handloom textiles production, and avoid regional imbalances across the federal system was discarded outrightly.

From the early 1990s, the discourse of liberalization came to monopolize economic discussion, just as planning had done in 1950 and 1960s. The real issues lay in towards other directions. What kind of participatory opportunities would economic growth actually provide – or fail to provide—for most Indians? Any agreed understanding of economic, and what it required and entailed, had faded from view; yet all the fundamental problems—poverty, illiteracy, deprivation, ill health, social inequalities—persisted. The liberalization and the growth pattern that India chartered after 1991 was 'unaimed liberalization' *a la* 'Brazilian path'—where high digit growth failed to alleviate poverty and social inequality. When the debate regarding liberalization and privatization was going on, this point was raised by many economists and some of the political outfits (Desai, *op. cit*).

'Centrally at issue in the debate about economic reforms were not growth rates but the kind of society in which the growth was expected to occur. If, as in India's case, it was scarred by poverty, illiteracy, poor health and sharp gender inequalities, then the likelihood of trampling 'Brazilian path'.......... would be high. Growth produced by 'unaimed liberalization'—which was not specifically targeted at improving the conditions of worse-off—could surely be expected to increase inequalities in three ways: across the country, it would widen the gap in social opportunities available to rich and poor; it would sharpen the divide between rural and urban India (urban incomes are around three times of rural ones, while female literacy rates in cities are more than double those in the countryside); and it would increase the already pronounced imbalances and differences among the regions, which gave the richest of them per capita incomes three times higher than the poorest ones.'[49]

This is what has happened after two decades of growth. The rich has become richer, while the poor has found himself further sliding down the abyss of poverty. The three fault lines of inequality and imbalances as existing between the rich and poor, urban and rural divide, and regional imbalances has been further accentuated. While the number of poor, hungry and malnourished children and people has increased substantially, the number of billionaires has grown accentuating the situation and concentration of wealth in a few hands.

A multi-pronged approach is needed to ensure that the benefits of high GDP growth trickle down to the remotest household in both urban and rural India. The higher GDP growth has not tickled down to the common people both in urban and rural areas. Moreover, it has led to a regional disparity that might endanger the very basis of democracy that is inclusiveness and economic equality. As for that matter, the per capita net domestic product varies significantly, ranging from Rs. 29, 137 for Delhi (2004-05, CSO estimates) to Rs. 6, 277 in Bihar. The per capita income of Delhi, one of the country's richest regions, is roughly five times that of Bihar, one of the poorest states. If the states are bunched into three categories—low, middle and high income—based on the level of their per capita income, it is evident 48 per cent of Indians live in low-income states, 30.6 per cent in middle-income ones, and the rest in high-income states.[50]

Out of 205.6 million household in the country, just 44.3 million of them – with a population of 220 million—earn annual average income of Rs. 89,288. In contrast, 91.7 million households—with 493.3 million population—that live in low income states of Assam, Bihar, Madhya Pradesh, Meghalya, Orissa, Rajasthan, Uttar Pradesh, Chhattisgarh, Uttarakhand and Jharkhand have an average income of just over half of that of households in high income states of Goa, Gujarat, Haryana, Maharashtra, Punjab, Pondicherry, Chandigarh and Delhi at Rs. 52,052 per annum. The high-income states have a share of just 21.5 per cent of all the households, but their contribution to total disposable income is nearly 30 per cent. In contrast, the low income states `have a share of nearly 45 per cent of all households and their share of total disposable income is about 35.7 per cent.

Low-income states have a higher concentration of rural population compared to middle and high-income states. While more than half the population of low-income states live in the villages 95.4 per cent), this is 29 per cent for middle-income states of Andhra Pradesh, Himachal Pradesh, Karnataka, Kerala, Tamilnadu and West Bengal, and just 16.4 per cent for high-income ones. The average annual rural household income in low-income states is much lower than those for both middle-and high-incomes states: Rs 44,999, Rs. 55,604 and Rs. 66,121 respectively. Urban household in middle- and high-income states to earn a lot more annually than those in lower-income states: Rs. 89,223, Rs. 116,421 and Rs. 80,948 respectively.[51]

'India is moving towards a situation where the ill-effects of economic growth will be magnified. The vigour and vitality of democratic institutions will be fully tested in coping with this situation'. The government is subject to many manipulations as liberalization and privatization have opened the Pandora's Box and the government agencies are liable to be manipulated by these. The constraints that government faces is best exemplified by the inability of government to ensure equitable distribution, as it warrants the control of government over economy, but the perceived or genuine fear of slowdown prevents it from doing it.[52]

The climate change and global warming is the cause and effect of such kind of poor governance and shortsightedness of the leadership. The disregard and gross negligence towards nature that human society shows towards their environment, nature and resources is but one of fundamental contradictions that betray the same attitude towards their fellow human beings. It is the same negligent and myopic governance that treat men and natural resources and environment as means to further their vested interests rather than considering these as end of themselves. This has endangered not only our life but very survival of our existence on the earth. It has resulted from 'a much larger system that of an unsubstantial pattern of development pursued in most countries.'

'Climate change, across the globe, has not received the attention it deserves. It is the result of a much larger system that of an unsubstantial pattern of development pursued in most countries. While technologies and processes can be altered to mitigate the emissions of the greenhouse gases, the challenge is actually much larger. It involves a change in value systems and lifestyles by which humans treat natural resources and their use with the value they carry. Unless the larger problem of maintaining and building up the Earth's natural resources is dealt with effectively, the cost to the world, both in human and economic terms, would become progressively higher and unbearable.'[53]

Thus lopsided and imbalanced growth and development is arch enemy of democracy both literally and metaphorically as it leads to steady and sure demise of democracy.

V

Poverty and Socio-Economic Inequality

Poverty and socio-economic inequality is another great enemy of democracy. It renders the meaning of democracy to a sham as existence of poverty and socio-economic equality is equivalent to its non-existence. If there is democracy or rule by the people or people's representative implying people's participation in the governance, there is no question of poverty existing or any kind of social and economic inequality existing. If poverty and social and economic inequality do exist, it means there is no democracy or democracy is in imminent danger of losing its status of being so or it has oligarchy or dictatorship.

The fact that there is poverty in India and it is growing, and so do the social and economic inequality, then democracy is endangered in loosing itself to oligarchy or any sort of dictatorship. There is hardened but misplaced belief that India is held back by casteism and rigid social hierarchy. It is touted as the prime reason for the reigning poverty and socio-economic and political inequality. However, this is a misnomer as 'caste has never stood in the way of political mobilization and secular demand for economic betterment.'

As no caste is large enough to form a political majority in any constituency; second, because caste and politics cannot be correlated as most voters are not 'professional casteist' and third; because no caste, as caste, thinks well of any other caste. As rural India votes outside the 'pure caste considerations, it is not responsible for India's inability to come to the top or to explain its lack of public infrastructure or its inability to provide quality level public goods….. caste identities are used to stake claims to jobs, educational opportunities as well as to positions of power..' caste and religious identities are obsessions of the politicians who stoke them for their own personal gains. The votaries of OBC (Other Backward Castes) reservation do not share the objective caste extirpation; instead they want its perpetuation to maintain personal vote-banks. 'It is so unfair to the millions of poor rural Indians who have had nothing to benefit from the caste politics of the rural rich.'[54]

Moreover, many scholars[55 56] have proved beyond doubt the traditional institutions such as castes, kinship play a vital role in strengthening and grounding of democracy. So it is wrong to blame casteism or caste for the prevalence of poverty and inequality and injustice. Caste, a functional division of the Indian society which later on came to be based on birth and became a rigid segregation of Indian society may be used as a convenient tool to maintain poverty and unjust social and economic order by vested interests. However, it cannot be held responsible for the prevalence of poverty, hunger and social and economic inequality.

The prevalence of poverty and socio-economic inequality and injustice emanate from the very constitution of social and economic structures of the Indian society. As Dr Ambedkar pointed this contradiction in 1948, "In politics we will be recognizing the principle of one man, one vote and one vote one value. In our social and economic life, we shall, by reason of our social and economic structure, continue to deny the principle of one man one value. How long shall we continue to live this life of contradiction?" (Ambedkar, 1948)

It is because of this contradiction that "Even today, despite laws and policies against caste discrimination, more than 165 million of Dalits (Downtrodden, lower caste, Scheduled Castes and Scheduled Tribes and exploited ones) are condemned to life time abuse simply because of their caste."[57] Despite elaborate provisions in the Constitution and other laws, it is unfortunate reality that there is social injustice and exploitation of Scheduled Castes and Scheduled Tribes and other weaker sections."[58] Over one-sixth of India's population, some 170 million people live a precarious existence, shunned by much of Indian society because of their rank as 'Untouchable' or Scheduled Castes at the bottom of society.[59]

If one critically analyzes various rural development, poverty alleviation and employment scheme such as NREGA, one would not fail to notice the continuity of the unjust social and economic organization and the structures that give rise to such type of poverty, inequality and injustice as mentioned by Dr. Ambedkar. All efforts and plans and counter plans point towards the fact that none has bothered to touch this unjust social and economic structures and organization of the society that has been at the root of the problem of poverty, inequality and injustice.

It is not surprising that India ranks 119th on Human Development Index (HDI), its loss in HDI due to equality is 30 per cent, gender equality index is 122 and multi-dimensional Poverty Index is 0.296. It is very poor record considering that China is ranked 89 on HDI rank, 23 per cent loss due to inequality, gender equality index is 38 and MPI is 0.056.[60]

In terms of inequality of opportunity, India may be one of the most unequal countries in the world. Much of the rise in inequality is likely to be due to these factors: Firstly, the increasing productivity gap between the rural and urban sector, and to a large extent between the formal and informal sector; secondly, the weaker bargaining power of over organized workers in the face of the increased threat of mobility of capital from one state to another and away from the country. Thirdly, there is the relative decline of agricultural sector where income inequality is somewhat lower than in the non-agricultural sector. Fourthly, there is relative expansion of capital and skill-intensive industries and fifthly the skill-based technical change, enhanced by global processes, which increases the rate of return to post-secondary education in a country where the overwhelming majority of the people are illiterate or social dropouts or never going beyond the secondary education. Finally there is usual agglomeration economies and clustering of non-agricultural growth, particularly with some of the populous backward states falling behind in the growth race (Bardhan, 2009).

Naxalism: Commentary on Unjust Social and Economic order

Naxalism or Left Wing Extremism (LEW) as is known in official parlance, whether it is viewed as law and order problem or developmental one or insurgency or people's movement, it is undoubtedly a commentary on unjust social and economic order. 'The mammoth Naxalites movement now sweeping across the countrywide, frequent attacks on people, police and infrastructure could be one of the biggest challenges before India. But the attacks are a result of injustice done for decades to the people behind the movement. The blessed, comfortable Indians refuse to accept that it has antagonized a sizable population of Dalits (Depressed class), tribal, and Adivasi (aborigines), looted their resources and turned them into Maoist extremists.'[61]

The biggest ever campaign has been launched against Naxalites assuming that it is a mere law and order problem. The attack against the Naxalites has been launched with helicopter as if they were enemy of our country. This is all being done for the benefit of corporate houses... (Rajendra Yadav, 2009).

Finally, the informational incompleteness and asymmetry in the actually existing capitalist societies have been responsible, along with the highly unequal distribution of inherited assets, for the enormous turbulence and unconscionably great and growing inequalities in those societies. The stock market has emerged as the fulcrum of neoliberal capitalism. However, in stock markets, information is systematically distorted by the very way the market, guided as it is by the actions and information generation of brokers, investment advisers, rating agencies and private equity funds. Destinies of the hundreds of millions of people are affected by institutions that are by their very nature non-transparent, generators of misleading information and subject to all manner of corrupt practices, as the latest global financial crisis has revealed so glaringly. ...[62]

On top of that in every major country, the laws of centralization and concentration of economic power has led to the control of most major media in fewer and fewer hands. This has led to the increasing constriction of the space for public reasoning that Amartya Sen has rightly picked out as a central feature of effective democracy. This was amply demonstrated when major media swallowed and propagated the Goebbelsian lie uttered by the Bush-Blair combine that Saddam Hussein had created and possessed Weapons of Mass Destruction…In many countries the influence of money power prevents the provision of basic requirements for the flowering of human capabilities which are throttled even in affluent capitalist countries (Bagchi, *ibid*).

VI

Colonial Mindset of State Apparatus

The colonial mindset of state apparatus is one of the greatest enemies of democracy. The system's apathy and callousness regarding people's plight and lack of basic necessities, resulting from colonial mindset infringe the enjoyment of the Fundamental Rights as enshrined in the Constitution of India. Approximately, 2/3 of populace who has been left out from the ambit of development and economic boom has been further shackled in the vicious circle of poverty and hunger. " In fact, India has inherited the legacy of Police Act of 1861 in letter and spirit which was a legal instrument meant to facilitate and legitimize oppression on the people of India by colonial power." (Singh, *op. cit,* para 4)

The intact state over which the Congress Party gained control in 1947 had been created by an alien power for its own extractive purposes; now, somehow it had to be made legitimate, it had to be able to require obligations of its population. The state's harming capacities would have to be seen to be restrained in favour of its population. (Khilnani, *op. cit.*) In Nehru's response to this task, what was required was a transformation of the state's formal identity, not merely a change in the colour of its administration: he mocked those for whom 'Swaraj' (Self government) means that everything continues as before, only with a darker side. (Nehru, Jawaharlal (1936) 'Autobiography': 417)

It implies that for such transformation a Constitution is needed, as Nehru averred that a constitution 'controls the making of the laws… protects liberties … checks the executive and provides democratic methods of bringing about changes in the political and economic structure. (Nehru, *ibid*). The colonial state nowhere approximated to these criteria: under colonial rule 'the term 'constitutional' was used mainly in support of the executive's more or less arbitrary actions.' The commitment to constitutionalism was to be the distinctive trait of the new Indian state, marking its break with the old political order (though he candidly admitted that to invoke constitutionalism and legality was after all to remain 'within the orbit of their [the colonial power's] ideology' (*ibid*, 427). It allowed state to make legitimate claim. In many respects the Constitution promulgated in 1950 did mark a departure from inherited forms (Khilnani, *op. cit.*).

However, basic structure of governance as decided by various Government of India Acts, particularly that of 1919 and 1935 was more or less left intact. Whatever changes were inserted was cosmetic in nature. Referring to imposition of President's rule, a relic of colonial ruler, which was imposed more frequently after 1967, Meghnad Desai has rightly said, 'All this was a continuation of the British Raj, where governor-general used to have extensive powers over the provinces and the viceroy could dismiss rulers of native states where disorder was likely to break out.' (Desai, *op. cit*)

The government machinery remains colonial in its functioning because it is not constituted to be accountable and responsible to the rights of citizens as citizens. Acquiring a foothold in the government machinery brings with it enormous clout and opportunities for upward mobility through means fair and foul. People perforce have to mobilize themselves as communities in order to gain a measure of protection and privilege. Those who cannot pull through their caste and family ties feel vulnerable and thwarted... The resultant vicious tussles over gaining a foothold in offices of power have made virtually every group feel aggrieved and insecure. Therefore, it does not take much effort to mobilize new groups to demand their share of the pie... The faults of our representative institutions and colonial-minded governance cannot really be corrected through the quota mechanism. Other more radical remedies are required involving far-reaching electoral and administrative reforms.[63]

The very fact that government machinery is not accountable and responsible to citizens or their representatives, points towards colonial nature of administration and governance. In a democratic government, the government and political authority is accountable and responsible to the people. However, in Indian democracy, it is very difficult to fix accountability, even if the concerned authority or person is responsible for the certain acts of commission and omission. Once the government machinery finds itself free from any sort of accountability and responsibility, then it becomes corrupt, irresponsible and more often than not despotic. This type of attitude is colonial which is not apt for democracy.

The colonial mindset of the government and other state apparatus has alienated the people. The common people find it very difficult to do business with government steeped in such anachronistic mindset. Either they have to grease the palm of the authority for getting the simple works such as birth or death certificate done or they have to find some intermediary or agent for this purpose. Moreover, the government servant or people representatives think themselves as 'ruler' not as the servant or service providers, this colonial mindset takes them far away from the people. Resultantly, both drift apart from each other leading to further alienation of the people and administration.

VII

Oligarchy

The growing arch of oligarchy and elitism is an imminent threat to democracy, and what is alarming is that it is becoming more a rule than exception. This menace now appears to have even gripped the mother of parliamentary democracy—Britain—as the recent elections and composition of Parliament is any indication. That is what some study conducted on the composition of New Parliament (2010) has found: 'Parliament as a whole remains very much social elite.'[64] In Russia, the government is being run by these oligarchs and has become so powerful that the President had to reportedly issue warning to them'.

Oligarchy is a form of government where most political power effectively rests with a small segment of society (most powerful, whether by wealth, military strength, ruthlessness or political influence). Oligarchies are often controlled by a few powerful families whose children are raised and mentored to become the inheritors of the power of the oligarchy, often at some sort of expense to those governed. In contrast to the aristocracy, this power may not always be exercised openly, the oligarchs preferring to remain 'the power behind the throne', exerting control through economic means. Unlike plutocracy, oligarchy is not always a rule by wealth, as oligarch can simply be a privileged cadre.[65]

A society may become an oligarchy by default as an outgrowth of the shifting alliances of warring tribal chieftains, although any form of government may transform into an oligarchy at some point in its evolution. The most likely mechanism for this transformation is a gradual accumulation of otherwise unchecked economic power. Oligarchies may also evolve into more classically authoritarian forms of government, sometimes as the result of one family gaining ascendancy over the others. Many of the European monarchies established during the late middle Ages began in this way. (*ibid*, 3rd para)

A report of *Forbes Asia Magazine* (2009) said that India's 100 richest people owning wealth of $276 billion account for almost 25 per cent of the country's GDP. This group holds substantial political clout as it is only through political connection they have been able to amass such disproportionate amount of wealth in their hands. That is why Narayan Murthy has termed the Budget making as the collective wish and demands of group of industrialists, businessmen, traders, financiers and Bankers (*TOI*, 2009).

A recent study of Alfaro and Chari (2009) on Indian corporate data over 1988-2007 shows that in spite of a great deal of new entry, particularly in the service sector, the dominance of incumbent state-owned and business house-controlled companies in the overall industrial scene continues unabated. The corrupt grip of the corporate oligarchy in Indian political life and in state allocation of access to land, monopoly rights on natural resources or telecommunication spectrum is much more evident (Bardhan, 2010).

'Indian democracy is in danger of subversion by a self confident, aggressive, articulate, patriotic and well meaning force, the oligarchy of successful.... Danger lies in the fact that this creamy layer of 20 per cent at the top has no interest in involving the froth of 80 per cent in decision-making. This emerging constituency, perhaps a maximum of 300 million, is keen to outsource its future to an oligarchy because it has sniffed the latter's success. It is strong enough to shift general elections towards one political party or other, but it is not strong enough to sustain governance. That leaves 800 million on goodwill.'[66]

This sums up the threat that this 'growing arch of oligarchy' is posing to democracy across the world in general and that of India in particular. It is they who decide who is going to win and who is getting what portfolio. It is they who decide what policy will be pursued in what respect and they are the real hands in making of the Budget and other important decisions. Moreover, they have great disdain and concealed hatred for the 80 per cent whom they want to be just living on fringes. This rather inhuman attitude of the oligarchy can be seen working overtime in keeping the 80 per cent just alive through various poverty alleviation programmes and rural development programmes which provides bare minimum necessities. Eminent social thinker and political scientist Dr. Dipankar Gupta from Jawaharlal Nehru University (JNU) has found this ironic fact that our policymakers do not want our poor uplifted from poverty, and rather provide them with bare minimum so they could be alive.[67]

VIII

Vote Politics and Politicization of Public Life

Vote politics and politicization of public life is another enemy of democracy, as in the race for garnering votes and securing the present and future political interest, the very basis of democracy is being sacrificed. In Indian democracy it is being done on daily basis; it has become a rule rather than exception. Days may not be far off when for the sake of vote politics and political interest, democracy may be consigned to the dustbin of history.

The spirit of the Constitution, in a constitutional democracy like India, and its provisions should be followed in true spirit. The vote politics should not and must not undermine the spirit of Constitution and democracy. The reservation issue, separate allocation of resources in the name of certain community, oversight of national issue and trivialization of important issues, bending before majoritarianism and prostrating before the minoritism, bartering national and public good for the sake of vote banks, etc, are some out of the numerous issues that prove this malady. "A more serious problem is the politicization of all aspects of public life. Indira Gandhi started the trend, aided and abetted by the communist parties, of claiming that the popular mandate gave her power to override conventions and even the Constitution…"[68]

The origin of vote politics and politicization of public life is traceable to Mrs. Indira Gandhi's era when she split the Congress in 1969, breaking the Syndicates and undermining regional 'satraps'. This internal engineering and her leftward moves, with bank nationalization and *Garibi hatao* (Removal of Poverty), ensured Congress the landslide majority in 1971 elections and the defeat of Pakistan and secession of Bangladesh further consolidated her triumph by sweeping the elections to the regional or state legislatures in 1972. However, she had done great damage to Congress as an organization, leading to unstoppable slide in the Indian politics. The party readily "degenerated" into an "unaudited company" for winning elections. Unlike in the past, when there used to be some ideological underpinnings to the factional tussle within the party, these became simply instrumental and the Congress just transformed into "a mechanism for collecting funds, distributing 'tickets' or nominations for seats, and conducting campaigns" (Khilnani, *op. cit.*).

This degeneration of Congress into 'an unaudited company' for winning elections has had cascading effects on the political map of India. As the Congress has been a dominant party ruling the country for all but few years, the lead that it gave to others in the vote bank politics and politicization of the public life was taken by all and sundry. The other parties followed with unprecedented vigour and zeal in acting as mechanism for collecting funds, distributing tickets and conducting campaigns, dumping democratic politics to hyperbole and rhetoric. "This politicization of public life has left only the army and the judiciary as trusted public institution in India. For the rest, the citizen's access to the goods and services provided by the state can be secured only by displaying a caste, religious or regional identity, the membership of viable vote bank, and only through agents who deploy the vote bank at higher levels. Everything that state has touched—education at the primary, secondary and tertiary levels, any public sector appointments, sports, medicine—has been corrupted" (Desai, *op. cit* p 63).

Winning election, by hook or by crook even throwing national interest and that of public good to the winds, and winning ability of the issues or candidates irrespective of the consideration that it is good or bad or in the interest of overall good of the society or whether it will be strengthening democracy or not, became overriding concern of all parties. Having taken lead form the Congress and Indira Gandhi, the situation has come to such a pass that even national interest and that of democracy are being thrown to the winds, just to stay in the power or grab power. In the name of winning majority, even the very principles of democracy and governance are being thrown to the winds.

This rather shortsightedness acts of making elections as center of activity symbolized rather a deeper change. The other essential aspects of politics such as courting support, follow up actions on promises made and other things were not attended to. Elections became "spasmodic, theatrical events," when Indians put their hopes and aspirations in anticipation. But these were never to materialize. In nutshell, Mrs. Gandhi just factored in a sea change in the meaning of "democracy for both the Indian state and its society" by making it election-centric. This led to rather tectonic shift within the state as the constitutional propriety, decorum and balance were made subordinate to arbitrarily interpreted "the will of the people" or the "popular mandate" as steeped in electoral majorities. This deviation was nothing sort of Jacobin view of direct popular sovereignty (Khilnani, *op. cit*).

This centrality of elections and its winning by any means subverted the democratic system in many respects. The constitutional arrangement, separation of power, check and balances and balance of institutional arrangement were blunted or subverted for political expediency. The governance and constitutional obligations were given a pass just to win election or keep their respective vote banks intact. Since then, it has become an established norm and there seems to be an undeclared competition among the parties to outdo each other for winning elections or keeping their respective vote banks. For that all constitutional arrangements, guidance and democratic norms are being given short shrift.

Electoral arithmetic in terms of 'vote banks' developed in a complex form whereby identifiable collectives—*Jatis* (Castes) religious minorities, linguistic or regional groups—could be appealed to through their leaders or agents to cast their vote for one party rather than another. For her return to power in 1980, Mrs. Gandhi manipulated the Muslim vote and Dalits vote bank. While holding on to her upper caste Hindu vote bank in north India, she joined forces with the anti-Brahmin forces in south India. This defied the very principal of liberal democracy which is based on the individual choice of selecting and electing candidates as judged by them. Nevertheless "the deepening of Indian democracy happened" more because of the rather simultaneous fiasco in the economic front. The Hindu rate of growth of 1 to 1.5 per cent that Indian economy grew per annum till 1991 which was the result of the policy that 'Congress under Nehru followed a statist, capital intensive development programmes' kept Indian democracy balanced (Desai, *op. cit*).

However, the 'unaimed liberalization' that followed after 1991 when the economy was liberalized and privatized and politics was unseated from the driving position has further accentuated this election centric malady, as it opened floodgates of opportunity in all possible sense of the term. Moreover, the growing cleavages between the rich and poor, urban and rural and regional imbalances that reckless liberalization and privatization has led to, might upset this deepening of democracy. This anomaly led to many far-reaching consequences. However, this centrality of election not only subverted the democratic process and constitution beyond recognition but led to violence, intolerance and regionalism undermining the national or societal interest. The violence in Bihar and UP resulting from this desperation to win elections testifies to this subversion of democracy. This has had cascading effects on Indian democracy introducing many distortions in the form of various narrow and sectional demands such as regional or caste or religious or linguistic identities

One of the most serious fallout of this centrality of election or the vote politics and politicization has been frequent use of invoking the President Rule in the states. While between 1950 and 1967, this draconian power was used only by ten times, between 1968 and 1999 the number swelled to eighty times. The slow and unabated encroachment of the state power by centre brought forth heady and "raucous amalgamation" of central and state politics. Unlike past practices when the regional or state matters were used to be solved at local level, with concentration of power at centre these matters or even the petty issues started coming to central level for resolution. This led to negligence of long-term national issues as central leadership was entangled in the petty issues of petty politicking and dissent or power equation.

This centrality of election and desperation to win the election led to political corruption in the public arena. The 'suitcase culture', 'suitcase politician' and 'briefcase grafters' came into being as fund raising, which was being done at local level for winning election also came to be centralized, ending transparency and accountability in this respect. This has subverted every democratic process and institutions, and thus, it is one of the great enemies of democracy.

IX

Unjust and Anti-people Legal System

Justice is a very important concept and it is one of the prerequisites of a democratic way of organizing society, economy and polity. Unjust and anti-people legal system is one of the great enemies of democracy. As independent and apolitical judiciary is one of the important pillars of democracy, its deviation or any dilution in its working may shake off people's confidence in democracy.

It is pertinent to discuss in brief as to what constitutes justice and how it is related to democracy. In this respect discussing Rawlsian concept of justice and that of Amartya Sen would be appropriate as these two sums up the justice in totality. Rawl's concept of justice is based on two principles—the Liberty principle and the Difference principle. His first principle is foundationally prior to all else and demands that each person is to have equal right to the most widespread liberty compatible with a likewise liberty for all. The second principle—Difference principle—puts emphasis on the primacy of maximizing the advantage of the people from the lower section or class or caste or the person who are disadvantaged. The advantage is maximized in terms of an index of primary goods such as incomes, wealth, opportunities and social bases for self respect. Specifically, 'social and economic inequalities are to be arranged so that they are both to the greatest benefit of the least advantaged, and attached to offices and positions open to all under conditions of fair equality of opportunity' (Rawl, 1971).

To secure the "the greatest benefit of the least advantaged" is a matter of "maximizing the minimum": Hence the often-employed characterization of Rawls' contribution in terms of the so-called "maximin principle" of justice. A just society is one which will address itself to the creation, design and promotion of social institutions (the "background structure") which will advance the cause of the criterion of public justice encompassing the twin principles. (Subramanian, 2010) Thus, Rawl theory of the justice is based on the correction of the liberal-utilitarian principles of the greatest happiness of the greatest number of the people. Differing from these principles, Rawl maintains that liberal-utilitarian view of the justice is morally wrong. He appreciates their contribution to the justice, it justifies the sacrifice of the good of some individuals for the happiness of the greatest number. Rawl criticizes the utilitarian for their neglect to the welfare and justice for each member of the society for the aggregate sum of the utility and happiness. It is more concerned about the happiness of the aggregate or the whole as against the each and every member of the society.

Rawl views it morally flawed and provides an alternative to the utilitarianism. His view of the justice is inspired by the Kantian Moral idea of equality of every man and freedom. Kant opines that all men are equal because they enjoy the same capacity to be moral and formulate moral laws. Hence, everyone should have equality in every possible respect, and all men are equal, they should be treated equally. As Rawls has maintained that justice is the first virtue of a society, and it should always take priority over other good. It is nothing but the Welfarism in another sense. Rawls put forward the theory of justice, which is in harmony with the needs and requirements of the welfare state. As he has aptly commented: " If law and government act effectively to keep the market competitive, resources fully employed, property and wealth widely distributed over time and to maintain the appropriate social minimum, then if there is equality of opportunity underwritten by education to all, the resulting distribution will be just." (1971, 51)

Rawls stands for the privileges and inequalities, not for the maximization of the social good as is the case with the utilitarian. He champions the privileges and inequalities and positive discrimination for the improvement of the least advantaged and downtrodden people. As he maintains that 'social and economic policies be aimed at maximizing the long term expectations of the least advantaged under conations of fair equality and opportunity.' Rawls justified the welfare state on the ground of the distributive justice. It harmonizes the relations between the state and market. As free market economy results into the concentration of wealth and inequality, which undermines the individual freedom and liberty, it must be regulated by the state. It gives importance to the individuals and does not allow the market forces to undermine his individuality. If the market forces narrow down these choices, it is the duty of the welfare state to do away with factors.

The welfare state is that increases the individual liberty. The welfare state has to act as catalyst of socio-economic change in the society. It not only distributes the national wealth and resources, but also provides services and goods to the society. The welfare state, with its interventionist ideology to attain the maximum welfare of the people, is based on the foundations of the equality. Citizenship is one of the foundations of the welfare state. If it strengthens this foundation, it benefits itself as well as enriching the citizenship.

But the welfare state has failed to deliver the desired result. All the problems of the society, for which welfare state was conceived – inequality, poverty, injustice, hunger and depredation, concentration of wealth, etc are far from being resolved. Some thinkers like Barry maintain that integration of the welfare theory with the philosophy of welfare state is an intellectual error. This is so because proper attention was not given to appropriate institutional mechanism, which resolves these burning issues of the humanity. This concept of the state activities takes its inspiration from his concept of the distributive justice. He maintains that conditions for the success of this model are to ensure equal opportunities to all. The state must provide and ensure equal opportunity. It insists that state should make investment in public health, education and other socio-economic infrastructures (Barry, 2001).

Amartya Sen in his book '*The idea of Justice*' (2009) views justice as 'social realization' of human capabilities. The capabilities that he refers to are the capabilities to function, a function being a state of being or doing. A functioning-bundle is a collection of specific functioning, and could, in some specific instance, be a more or less precise description of an individual's nutritional status, his or her mobility status; his or her housing status and his or her status in respect of what Adam Smith called the ability to appear in public without shame. Like Rawls' theory of justice in which liberty and equality are integral aspects of the justice, the capability perspective also puts emphasis on the importance of both freedom and equality in overall assessment of the demands of the justice. However, he puts stress on "positive freedom" which is concerned with the actual capability of an individual to be or do this or that rather than only with his ability to pursue his desired ends in his protected personal sphere without hindrance or restraint. (Subramanian, *ibid*)

Another important aspect of Sen's contribution to the concept of justice is that he puts emphasis on *Nayay* (substantial aspect of justice) aspect of it, while Rawls' proclivity is towards the *niti* (procedural aspect of justice). One can understand two aspects of the justice when Indian system is juxtaposed with that of Chinese. While India has good *niti* with parliamentary democracy, free press, duly elected executive and free and fair elections, there is poverty, inequality and exploitation. On the other hand China is not a free society with rights and freedoms restricted; however, it has good record in *nayay* or substantial aspect of justice with no hunger death, no baffling inequalities and disparity. (Sen, *op.cit*)

How the Indian legal system is anti-people and pro-rich is reflected from self-acceptance within the system. The Chief Justice of India has commented that in India, the rich, powerful and influential resorted to every method available to them in the system to delay the trial… "The prosecution does not care if there is delay… They do not realize that delay benefits the accused…" The Chief Justice of India criticized the favoritism in higher courts. Dalai Lama, the spiritual leader of Tibet mentioned about corruption in Judiciary.[69]

However, the most serious matter is that judiciary is losing trust and credibility among the people. The situation has come to such a pass that the cases linger for years, without any hope for the judgment. Judgment is deferred for unlimited period with no hope of its fruition, delay and deferment are the norms, the witnesses are bought or sold or tamed or forced to be hostile or silenced. While victim is neutralized by delay, the accused keeps on doing what he has been doing unhindered. The justice system is lost amidst these procedural and non-procedural hurdles, with adjournments and incessant dates for hearing in toes. The justice system has become classic case of differend as propounded by Jean-Francois Lyotard.

"I would like to call a differend the case where the plaintiff is divested of the means to argue and becomes for that reason a victim. If the addressor, the addressee, and the sense of the testimony are neutralized, everything takes place as if there were no damages. A case of differend between two parties take place when the regulation of the conflict that opposes them is done in the idiom of one of the parties while the wrong suffered by the other is not signified in that idiom. The differend is signalled by this inability to prove. The one who lodges a complaint is heard, but the one who is a victim, and who is perhaps the same one, is reduced to silence. The differend is most unstable state and instance of language wherein something must be able to be put into phrases cannot yet be. The state is signalled by what one ordinarily calls a feeling."[70]

This is what justice has come to be in the postmodern arena, where it has become a mere phrase game. This is what is called as differend where plaintiff becomes victim as he or she divested of the means to argue. It has become quite easy to subvert the justice, whether through differend or delaying the process – it is also a part of silencing the victim. What one has to do is to neutralize the addressor, addressee and the sense of testimony, and then everything would seem as if there was no injustice or any damage or victimization. This is what justice has been reduced to.

This case of differend as the phrases in dispute has become common practice and justice and injustice has become dispute of phrases. However, a victim may be silenced or the addressor, addressee and sense of testimony may be neutralized, but it is very difficult to mitigate the effects it has on the system. It hollows the system where the justice becomes the prerogative of the riches, powerful and well-connected, and there reign a regime of lawlessness and indiscipline. 'This symptom of a near-complete loss of faith in the justice-system is indeed at the root of most of the present day national ills... unfortunately the political and social climate in the country is conducive to the growth of a such feeling. The result is that the remedial measures adopted have merely the appearance of an attempt to jump out of the morass in which the society is fast sinking...'[71]

Moreover, the anti-people and pro-rich and influential justice system gives rise to such lawlessness and indiscipline that people loose faith in the system. As people lose faith in state for providing justice and judiciary delivering fair justice, the people more often than not are resorting to their own justice mechanism. The growing incidence of lawlessness, violent demonstrations, mob violence and the organized violence, the private armies, even the Naxalites are outcom of such loss of faith in the system. "The legal system delivers little justice to the poor, even as the rich and powerful seem beyond its reach. While the homeless are heartlessly evicted—in the middle of night for the Commonwealth Games, in the very same city the government admits that it can do nothing about a well-known colony (Sainik Farms) which is completely illegal. Needless to say, the latter houses many of the Capital's educated, prosperous and obviously the powerful. Can such inequitable justice be a part of our vision for future?".[72]

It is said that justice delayed is justice denied. What would one say if justice is deferred for unlimited period? "It appears as if there is an understanding between the courts and advocates that come what may the orders of trial courts refusing adjournments shall be set aside on mercy pleas and one more opportunity shall be granted... A separate breed of advocates has cropped up. They are experts in pleading for adjournments. This culture has to be stopped... This whole culture of adjournment is a major reason why a case or a petition, which should be decided in two or three hearings, is disposed of in more than 100 hearings."[73]

From the mid-1990s, we can see that the court has often sacrificed civil liberties on the ground of "state security". This is apparent in the manner in which it has upheld the constitutional validity of several highly draconian legislations such as the Armed Forces Special Powers Act (AFSPA), the Terrorist and Disruptive Activities Act (TADA) and the Prevention of Terrorism Act (POTA).[74] Millions of people are being deprived of or forcibly evicted from their homes, hearth, jungles, tribal areas rich with minerals and means of their livelihood in the name of environment protection and development. Courts are sitting silently or taking active role in such inhuman and undemocratic acts. This deprives the people of their shelter and livelihood, violating their rights as declared by the Supreme Court in Chameli Singh's case.[75]

The trend of recent judicial pronouncements suggests that court has often subordinated civil liberties to the perceived imperative of state security, particularly in the context of the recent war on terror. The court's liberal and expansive pronouncements on socio-economic rights under Article 21 have not been matched by a determination to implement those rights. Since the liberalization of Indian economy, even the court's rhetoric on socio-economic rights has been weakening. Very often the court has itself ordered the violation of those rights, and in the process violating the principles of natural justice. Whenever socio-economic rights of the poor come into conflict with environmental protection, the court has usually subordinated those rights to environmental protection. Whenever environmental protection comes into with what is perceived by the court to be "development" or powerful commercial interests, environmental protection is usually subordinated at the altar of "development", or such powerful interests. There are of course exceptional judgments which defy these trends, particularly from high courts. (Bhushan, 2009).

These acts of omission and commission calls into question the commitment of the Indian courts to the rights of the poor and to the constitutional imperative of creating an egalitarian socialist republic. There can be little doubt that the Indian courts have failed to protect the socio-economic rights of the common people of India who constitute the vast majority of the Indian population. Part of the reason for this, undoubtedly, lies in the class structure of the Indian judiciary. The higher judiciary in India almost invariably comes from the elite section of the society and has become a self-appointing and self-perpetuating oligarchy. The Indian judges appoint themselves with the help of remarkably self-serving judgment by which the power of appointment was appropriated from the government by judiciary (*ibid*, 2009).

X

Undemocratic Political Parties

Congress centric politics or politics dominated by Congress borders on one party rule, whether there is internal democracy or not which has been exception rather than rule. If all the coverings and toppings of democracy or façade of democracy is removed, then one would find the clear imprint of one party rule behind all ills afflicting our polity and society. The subversion of democracy in the form of dynastic politics, oligarchy, vote bank politics, 'Suitcase Culture', corruption, lower participation and all the ills seem to have emanated from it. No wonder, Gandhiji foretold about this when 'He wanted the Congress to disband itself as a political movement (which institutionalized form is the Congress party) and become a vehicle for constructive work in the villages. He favoured an indirect democracy wherein villages would have their own elected Panchayats and then send someone to a central body. The center was to be weak and power was to be devolved downwards.'[76]

From temporary start in America, "by the close of century (19th century) parties have become permanent organization with professional staffs and offices that remained active between elections. They had evolved from gentlemen's parliamentary coalitions into disciplined organizations that kept in touch with constituencies... European political observers found the frank dominance of party in American life the key to understanding modern democratic politics. 'The spirit of and force of the party', wrote Lord Bryce in the 1890s, 'has in America been as essential to the action of the machinery of government as steam is to a locomotive engine' (The American Commonwealth, as cited in Hofstadter 1969; 71). Max Webber, Moisei Ostrogorski and others examined American parties, then discovered that the political machines so prominent in the New World also characterized the old.

In the generation after the second Reform Bill (1867), British parliamentary life fell into a routine rivalry organized by Conservatives and Liberals, occasionally racked by internal conflict and increasingly perturbed by the Irish representatives who sought to swing the balance. By the end of the century French Radical Socialists, middle-of-the-road socialists all organized parties to contest the Chamber elections and cope with polarized issues of Church and State. Even in Germany, where the federal Reichstag exerted less influence, strong party organizations grew up around religious and class cleavages... "By the end of the nineteenth century, democracy meant party government. Those at odds with its triumph worried less about any revolutionary danger than its alleged debasing of public life."[77]

It is quite ironic that the conduct and affairs of democracy in general and in India particularly is being carried out by the undemocratic parties. Most of the parties in India and to some extent all other democracies (in countries like USA and some European nations, despite organizational election, there are some undemocratic derivatives such as use of money or muscles power, pulls and pressures, managed or fixed elections etc.) do not follow democratic norms of organizational election. The decision making is undemocratic as it is centralized and imposed from above. Even if the election is held, it is stage-managed or its results are foregone conclusion or decided in advance by dominant faction or clique.

The party leaders and functionaries are nominated and imposed from above. The grassroot leaders and functionaries are left out most often than not to fend for themselves as they have no chance of making it to the top. The debates, discussions, articulation of issues pertaining to nation, society and general well-being of the people are given short shrift; while personality cult, groupism, factionalism, clique and 'Iron Law of Oligarchy' takes the center stage. 'A few recent important political happenings have revealed that the party system, which is the mainstay of any parliamentary competitive electoral, is facing a serious internal crisis and that the style of management of inner party challenges has given the impression of either adhocism or crude party bossism... a party system in a democracy based on a written constitution should have a constitutional and institutional mechanism of admitting and kicking out its dissenting members.'[78]

Every 'regional party' whether religion-based or culture-based or caste-based is all based on the principle of a leadership which is authoritarian because all regional (and some so called national parties also) are personality-based outfits. It is the writ of the leader which runs in the party... Supreme leader-based party system has shown its utter incapacity to take important public decisions and the result is that party pronouncements and announcements have lost any public credibility... Parties do not seem to have any institutional mechanism of creating a consensus through debate and discussion. Every political party is led by a leader who is surrounded by coteries of favourites. India is ruled by authoritarian party bosses and coteries of political favourites. Indian democracy is threatened because the completely undemocratic party system cannot be expected to practice democracy in governance.' (Bhambri, *ibid*, 3 para)

Once the parties come to power, their only interest is to stay in power, and they stick to power by hook or by crook. For it, these parties can go to any extent, even compromising or undermining national interest or social good or economic or social interest, national security or social harmony or for that matter democratic values or norms can be thrown unto the altar of their selfish motive to stay put in power. In addition to these maladies afflicting the political parties, dynastic politics has taken almost all parties in its malevolent fold. The perpetuation of family rule and one's dynasty has taken such strong hold that it has undercut their democratic credentials.

The way political parties have evolved has endangered democracy in general and future prospect of evolution of democracy in India – vote politics, caste and communal cauldron, criminalization of political parties and politicization of crime, lopsided viewpoint, emasculated and short-sighted leaders, dynastic grip, non-circulation of elite, becoming more of propaganda tool than a veritable carrier of democracy and facilitator of democratic ideals, mismatch between their promises during elections and real performance. Instead of becoming an aid to carrying conduct of democracy, the parties have become a tool for vested interests.

The most ironic situation is that in the largest democracy of the world, which has surprised world as well as given rise to envy among non-democratic nation bordering on jealousy, all parties are undemocratic in their organizational structure (*TOI, ET* and other Newspapers, 2010). Barring communist parties, whose democratic credential are point of debate; no Indian party follows the democratic norms so far organizational structure and selection of leadership are concerned.

Gandhi has commented soon after Independence that Congress as a party should be wound up (*Young India*, 1947). Why? He was aware that in the name of Independence it would seek its pound of flesh, while the national and social interests would be put on backburner. That is exactly what has happened, giving rise to many undemocratic tendencies, systemic distortions and imbalances. To view it in a more Machiavellian light: the Congress Party then appears as a league of aspiring groups and power-broking individuals, initially created by the 'collaborative' strategy of British rule. The political dynamism of the movement owed little to ideological conviction: rather, driven by internal jostling and competition into faction-building, it was pushed into grubby world of local politics in order to enlist support from the inert urban and rural populations… The intact state over which the Congress Party gained control in 1947 had been created by an alien power for its own extractive purposes; now, it had to somehow be made legitimate, it had to be able to require obligations of its population.[79]

Hence started a deliberate and well-calculated strategy in perception management that later turned into a mere propaganda. This league of aspiring groups and power-broking individuals initially created by 'collaborative' strategy of British rule started taking their pound of flesh in various ways, subverting democracy and democratic principle. 'One major socialist leader, Ram Manohar Lohia articulated a doctrine that only by weakening the Congress would India thrive. Anti-Congressism as political programmes was born then and was to influence politics in subsequent decades.'[80]

However, it is impossible to think that real democracy can be ingrained through undemocratic parties. As most of the parties are undemocratic and it is the party or the parties that carry or conduct the affairs of democracy,

democracy as prevailing in India is bound to be a sham. 'India's chaotic politics can sometimes seem democratic to a fault: the election cycle rarely pauses and the country has roughly 1050 registered national and regional parties. But most of the major parties, including the majority Congress Party, are internally undemocratic, there are no primaries and party leaders discourage dissent. Party bosses select candidates and have shown increasing tendency to select their own relatives.'[81]

XI

Insecurity and Lopsided Foreign Policy

Security or the feeling of security among general people is an important aspect in reinforcing belief in democracy. If people feel secured—internally and externally, their faith in democracy is reinforced, which strengthens democracy substantially. However, if people feel unsecured and let down by the leadership and the system, they start loosing interest in the state of affairs of the country, directly or indirectly. And this is the starting point in the decline of democracy. There has been substantial loss of territory in Leh-Laddkh sector and numerous incursions by China, without any befitting reply from Indian side. (Reports in *TOI* and other national newpapers,15th January, 2010) If you cannot defend your territory, how can people be defended? This is cause and effect of insecurity and lopsided foreign policy.

The image of Soft State and arch of enemies slowly encircling us, bid of sole super power to hamstring us in regional context and the regional power that is fast emerging as world power efforts to downsize us to the sub-continent. The weak, myopic, impulsive and knee-jerking leaders are unable to see beyond appearances and platitudes. While career diplomats are more concerned about their upward mobile careers, the people are left to fend for themselves as there is veil of secrecy and unilateralism surrounding our foreign policy. It appears that we have not learnt from thousand years of foreign rule.

The present state of our foreign policy is the continuation of the policy followed by the past leaders. 'The tryst was betrayed by many (leaders), with result that India has performed dismally… The one overriding has been of our civil servants abdicating the obligation to volunteer advice in the long-term interest of the country… Honest opinion given in the national interest has its won reward… The responsibility of ensuring a just democracy hinges on the activism of an unselfish voluntary effort.'[82]

It is a great regret that our nation and leadership failed to see the equality of nationalism; India did not perceive that the Cold War as mutually reinforced and that outside the Cold War, the Soviet Union would be neutral. Many years of Nehru's eras were wasted (in chasing chimera of world peace, disarmament and fraternity for developing countries while neglecting our national interest and foreign policy goals). Nehru wrongly assumed countries like China would appreciate India's non-hostility through non-alignment. After 1980, mistakes by Indira Gandhi in Afghan policy alienated India from the Afghan nationalists. On Pakistan, the policy of knee-jerk reaction and considering the problem with Pakistan an unique is wrong.[83]

The same policy of 'myopia, sacrificing long term interest for short term goal of buying peace or knee-jerk reaction' is being followed with impunity, secured as they are in the coterie of non-visionary leaders, bookish diplomats with 'yes-man approach', far from the debate and discussion. There are many vital policy decisions such as Kashmir policy, Nuclear Deal, terrorism and other matter of national security such as Chinese brazenness in claiming their sovereignty on Arunachal, etc., are kept away from public eye. Even Parliament is not being kept in loop in this vital aspect of foreign policy.

How India is following the old policy of brinkmanship, discarding public opinion for whims and fancies of the leaders who are guided by their short-term interests and goals are witnessed in case of China vis-à-vis Arunachal Pradesh. A World Bank document says external affair minister S M Krishna has stated that "India will not pose any Arunachal Pradesh specific project" to the Bank.[84] This is virtual granting suzerainty to China and it is not historic mistake that our immature and idealistic leader gifted Tibet to China on platter without any quid pro quo.

There is series of mistakes for which there is no one accountable and even if the person concerned is found to be guilty, the person instead of being punished is rewarded with plum post and post retirement job. The example is that of K. Menon who made blunder at Sharm-al-Sheikh when Indian interference in Baluchistan is acceded by making commitment that India would not interfere in it. Or a minister of state for external affairs announcing a 360 degree shift inadvertently on Kashmir issue when he proposed a mediation or interlocution by Saudi Arabia which is against our stated stand on the issue and retracting his stand next day symbolizes the undemocratic nature of foreign policy.

It is no wonder that the undemocratic, secretive, unaccountable and untransparent foreign policy is reflected in the uninspiring diplomatic service, think tanks and universities. 'India's diplomatic service, think tanks and universities are not up to the task of managing an agenda befitting a great power. Instead of acting as a catalyst for India's transformation into a world power, the foreign ministry establishment may be a drag on the nation, preventing it from moving up on the international power ladder.'[85] It is in this context that Subrahmanyam, the strategic guru of India has commented that strategic naiveté is a national weakness (*TOI*, 2011).

XII

Criminalization of Politics and Politicization of Crime, Politicization of Business and Corporatization of Politics

The Criminalization of politics and the politicization of the crime, and the politicization of business and corporatization of politics is another enemy of democracy as it is eating into vitals and essentials of democracy.

Criminalization has posed a grave threat to our democracy and the very existence of the country. History sheeters, mafia don, leaders of criminal gangs, bandit queens and petty criminals have entered the politics in a big way. Though they seem to champion the cause of their respective community, class, caste, region, religion, etc, their focus changes once they are well-entrenched in Parliament or the Legislative Assembly. 'Politics in India has become a profession rather than a vocation; we do not have political culture, only uncultured politics are found in the country. The public realm is increasingly and sharply in the risk of being overtaken by the greedy, exploitative private realm. Naturally, there is to be seen a glaring disjunction between the policy formulation and policy implementation. Political corruption is the mother of all corruption.'[86]

In the 14th Lok Sabha, out of 542 members there were no less than 100 MPs who had been charge sheeted in criminal cases, ranging from minor misdemeanors like 'disturbing the peace' to the omnibus charge of 'rioting' to serious offences like murder, rape, and dacoity. Out of these five-score MPs across the political spectrum, roughly one third could be described as those involved in heinous crimes. A dozen have murder charges against them, another 10 have been charged with attempted murder. Around 11 of them in public perception were known as dons. And at the state level, nearly 700 members of the state legislative assemblies are involved in criminal cases and trials are pending against them... Criminals and mafia gangs in large numbers in the garb of politicians are now occupying seats of power. Communal and caste identities are being highlighted by them to gain political power. It is for this reason that ex-Chief Election Commissioner JS Lyngdoh has commented that the politicians are the cancer of the society.[87]

The criminalization of politics and politicization of the crime has been made possible due to lacunae in the Representation of People's Act 1951. Moreover, the Constitution of India does not directly mention or explain disqualification or ineligibility of criminals from contesting elections. This lacuna has been there, but nobody dares to amend it as it is akin to as who would bell the cat. The authority for amendment lies with Parliament and legislative assemblies and they do not seem to have will power to correct this for obvious reason. The contradiction is galore in this respect when one analyzes the various articles and provisions in this regard. Article 102(1) (e) in respect of Parliament and Article 191 (1) (e) in case of State Legislatures the matter regarding disqualification is to be decided by the Act of Parliament.

The Representation of People's Act 1951 vide Section 8 provides for the disqualification as consequence of conviction in certain offences. Subsection (1) provides for immediate disqualification for a period of six years from the date of conviction for offences mentioned in the section. Subsection (2) of Section 8 provides for disqualification on conviction of offences of hoarding, adulteration, dowry and *sati* but with caveat requiring that conviction must be followed by a sentence of imprisonment for a period of not less than two years.

Subsection (3) of Section 8 provides for disqualification due to conviction or any other offence, but it requires that conviction must be followed by a sentence of imprisonment for a period not less than two years. This subsection also mentions that disqualification under Subsections (1), (2) and (3) will not be valid in case of a Member of any of the Houses, for a period of three months, even if an appeal or revision application is filed in meantime; the disqualification will not be operational further till decision on such appeal or revision vide Subsection (4). Thus, the provision of disqualification on conviction as mentioned in Subsections (1), (2), and (3) gets nullified by Subsection 8. Apart from it, there is another contradiction regarding disqualification under 103 (1) of Article 192 of the Constitution whereby the disqualification process can be initiated by the President of India or Governor only after the person has been elected to the House.

The disqualification before election is to be decided by an election petition and the election petition comes into effect only after the election. The criminals aspiring to enter politics make use of this pitfall in the Act. Hence a criminal who should be disqualified is allowed to be elected and become the member of the House till the decision is made in respect of his or her election petition. And it takes years to decide on the election petition, sometimes the member completes his or her full term even then the decision does not come.

There are many nexuses undercutting the nexus of politicians, criminals, business or all other nexuses are being undercut by these nexuses of politicians, criminals and business. But of course there is a nexus between big money, journalism and politics and not every journalist is independent. The size of the press, however, does matter and it can be a constant irritant to the politicians (Desai, *op.cit*). The most threatening aspect is that criminalization of politics, politicization of crime and corporatization of politics has taken our system in such a vicious circle that it seems impossible to come out of their clutches. While criminalization of politics and politicization of crime limit the democratic space and scare people from public sphere, corporatization of politics transform democracy into oligarchy and then tyrannical monarchy.

It is because of the clout of this nexus, there is no provision for criminal prosecution for cartelization in Indian law as is the case in US and Australia, and other countries of the world that has declared cartel as criminal offence. Resultantly, it has led to formation of cartel in almost every sector of economy. As cartel operates secretly, it is very difficult to detect them even if there is law there. In a country like India which has no law for declaring cartel formation as an offence, there is no scope for doing anything in this regard.

The most serious repercussion of this layered nexus is that protest, demonstration, dissent, free debate and discussion has become scarce and spasmodic, leading to virtual strangulation of democratic norms and values. If anyone or any organization or association or party dares to raise voice against them, they are silenced with vast pool of intimidating resources these nexus have. Perhaps no other issue poses as big threat to the safety and security of citizens (and ultimately democracy) as the growing criminalization of politics in the country. Criminals masquerading as politicians and taking advantage of the lax laws are playing havoc in the country (Tharoor, 1997).

These criminals masquerading as politicians have acquired formidable powers and have compromised the police agencies (and other administrative and democratic institutions) to the extent that they have become immune to legal restraints. For too long the political class has resisted the demands to enact suitable laws to deal with this phenomenon. While it is well understood what needs to be done, no political party has shown willingness and determination to deal with this threat. This body (police leadership, IPS) demands that people charge-sheeted in serious offences be debarred from entering the political arena (Verma, 2010).

Politician-bureaucrat-contractor or Businessman-criminal nexus

The politician-bureaucrat-business or contractor-criminal nexus (PBCBC) has emerged as the most threatening element for democracy. Recently particularly after the liberalization and privatization of the Indian economy, the PBCBC nexus has virtually suffocated the democratic norms and values of accountability, debate and discussion, protest and probity in the public conduct and responsibility. Moreover, this nexus has edged out the people form the democratic space through their muscles and money power. This has not only shrunk the space of democratic movement and people's view being aired without any genuine or perceived threats but also forced people from their natural habits, robbed of their rights over jungle, greensands, pasture lands, rivers, hills and mountains.

It was promised that abolition of licensing and the deregulation of the economy would remove the scope for an entwining of business and politics. Far from it, the impregnation of politics in business has deepened and is now qualitatively different from before. Two things have changed. First, deregulation has meant that while micro-rules are no longer important, the terms of the larger policy become all the more so. Hence the twist to the policy to suit one's interests (the tussles over the telecom licensing, gas pricing policy and the creating of special economic zones are good examples). Second, oligarchs and entrepreneurs, far from working in the background, are now active participants in politics. Of course, the usual explanation is that resources are needed to fight elections in ever growing amounts and hence the growing influence of money in politics. What is not acknowledged is that more and more money is flowing into contesting elections because once elected even there is more money.[88]

The net result of such obnoxious nexuses is: The right to life has been emptied out of its contents and facilitating elements with only level being intact. The air has been polluted, water which nature has provided in plenty has become intoxicated and unhygienic for making money and business ventures, the land and hills and jungles are being plundered for the mining lobby, and perishable resources are being plundered to the hilt. The freedom of expression has been reduced to sham in the face of this nexus. While equality and justice has remained only on the paper, rosy pictures are being stuffed in public space through media and traditional channels of communication and Goebbelsian propaganda.

This nexus is threatening the people and democratic value of protest and movement. If one tries to raise voice against this or attempt to mobilize, the threat or very prospect of it deters person or group or association to fill up the gap left by this nexus. What is more that all political parties with a few notable exceptions have put their men in the different segments and layers of civil society such as resident welfare association, various unions, associations, groups and other forums of civil society who act as double agent. On one side these people, usually of dubious or shady characters or the criminal or person with low IQ but strong loyalty to the party hooked through baits of the vested interests, act as agent of the concerned parties and side by side forcibly occupy the space in civil society, with tacit support from these parties.

Once they occupy the space or the posts, they don't vacate it and pass it to their kith and kin or other henchmen of the concerned parties. The same structures and patterns exist in rural areas where these criminals, henchmen, muscles with shady and criminal background dot the heads of governmental and non-governmental organizations, and different segments of the civil society.

This obnoxious nexus, minus criminal came into being after the second Five-Year Plan was mooted in 1956. In this plan, the priority was given to industries. Hence, for the first time, politicians, bureaucrats and business tested the advantage of forming such nexus. Afterwards, their nefarious bond got further cemented with advantages accruing to all without any collateral risk. The businessmen required licence to do business, the Minister or the politicians had the granting authority and bureaucrats or the civil servants were the one who used to process the papers and necessary formalities.

When this 'licence-permit' Raj was done away with the introduction of the liberalization of the Indian economy in 1991, it hardly made any difference to their nexus. On the contrary, it provided mind-boggling opportunities for their aggrandizement. The only difference was that criminals were added to their nexus, making it more deadly and hardened. By the time the liberalization and privatization of the Indian economy completed two decades, this politicians-bureaucrats-businessmen-criminals nexus fortified itself into impregnable force which is looting the public money and resources, making our democracy sham and hollowed.

This nexus has been facilitated by decay of institutions such as CBI, Judiciary and institutionalization of kickbacks in government contracts, political patronage, and no provision to book errant bureaucrats. For initiating any criminal proceedings in the corruption or graft case against the Joint secretary and above level, there is provision of prior permission, and unless it is granted nothing can be done. It is worth mentioning that it is these ranks and file who are involved in the corruption and swindling of public money. By the time permission is sought and granted, the concerned official wipes out every proof and stymie the case in such a manner that nothing happens.

Administrators (civil servants or the bureaucrats) are adept in interpretation and application of rules and regulations and astute enough to manipulate government policies, decisions and actions in a manner that these would appear in consonance with the formal laws and rules, although in this process, there may be a gross violation of norms of fair, equitable and moral conduct. The politicians and bureaucrats in India are partners in bending rules. Both provide support to each other for their common benefits at individual level.[89]

It is not to deny that 'politics and business together constitute the fount of a corrupt system, but if they are the twin head of the corruption, the professionals (Civil servants and criminals) constitute the limbs. It has been proven time and again that no case of major corruption is possible without mutual collaboration between the politicians and the civil servants. There is no dearth of such misconducts of the Ministers. There are many cases of Ministers colluding with servants in misappropriation of the government money and misuse of the office for private gains. However, without the acquiescence of the civil servants, the ministers could not indulge in corruption.[90] That is why Dr. Kiran Bedi, the first Indian woman Police Officer has said 'the country has been ruined by IAS, IPS and Politicians, with top slot shared by IAS followed by IPS and politicians'.[91]

The politicization of every sphere of public life has made it tough for democracy. While these politicians, who are mostly third graders of every field where they could not make any mark or any money and rest are progenies of the politicians, do not give any space for dedicated workers, they force them to soil their hands with cuts and commissions. Even if they want to do the work or implement the project seriously and honestly, they are not allowed to do so. "Politicians really forced junior engineers to raise illicit funds through distributors of canal water and allocation of maintenance contracts and offer them a share of these."[92]

The problem in this regard is that our mindset and lack of institutional arrangement that should have been there considering ours being a constitutional democracy has made things very complicated. Although the Indian Constitution provides detailed function and powers of each and every institution and organization, yet there is no mention about as to how state would operate or execute various laws and policies. It was this lacuna that gave the bureaucracy tremendous power to bend the rules and regulations framed by them. Anticipating this negative aspect, Pt Nehru tried to put up a system based on planned economy and tolerance, but the fast paced changes taking country in its whirlwind did not give him enough time and scope for this. The internal wrangling in Congress forced Nehru to rely on civil servants, and "the diffuse aspirations of the pre-independence period was thus formalized and handed over to the bureaucracy's rule-bound incompetence" (Khilnani, *op.cit*).

This is how bureaucracy started gaining ascendancy and accumulated vast power within it. Under its tutelage, it coalesced a powerful, dangerous, and intimidating nexus – Politician-bureaucrat-contractor or Businessman-criminal nexus which is playing havoc with democracy, democratic institutions and democratic values and norms as dictated by their vested interests.

XIII

Violence

Last but not least is the violence which is anathema to democracy as it attacks on the very basis of democracy—freedom and debate and discussion. Once violence is let loose, it has cascading effects on the individual and collective psyche. Not only it invokes fear among the populace acting as spoke on their freedom, but also restricts personal and collective growth of the society by strangulating creativity and innovation. Hence, it should not be and must not be used except as measure of the last resort. Even if it is used or even threat of its use is to be resorted to, it should be done in very restraint way, without causing irreversible damage to physical and psychological well-being.

The term 'violence' has attained wider meaning in all type of discourse as the thin line dividing the political violence from that of non-political one has been blurred as scope and intensity of violence has transcended all barriers. The famous feminist contention that nothing is personal can be used in case of violence: no violent act is personal as it has social and political inputs.

Likewise, the United Nations Development Program, in its path-breaking 2005 Human Development Report (HDR), devotes special attention to the analysis of violent conflict and brings the real threat into focus. It identifies violent conflict as the most brutal suppression of human development. Every civilian death linked to conflict is a violation of human rights. The risk is heavily weighted against people living in the world's poorest countries. Humanity cannot enjoy security without development or development without security, and neither without respect for human rights (UNDP, 2005).

The 1994 HDR attempted a framework for security beyond military concerns. It called for safety from chronic threats and protection from sudden disruptions in the patterns of daily life. The 2005 HDR holds that violent conflict undermines human security in both dimensions. It notes a strong association between violent conflict and low human development. A security framework is needed which recognizes poverty, social breakdown and civil conflicts as the core components of the global security. Prevention of violent conflict must be at the centre of planning for poverty reduction. Comprehensive risk assessments must be taken up to evaluate how specific conflicts affect policies (Subramanian, 2007).

Violence of the oppressed against the state is often of the physical kind. State violence is defined as legitimate, but violence of the oppressed is regarded as illegitimate. Structural and symbolic violence are also relevant and cannot be ignored in the analysis of violence. (Oommen, 2006) Structural violence occurs when the oppressed are culturally stigmatized and ideologically regulated or marginalized. Symbolic violence is used by the state and the cultural mainstream to perpetuate their hegemony. Both kinds of violence are invoked against those in the lowest rungs of the social order. Physical violence manifests itself as the weapon of the oppressed against the structural and symbolic violence (Subramanian, *op. cit*).

Even if the violence seems to be wired in human nature, it is not justified as very evolution of politics, diplomacy, dialogue and democracy as form of government negates any doubt in this regard. 'When the well preserved body of a 5,000-year old man was found in a glacier in Austria in 1991, it had an arrowhead in its back. When the 2000-year old 'Tolland Man' was found in a Danish Peat-bog in 1950, he had been strangulated. The earliest recoded civilization were founded on conquest and slaughter, and the vast war cemeteries strung along the former front lines of first world war remind us that capitalist civilization has not been different in this respect, except for its industrialization of the means of destruction. But whereas earlier cultures tool of violence and even cruelty were taken for granted, in our own times violence may be no less bloody (and glorified in movies and video games), but it is no longer taken for granted – or at least much less than formerly' (Bernstein, 2009).

Everyone has underlined the prevalence of violence and how to avoid it or control it. Even Marx could not but had to concede: "Capital comes dripping from head to foot, from every pore, with blood and dirt. The discovery of gold and silver in America, the extirpation, enslavements and entombment in mines of the aboriginal population, the beginning of conquest and looting of the East, the turning of Africa in a warren commercial hunting of black skin, signalize the rosy down of the era of capital production". History is replete with numerous horrific saga of blood, extermination, Gulag and dirt of communist regime.

One of the most widespread kinds of violence today is between people who are all themselves victim, in one way or other, of global capitalism, imperialism and attendant local form of inequality and injustice. An instance is the African conflict zones of Rwanda and the eastern Congo, Sudan/Darfur and Liberia/Sierra Lone, 'when victims become killers' as Mahmood Madani puts it. The Congo, in which disease and malnutrition caused by almost a decade of political violence, has since 2003 been killing an average of 40,000 people a month, half of them children, is possibly the most appalling example in the world at this moment (*ibid*).

However, there is another type of violence which is not less lethal and damaging than any other type of violence being perpetrated in human society. This can be termed as 'systemic violence'. In the past six years more children have died globally as a result of starvation and preventable diseases than humans perished in the six years of Second World War. Every three seconds a human life that just began ceases to exist in a cruel way. At the same time in these three second $ 120,000 are being spent on military armament worldwide (Brie, 2009).

Modern imperialism has nothing to offer to the large majorities of peoples in Asia, Africa and Latin America (75 per cent of the population). The continuation of the domination of capital over the totality of these peripheries requires the militarization of the globalization. This rules out any genuine democratization or the social progress for these peoples. The deployment of over 600 US military bases distributed over the whole planet is intended to establish the domination of Washington over the whole world (Amin, 2009).

However, it is the duty of the state, society and government that people or group or section of people is not pushed to the extent that they resort to the violence. The cult of violence that has swept our nation is cause and effect of the poor or no governance at all that is pushing them to resort to violence. There is no mechanism to filter such demand or issue that has the potentiality of sliding into a violence or violent form of agitation at regional level or micro level. The power and institutions are centralized, and decentralization and regional mechanism that were in place during Nehru era, which was broken by Mrs. Gandhi to get complete control over the party and government, had been done away with. It is because of this that every local or regional issue is made national, whereas the national issues are relegated to back burner.

What is more dangerous for democracy is that violence is acquiring some sort of legitimacy as a means of grievance redressal. Be it petty local issue or any sectarian or sectional issue, violence is more often than not used for getting things done. The government and other democratic institutions, handicapped as these are with corruption; nepotism and colonial mindset are unable to solve the problems of common people unless goaded by violence or threat of violence or the possibility of violence. This type of response from the democratic institutions reinforces the faith in violence which is very dangerous for democracy. Be it Naxal problem or police problem this mindset is getting ingrained in our system which is taking toll of faith in democracy.

XIV

Procedural Deviation

Procedural deviation is one of the enemies of democracy as it hollows the politics and political actors, and institutions find caught in the logjam of this procedural deviation. Over the period, particularly after Indira regime when the politics and democratic institutions were reduced to personal 'fiefdom' and 'political expediency', procedural deviation has set in to the extent that executive, parliament and party system has been weakened and marginalized.

Consequently, there has been shift of power to Supreme Court, Election Commission and President, moderating the damages caused by fragmentation of polity. Though these institutions have worked to reinvigorate institutional capital and check undemocratic excesses partly, the weakening of executive, Parliament and party system due to fragmentation of politics has certainly weakened the case for democracy. Particularly the decreasing credibility of political institutions such as legislature and political parties as effective institutions of democracy which is vital for delivering public good and good governance is not good for democracy (Rudolphs, 2008).

However, the most debilitating blow that democracy has received, particularly during the last two decades has been the pitiable condition of political parties. The political parties have been reduced to 'family fiefdom and without a trace of internal democracy'. It is for this reason that political parties have become weak and incapable to formulate and debate policies reflecting people's needs, hopes and aspirations. For obtaining power or some pecuniary gain, the party leaders have no qualm for dumping the ideology of the party or issues on which they have sought mandate from the people. It is no wonder that for many political leaders a career in politics has become a means for 'amassing a fortune or promoting personal interest at the expense of public interest.' The all pervasive coalition logic based on winning formulas and post poll alliances has furthered the destruction of politics and heightened the tendency of leaving the people out of political discourse (*ibid*, 2008).

Consequently, political processes have much less power over the policy decisions and implementation which is critical in shaping people's lives and livelihood. The divergence between election rhetoric and actual implementation of government policy remains at large, particularly with regard to policies that have distributive and welfare outcomes. In more recent years, the increasing focus on economic growth has led to an insulation of decision-making from popular pressure and focus instead on preserving the status quo for the sake of the current economic boom. Most governments end up attending to the demands and anxieties of powerful and articulate sections of the upper and middle classes (Hasan, 2009).

Systemic imbalance, election centric political obsession, vote bank politics, faulty electoral system where 200 million voters out of 600 million decide who would win the system (Election Commission Report, 2009), first-past-the-post based electoral system which elects a person who just passes the post by getting the maximum number of votes as compared to other candidates which is not majority of the total votes – all these render democracy to mere name. The democratic institutions have been reduced to mere puppet in the grand game of politics of aggrandizement and vested interest which is being paled out in the name of democracy. "The hoary institutions of Indian Democracy—the judiciary, the police, the 'free' press and of, course elections—far from working as a system of checks and balances, quite often do the opposite."[93]

While we have a vibrant electoral democracy, participatory democracy is very weak, despite the very positive structural elements of the local self-governance brought in through the 73rd and 74th amendments in the Constitution... Sadly, democracy occasionally degenerates into majoritarianism. A majority riding roughshod over the rights or views of the minority certainly cannot be the vision of India; nor an aggressive, organized minority coercing other by threats. Unfortunately, while the former sometimes rears its head, we see increasing examples of the latter too. Today, many groups—particularly the poor, tribal and woman—do not get justice and are often oppressed and exploited. Traditional stoicism of the voiceless is now giving way to activism, which takes different forms—including Naxalism (Karnik, 2010).

XV

Neoliberalism of Crony and Erstraz Capitalism Version

Neoliberalism of crony and Erstraz capitalism version is the most versatile invisible enemy of democracy which eats its vitals slowly but steadily.

The term 'Neoliberalism' was used first time in Germany during interwar period for a 'Third way' apart from laissez-faire capitalism and socialism. Later on, it came to be known as 'social market economy' in post war period (Hartwich, 2009). Recently, the term Neoliberalism was viewed as admixture or blend of economic policies like privatization, trade liberalization, deregulation, removal of subsidies and free flow of capital and goods. Gradually, the term came to be associated with 'Washington Consensus' (Williamson, 1990). Later it was put to variegated criticism and came to be known as 'Market Fundamentalism' (Stilgitz, 2002).

The Marxist critique views social content of Neoliberalism as 'accumulation by dispossession' (Harvey, 2003). While some see neoliberalism as 'accumulation through encroachment' (Patnaik, 2008), others view it as 'accumulation by displacement' (Araghi, 2009). Indeed those who extract a theory of 'cyclical determinism' or 'Pendulum Shift' from Polanyi's historical account of the 'double movement' (from economic liberalism to protective regulation) constrict the neoliberalism as the opposite of Keynesianism (Araghi, 2010). Recently, particularly in the wake of financial crisis and related social strife, the Keynesianism has been seen as an alternative to neoliberalism (Davidson, 2009).

The "great lacuna" in Keynesianism, to borrow Bello's words (2009), is that it has never understood (or never had to understand) the ecological contradiction of high consumption capitalism. National Keynesianism was always a model that worked within a definite "time-space". Over the "long time", as Kalecki (1943) presciently predicted, it would lead to wage inflation and over the "long space", it would lead to ecological disaster (Araghi, *op. cit*) 'Global Keynesianism', in these accounts, appears as a rational alternative to global neoliberalism (Mead, 1989).

Challenging these positions, Araghi (2010) argues that neoliberalism is neither opposite of Keynesianism, nor is global Keynesianism a possible alternative to global neoliberalism as a moment within Keynesianism and being anti-thesis to it, neoliberalism was the Keynesian response to its own contradictions. Reacting to wage inflation and stagflation at home and unruly developmentism abroad, (Araghi, 1994; McMichael, 2008) it used the state (supra state) intervention to shift the basis of demand management from wage contracts and 'development compromise' to micro and macro credit and debt-based globalization. (Araghi, 2009) It was this strategic shift from 'positive' to 'negative' means of managing effective demand, rather than abandoning the Keynesian system altogether that was a core element of the 'neoliberal innovation' (Araghi, 2010).

Neo-liberalism of Crony and Erstraz capitalism brand is another great enemy of democracy. The crony and Erstraz capitalism uses democracy and its institution to further their interest at the cost of people and the principles of equality and freedom.

One can get the glimpse of the grip that this crony and Erstraz version of neoliberalism have on democratic institution across the democratic countries of the world, whether be it USA or UK or Australia or India. In the wake of the recession and slowdown that hit the world economies across the board in 2008 and its aftermath, this contradiction came to fore when the democratic governments across the world provided hefty stimulus package in the form of financial bailout and tax concession to the financiers, industrialists and business houses, from the money garnered from the people, while the same people were left to fend for themselves in the wake of economic crisis hitting below their belt in the form of loss of job, reduced income, spiralling inflation, shooting prices and what not.

This contradiction becomes more glaring when one considers the fact that these liberal capitalists ferociously oppose any transfer of money to the poor, and any government control or extra-governmental control. But when the crisis hits them devouring their profits, they beg for government assistance and the government of this crony or Erstraz capitalist readily oblige, generously disbursing the money collected from poor in the form of tax. 'Under the threat of a collapse of the entire system, the safety net – intended to help unfortunate individuals meet the exigencies of life—was generously extended to commercial banks, then to investment banks, insurance firms, auto firms even car loan companies. Never has so much money transferred from so many to a so few.

'We are accustomed to thinking of government transferring money from the well off to the poor. Here, it was the poor and average transferring money to the rich. Already heavily burdened taxpayers saw their money—intended to help banks lend so that economy be revived—go to pay outsized bonuses and dividends. Dividends are supposed to be a share of profits; here it was simply a share of government largesse... The bailout exposed deep hypocrisy all around. Those who had preached fiscal restraint when it came to small welfare programmes for the poor now clamoured for the world's largest welfare programmes. Those who argued for the free market's virtue of "transparency" ended up creating financial systems so opaque that banks could not make sense of their own balance sheets. And then the government, too, was induced to engage decreasingly transparent forms of bailouts to cover up its largesse to the banks. Those who had argued for "accountability" and "responsibility" now sought debt forgiveness for the financial sector' (Stilgitz, *ibid*).

This is what crony and Erstraz version of neoliberalism stands for wherein profit is privatized and losses of the industries and businesses are nationalized. In the case of India, the stimulus was a very hush-hush affair, where transparency and accountability was thrown to winds. While in most countries on both side of Atlantic it was open affair without any pinch of their democratic conscience.

Endnotes

1 Popper, Karl, *The Open Society and its Enemies*, Routledge Classics: New York & London, One Volume Edition. 1995.

2 *See* Sunil Khilnani

3 *See* Lloyd Rudolph and Susanne Hoeber

4 World Bank, 2008

5 Tandon, Rajesh and Mohanty, Ranjita, *ibid*, pp 8, para 3

6 Mudraraksha , 3/15 as quoted in 'Chanakyaniti' by Swami Jagadishwaranand Saraswati

7 Ludwig (ed.), 'Chanakya Policy mirror (Chanakyanitidarpan) page 8

8 Mukhopadhyay, Amal Kumar, '*Superpowering India*,' Manas Publications, New Delhi, 2009

9 *See* www.wikileaks.com : India related news

10 Kampfner, John, 'India's selfish elite hold the Republic back' *Times of India*, dated 24.01.2010.

11 Kampfner, John, *ibid*

12 Khilnani, Sunil, *op. cit* p 65

13 Gupta, Dipankar, *op. cit*, page 46

14 Rifkin, Jeremy, '*The Emphatic Civilization*', Penguin, 2009

15 Yamini Mishra, woman member of Planning Commission as quoted in *Sunday Jansatta*, dated 14.02.10.

16 Prasoon Latant, 'Alakh Jagati Nanhi Duniya' *Janstatta*, dated 14.02.2010

17 Prasoon Latant, *ibid*, para 5

18 Pankaj Mishra: en.wikipedia.org/wiki/Pankaj_Mishra link pages 29/03/2011

19 Kamfner, *op. cit.* p 65

20 'Elections have become the biggest source of corruption', said chief election commissioner S.Y Qurashi. According to him, one of new missions for the Election Commission (EC) is to fight against money power in polls..... Candidates' spending spree during election is a competitive phenomenon. "Anecdotally, we know that if a candidate spends Rs. 2 crore, he wants, say, Rs. 10 crore in return. He has to take the help of criminals and moneybags. Once elected, he twists policies to favour the moneybags," in *The Times of India*, "CEC: Elections biggest source of Corruption". Dated: 27.03.2011.

21 http://eci.nic.in/eci_main/faq/Contesting.asp 28.10.2010

22 *The Economic Times*, *The Times of India*, and other national newspapers dated 15.01.21010

23 Budget Papers, 2010-11 and Economic Survey, 2009-10 and 2010-11

24 Comptroller Auditor General Report 2009-10

25 Kishwar, Madhu Purnima, 'The flawed Logic of Quota', *The Times of India*, 20.03.2010.

26 Patil, Sanjay 'Feudal Forces: Reform Delayed, Moving from Force to Service in South Asian Policy', Commonwealth Human Right Initiative, 2008.

27 Aikin, C, 'Corruption', *Dictionary of Social Science*, New York, 1964, p 142

28 World Bank Report, The World Bank, Washington DC, 1989

29 Report of Committee on Prevention of Corruption , Government of India, Ministry of Home Affairs, New Delhi, p.5

30 Friedrich, Carl J., 'Corruption Concepts in Historical Perspective', in Arnold J. Heidenheimer, Michael Johnson and Victor T. Levine, (Eds), *Political Corruption: A Handbook*, Transaction Publishers, New Brunswick, 1989, p:15

31 Scott, J.C, '*Comparative Politcal Corruption*', Englewood Cliffs, N.J. Prentice –Hall, 1972, p.3

32 Braibanti, Ralph, '*Reflections on Bureaucratic Corruption*', Public Administration, winter 1962, p.357

33 *Kautilya's Arthshastra*, translated and edited by R. Shamsastri, Mysore Printing and Publishing House, Mysore, 1967p. 67.

34 Ahmad Shamshad and Nafees Ahmad Ansari, '*Corruption, Criminalization of politics and Development*', Indian Journal of Public Administration, vol. LIV, No. 4, October-December, 2008 p.868

35 *See* Corruption Perception Index as issued by Transparency International

36 *Social issues in India*, Chronicle Books, New Delhi, 2004 p.6

37 Basu, Kaushik, *Economic Graffiti: Essays for Everyone*, Oxford University Press, New Delhi, 1994, p56

38 Mitra, Chandan, *The Corrupt Society*, Viking Publications, New Delhi, 1998, p.76

39 Arora, Ramesh K., *Challenging Corruption in Indian Public Service, in Public Governance and Decentralization*, Mittal Publications, New Delhi, 2003 p. 111

40 Editorial, *Economic & Political Weekly*, January 31, Vol. XLIV No 4

41 Vittal, N, '*Fighting Corruption in daily life*'. Paper presented in the Forum of Public Causes, New Delhi, 25th September, 2000, p.2.

42 Ahmad, Shamshad and Nafees Ahmad Ansari, *op. cit.* p. 60

43 Prof. Vaidyanathan R, Professor, IIM, Bangalore, as quoted in News Report '$1.4tn Parked in Safe Heavens Abroad : Stash way over National Income of Around Rs. 50 Lakh Crore, says Expert' *The Times of India,* 10.08.2009

44 Peter Eigen, Chairman of Transparency International as quoted in 'Corruption Perception Index 2002 : Where are we heading to? By Mervin Alexander, *CBI Bulletin*, Special issue, August 2009

45 Yardley, Jim, 'Family ties Dominate Political Life in India', *New York Times – Asian Age*, dated 24.10.2009.

46 UNESCO World Summit for Social Development Position Paper, Paris, 1994

47 Ghosh, Maya, 'Institutionalizing Democracy at the Grassroots for People's participation in Development Planning – An Experiment in West Bengal', *The Indian Journal of Public Administration*, Vol. LV, no2 , pn. 2009.

48 Gupta, Dipanakar, '*The Caged Phoenix: Can India Fly?*', Penguin. 2010

49 Khilnani, *ibid*, p. 101

50 Rajesh Shukla, 'Inclusive Growth and Regional disparity', *The Economic Times*, dated 04.01.10

51 NCEAR Data as quoted in article of Rajesh Shukla, *ibid*

52 Roy, Ramashray, *Economy, Democracy and the State: The Indian Experience,* Sage, New Delhi. 2009.

53 Dr.Pachauri, R. K. 'Cope & Haggle Year', *The Pioneer*, 27th.12.2009

54 Gupta, Dipanakar, *op. cit*, p 45

55 *See* Khilnani, 1997, 1992

56 *See* Rudolphs, 2008

57 National Human Right Commission Report, 2002

58 NHRC, 2004

59 Darshan Singh, 'Atrocities against Scheduled caste: Highlights the role of Police'. *Indian Police Journal*, Vol.LVII, No1,. New Delhi

60 UNDP Human Development Index, 2010.

61 Ashis Nandy, *AsianAge*, dated 27.12.09

62 Bagchi, Amiya Kumar, 'Capabilities, Informational bases and Global Justice', *Statesman* Review (11.10.2009) of Amartya Sen's '*The Idea of Justice*', Penguin\Allen Lane London, 2009.

63 Kishwar, *op. cit.*

64 Study by Sutton Trust on composition of New Parliament (2010) as quoted by *The Economic Times*, dated 11.05.10

65 http://www.wisegeek.com/what-is-an-oligarchy.htm11.9.2010

66 Akbar, M. J, 'Danger from the New Brahmins', *The Times of India,* dated 07.02.2010

67 Dipankar Gupta, *The Times of India,* 06.02. 2010, edit page

68 Desai, Meghnad, 'Divided by Democracy', (Ed.) David Page, Roli Books, New Delhi 2005.

69 *The Times of India,* dated 11.01.2010, 13,11 Nov. 2009, 23.11.09

70 Lyotard, Jean-Francois, '*The Differend: Phrases in dispute.*' University of Minnesota Press. Pp 9. 1988

71 Nath, Triloki, '*State of the Nation*', Marwah Publications, New Delhi. 1986

72 Karnik, Kiran , 'Envisioning a Civilized Democracy', *The Economic Times*, 4.2.2010

73 Justice Dhingra, S. N., as quoted in 'HC Judge slams culture of adjournments', *The Times of India,* 28.01.2010

74 Kartar Singh vs. State of Punjab (1994), 3 SCC 569; People's Union for Civil Liberties & Anr vs. Union of India (2004), 9SCC580.

75 Chameli Singh vs. State of Uttar Pradesh, AIR 1996 SC 1051

76 Desai, *op. cit.*

77 Maier (1992), *op. cit*, pp 45

78 Bhambri, *op. cit*.

79 Khilnani, *op. cit*

80 Desai, Meghnad, *op. cit*, p 31

81 Yardley, Jim, 'Family Ties dominate Political Life in India,' *New York Times-Asian Age*, dated 24.10.2009.

82 Mehta, Jagat S, '*The Tryst Betrayed: Reflections on Diplomacy and Development*', Penguin, 2010.

83 Mehta, *ibid*

84 Jain Bharti, 'India Succumbs to Chinese Pressure on Arunachal, *Economic Times*, dated 06.03.2010

85 Markey, Daniel, 'Developing Foreign Policy software', *The Times of India,* dated 27.07.2009.

86 Ahmad Shamshad and Nafees Ahmad Ansari, *op. cit.*, p60

87 *India Today*, New Delhi, June 21, 2004.

88 Editorial, *Economic & Political Weekly*, November 7, 2009, Vol XLIV No 45, Page no 5 Para II

89 Bhambri, C.P. *Indian Politics since Independence*, Shipra Publications, New Delhi, 1994 311-315

90 Noorani A.G., *Ministers' Misconduct*, Vikas Publications, New Delhi, 1973

91 Bedi, Dr. Kiran, 2007

92 Wade, Robert, "The System of Administrative and Political Corruption: Canal Irrigation in South India" *Journal of Development Studies*, Vol. 18, 1982,pp 287-322.

93 Roy, *op. cit*, p5

References

Amin, Samir (2009) 'The Defense of Humanity Requires the Radicalization of Popular Struggles' in Panitch, Leo and Colin, Leys (ed.) *Violence Today: Actually Existing Barbarism—Socialist Register 2009*: Left Word Books; New Delhi

Araghi, Farshad (2009) 'The Invisible Hand and Visible Foot: Peasants, Dispossession and Globalization', A Haroon, Akram Lodhi and Christobel Kay (Ed.) *Peasants and Globalization: Political Economy, Rural Transformation and the Agrarian Question*: Routledge: New York.

------------------(2010) 'The End of 'Cheap Ecology' and the crisis of 'Long Keynesianism' *Economic and Political Weekly*, Vol. XLV No.4, Jan 23

Araghi, Giovaum (1994): *The long twentieth Century: Money, Power and the origins of Our Times*, Verso: London.

Arnold, David, 'Police Power and Colonial Rule: Madras 1859-1943

Bardhan, Pranab (2009) 'Notes on the Political Economy of India's Tortuous Transition,' *Economic and Political Weekly*, Vol.LVII, no 49, Dec. 5

Barry, Andrew (2001) *Political Machines: Governing a Technological Society* [Paperback] Kindle edition: London

Baxi, Upendra (1982) *Crisis of Indian Legal System*: Vikas Publications; New Delhi

Bernstein, Henry (2009) 'Reflection on Violence', in Panitch, Leo and Colin, Leys (ed.)

Violence Today: Actually Existing Barbarism—Socialist Register 2009: Left Word Books; New Delhi

Bhushan, Prashant, (2009) 'Misplaced Priorities and Class Bias of Judiciary', *Economic and Political Weekly*, Vol. XLIV No 14, April, 24, 2009

Brie, Michael (2009) 'Emancipation and the Left: The Issue of Violence' in Panitch, Leo and Colin, Leys (ed.) *Violence Today: Actually Existing Barbarism—Socialist Register 2009*: Left Word Books; New Delhi

Dali, Vidyadhar (2009) 'Is the CEO Model of Political Leadership the Answer?' *Economic and Political Weekly*, Vol.LVII no. 8 Feb

Davidson, Paul (2009): *The Keynes Solution: The Path to Global Economic Prosperity*, Palgrave Macmillan: New York

Harvey, David (2003) *The New Imperialism*, Oxford University Press: Oxford

----------------(2005) *A Brief history of Neoliberalism*, Oxford University Press, London

Hartwich, Oliver Marc (2009): 'Neoliberalism: The Genesis of a Political Swearword,' The *Center for Independent Studies* (http://www.cis.org.au/tem/op114_neoliberalism.pdf dated 27/12/2010)

Hasan, Zoya, (2009) 'The Enduring Challenge of Building a Just Society', *Economic and Political Weekly*, Vol XLIV No. 22, May 30, p 24

Khilnani, Sunil (1997) *The Idea of India*, Hamish Hamilton, London

Karnik, Kiran (2010, "Envisioning a Civilized Democracy" *The Economic Times*, 4.02.2010

McMichael, Philip (2008): *Development and Social Change: A Global Perspective*, Pine Forge Press: Thousand Oaks.

Mead, WR (1989) 'American Economic Policy in the Antemillenial Era', *World Policy Journal*, Vol 6, no 3 pp385-468

Oommen, TK (2006) *Understanding Security: A New Perspective*. :Macmillan, New Delhi

Patnaik, Prabhat (2008) 'The Accumulation Process in the Period of Globalization' *Economic and Political Weekly*, Vol.43, No. 26 pp108-113

Rudolph, Lloyd and Rudolph, Susanne Hoeber (2008) *Explaining Indian Democracy: A Fifty Year Perspective*, 1956-2006, Oxford: Delhi

Samaddar, Ranbir (2009): 'The Limits of Lokniti' *Economic and Political Weekly*. Vol. XLIV No 7 Page 73

Skidelsky, Robert (2009): *Keynes: The Return of the Master*, Perseus: New York

Stilgitz, Joseph (2002) 'Information and the Change in the Paradigm', *American Economic Review*, Vol 92, No. 3, pp 460-501

Subramanian, K.S. (2007) *Political Violence and Police in India*, Sage Publication, New Delhi

Tharoor, Shashi (1997) *India: From Midnight to the Millennium*, Arcade Publishing, New York.

Verma, Arvind (2010) 'War on Terror: The Road Ahead' *The Indian Police Journal* Vol. LVII, July-September, 2010.

-------------------(2005) *Indian Police: a Critical Evaluation*, Regency Publications, New Delhi

Williamson, John (1990) 'What Washington Means by Policy Reform', in John Williamson (Ed) *Latin American Adjustment: how much has happened?* Institute of International Economics: Washington DC.

Section Five

Political Auditing

The term political auditing is used in various ways and for various purposes. The term is being used in Japan for auditing political fund received by political parties. 'The system requires audits of expenses flowing out of political groups tied to Diet members, but excludes revenues flowing into such groups..... Though the system aims to disclose to the public how political funds were spent – down to the very last yen—politicians' revenues are not subject to the Auditor's check.'[1]

While in America and Europe it is being used for auditing political hierarchy in Supreme Court's Certiorari decisions and Executive decisions. In an article published in American *Political Science Review* (2000), this concept has been elaborated as 'We examine how the Supreme Court uses signals and indices from lower courts to determine which case to review. In our game theoretic model, a higher court cues from publicly observable case facts, the known preferences of a lower court and its decision. The lower court attempts to enforce its preferences, exploiting ambiguity in cases' facts patterns. In equilibrium, a conservative higher court declines to review conservative decisions from lower courts regardless of the facts of the case or the relative ideology of the judges. But a conservative higher court probabilistically review liberal decisions, with the "audit rate" ties to observable facts and ideologies of the lower court judge.[2] There has been some proposal for "democratic audit of a country's public life and institutions" and some work has been published in this regard.[3]

Some, particularly in Europe, use the term political auditing in auditing executive discretion. Similarly, a research paper published in *Notre Dame Law Review* (2006) maintains, "...Reliance on judicial review to generate information about executive discretions makes it difficult to address these concerns because courts routinely define much of their work in terms of applying the same standard of deference to every case in a particular class, limiting the possibility to increase the stringency of review in some policy domains without making the costs allegedly prohibitive as a conceptual alternative for monitoring executive discretion, this article develops a framework akin to that employed by courts engaged in the sample adjudication of class action and governmental fraud cases. It relies on the possibility of systematically auditing samples of discretionary decisions and making those results public. Although the efficacy of such a system depends on the political context and details of its institutional, audits have the potential to sever the connection between the perceived costs of encroaching on discretionary and the stringency of review."[4]

In some Asian countries like Israel, auditing has been undertaken in the context of political behaviours of elected representatives, which has been termed as political auditing. As Ms. Ira Sharkansky, Department of Political Science, Hebrew University of Jerusalem has observed in her research paper, "Israel's State Comptroller has audited the political behaviours of elected officials and private citizens, in what are departures from its own tradition and those of other state auditors. Political auditing seems likely to appear among other auditors, sooner or later. Auditing is likely to attract more attention from political scientists and politics of auditing is likely to become an increasing topic of inquiry as politics becomes more prominent on the auditor's agenda."[5]

Whatever proposals and works have been undertaken in respect of political auditing has been partial, and even if there has been some proposal which is comprehensive, taking into account "a country's public life and institutions", it has been on ideational level. What is needed is the institutionalization of political auditing with some sort of democratic input so that there is no objection on ground of popular mandate.

I

Auditing

Before discussing what is political auditing, and how it should be institutionalized and democratized, it is pertinent to delve into what is auditing and what is its scope. Generally speaking the audit refers to evaluation of a person, organization, system, process, project or product. Audit is generally undertaken to ascertain the reliability and validity of the information, providing an assessment of a system's internal control. The aim of an audit is to provide an opinion on the system/organization and person evaluated on the basis of work done or executed. As auditing is done by the person or a group of persons, there is likelihood of subjectivity creeping into the evaluation work. To neutralize such chance or intentional subjectivity, various statistical methods are used to make it objective and empirical. The statistical sampling is used for such purpose.

Traditionally, auditing has been associated with gathering information about finaces and financial systems in general and financial records of a company or business. Lately, the scope of auditing has been enlarged with inclusion of the environmental performance, health, general well-being, etc. Consequently, separate auditing is being done for environment and other points as desired by the concerned authority. In financial accounting, an audit is an independent assessment of the fairness by which a company's financial statements are placed by management. This assessment is done by competent, independent and objective person or a group of persons. Such person or a group of persons are known as auditors or accountants, and after doing the assessment or auditing, they issue an auditor's report regarding the results of the audit. Such systems must adhere to generally accepted standards set by governing bodies which regulate the business or the company. It is a kind of assurance for the third parties or external users that such statements present a true picture of the company's financial condition and results of operations.

The word 'audit' is derived from Latin word 'audire' which literally means 'to hear'. Auditing existed in ancient India, Egypt, Greek and Roman Civilizations. The aim was to know whether there existed any fraud. However, the scope of audit was very limited as most businesses were small and owner-operated. As this owner-manager had hands on knowledge of the business and its entire operations, there was no need of independent auditor. As the owners or the mangers were interested only in ensuring whether all cash receipts and payment had been properly accounted or not and checking of possible frauds. Broadly speaking, they were interested only in checking whether any embezzlement of cash or fund has happened and if it did happen; to what extent the amount had been embezzled.

However, with the growth of businesses in terms of size and complexity, it was difficult for owners to keep abreast of all aspects of the businesses. Especially with the advent of the company form of business organization, a need arose to appoint an independent person who would examine the company's affairs on behalf of the shareholders, who had no hand in the running of the company. This led to the demand for independent auditor. 'The principal objective of modern auditing is not limited to cash verification; it is to report on the financial position of a business undertaking under the audit as by its financial statement i.e the balance sheet and the profit and loss account. Detection of frauds and irregularities became the objective of the independent financial audit. Lately, auditing has switched its emphasis from searching fraud to judging the fair presentation of financial statement.

II

Why Political Auditing

Political auditing has been tried by some countries and Non-Governmental Organizations (NGOs), and some human rights groups such as International Institute for Democracy and Electoral Assistance Democratic Audit (IDEA) by Human Rights Centre, University of Essex. However, these have been limited to some aspect of democracy. There have not been any organized efforts to institutionalize political auditing to make politics more accountable and transparent. But there has not been any dearth of scattered attempts being made to conceive and conceptualize the concept of political auditing. For example, Israel's State Comptroller has audited the political behaviours of elected officials and private citizens, in what are departures from its own traditions and those of the other state auditors. Political auditing seems likely to appear among other auditors, sooner or later. Auditing is likely to attract more attention from political scientists and politics of auditing is likely to become an increasing topic of inquiry as politics becomes more prominent on the auditor's agenda.[6]

Democratized Political Auditing (PA) and its institutionalization is the only hope for democracy that has lost its sheen, ideals and principles in quagmire of rule of few, or certain group or cliques, dynasty, corruption, big money, appalling poverty and cartelization of economy and society. The leftover effects of colonialism or imperialism are getting accentuated, and these are regrouping and recuperating to eclipse the democratic society. Democratized PA seems to be beacon amidst all round gloom that has descended in society, polity and economy. Despite the recovery of world economy back on the road to normalization, the global capitalism and their satellite states will continue to face the glut, recession, glitches and market upheavals. This is only surface like the iceberg of which only one third is visible while three fourth is hidden under deep water. While the boom is for few—for chosen few, groups, cliques, interests, few countries, the crisis ensnares all and sundry. Whether boom or bust for the underbelly – the people and masses—it is the same saga of poverty, inequality and exploitation and deliberate attempt to keep nations, societies, groups, class and masses ensnared in daily struggle for survival.

Civil Society: Highjacked and Neutralized

Lately civil society has been highjacked, if not, then neutralized by the vested interests in cahoots with state apparatus. The public space, independent of state and government, political parties, etc that is for people and their associations for airing their grievances, articulating their demands and mobilizing people on issue of common good has been captured by the vested interests and their agents (Tandon and Mohanty; 2002). The political parties and their agents, in collaboration with neo-liberal predatory capitalists, have tacitly occupied the space by crowding it with too many issues or non-issues, by infiltrating with their own agents and controlling the public space through their proxy and remote controlling these with their agents and issues. The media too has been neutralized by trivializing the issues of public concern and seems to have become willing partner in an open show of consumerism and mass culture.

So the civil society seems to have courted the same fate that the public sphere or space of Jugen Habermas has done. In *The Structural transformation of public sphere*, Habermas developed the influential concept of the public sphere, which emerged in the 18th century Europe as a space of critical discussion, open to all, where private people came together to form a public whose 'public reason' would work as a check on state power. Habermas argues that prior to the 18th century; European culture has been dominated by a 'representational' culture, where one party sought to "represent" itself on its audience by overwhelming its subjects. (Blanning, 1998)

Habermas has mentioned that a variety of factors resulted in the eventual decay of the public sphere, including the growth of a commercial mass media, which turned the critical public into a passive consumer public; and the welfare state, which merged the state with society thoroughly, squeezing public sphere out of its life. Moreover, it turned the "public sphere" into a site of self-interested contestation for the resources of the state rather than a space for the development of a public minded rational consensus (Edgar, 2005). Habermas has urged that the public sphere should be reinvented, not only at national but international level also so that postnational society should be resurrected (Flyvbjerg, 1998)

Michael Foucault has made clarion call that (civil) society must be defended from all sorts of visible and invisible onslaught launched by the power and discipline based state and its agencies (Foucault, 2003). 'As soon as there is a power relation, there is a possibility of the resistance. We can never be ensnared by power: we can always modify its grip in determinate conditions and according to a precise strategy.' (Kritzman, 1988) The field in which power is deployed is therefore not that of a doleful and stable domination: "The struggle is everywhere... at every moment, we move from rebellion to domination, from domination to rebellion, and is all this perpetual agitation that I would like to bring out."[7]

Even conceding the fact that these are west-centric opinions having not much relevance to non-western societies, it may act as point of reference for analyzing the civil society and its constraints as existing in these countries. Steering clear of the debate whether civil society exists in India or not, what is important is how its dynamics and forces can be harnessed in strengthening democracy and empowering the people on margin. However, it would be pertinent to have a glance over the debate regarding civil society in India and non-western countries.

According to some thinkers the civil society does not exist in India except as narrow bourgeoisie enclave, excluding the vast majority of the people (Chatterjee, 1983; Kaviraj, 2001). The communities in India act and operate under the state as a political society rather than civil society. As they negotiate with government for privileges and rights which is generally granted on the ground of democracy and electoral compulsion, they are controlled and looked after by the government as per Foucault thesis. Hence they constitute the political society not civil one (Chatterjee, 2004).

Lately, the conflict between corporate and non-corporate capital under the conditions of post-colonial primitive accumulation of the capital has been added to this division between the political society and civil society. However, the government has to intervene to offset the effects of post-colonial primitive accumulation by doling out the 'livelihood needs' to the people who have been dispossessed and uprooted, particularly in democracy. These provisions are "culturally determined sense of what is minimally necessary for a decent life, one that is neither unacceptably impoverished nor excessive and luxurious" (Chatterjee, 2008).

Those in political society make their claims on government, and in turn are governed, not within the framework of stable constitutionally defined rights and laws, but rather through temporary, contextual and unstable arrangements arrived at through direct political negotiations. The latter domain, which represents the vast bulk of democratic politics in India, is not under the moral-political leadership of the capitalist class (*ibid*). There is no denying the fact this has been happening, particularly after globalization and liberalization of political economy of India. But this seems to be a tactical strategy of the state to temporarily ward off any major upheavals and uprisings in the society, and it may be hidden agenda to stymie any consolidation of the civil society with force and power.

However, any stretching of this concept of political society may lead to many dangers and anomalies to democracy. It has already led to subversion of democratic principles and institutions. Moreover, it has further increased the fragmentation of Indian society and polity on sectarian basis such as caste, religion, language, etc. This organization of a certain group on such narrow issues and negotiation with State thereof, which it concedes due to electoral compulsion acts as red herring for other groups. In this process democratic norms are being sacrificed and the democratic institutions stymied, it does not matter as it ensures the winning of next election.

As this concept is based on identification of democracy and its fundamental conflict with modernity as the framing question under the conditions of post-colonialism and globalization (Chatterjee, 2003), it may catapult this conflict between the modernity and democracy as conflict between civil society and political society, which is posited as an elite-subaltern conflict. This has resulted in the emergence of "a modern civil society, consistent with the idea of freedom and equality, is a project that is located in the historical desire of certain elite sections of India", which has reportedly led to a situation which has been termed as lumpenization and criminalization of the polity (*ibid*).

Notwithstanding the emerging scenario wherein the state and global capital has embarked on project akin to what Marx called the primitive accumulation of capital and in the process is dispossessing peasants of their rights over lands and other natural resources (Sanyal: 2007). This violation of poor's rights by the state warrants that these should be included in the civil society. Thus, we need to highlight the thicker meaning of democracy, to include institution-building and institutional norms, like the rule of law and rights and respect for dissent, instead of celebrating the populist democratic assertions. In the absence of these norms and values, democracy slides from majoritarianism to authoritarianism, fundamentalism or fascism. This is a well-known experience in most parts of the world (Mukherjee, 2010).

Hence there is a need to conceptualize and demarcate new areas of government outside the classic trinity—legislature, executive and judiciary. The so-called welfare functions are central to the modern state; they have to be recognized and subjected to the discourse and canons of justice, rights and democracy. Putting it differently, they have to be transformed from issues of management and control into matters of democratic politics (*ibid*). So there is a need to introduce democratized political auditing as institutionalized mechanism to ensure accountability and transparency in governance. The political auditing in general and institutionalized in particular would give civil society a new, effective and permanent leverage to subject the welfare activities of the modern state to the discourse and canons of justice, rights and democracy.

Since its rediscovery and reinvention in 1970s but more particularly in 1980s (Chandhoke, 2009) after stellar performance in 1960s when it forced the democratic governments across the world to give legitimacy to dissent and new rights, including India where it did away the one party rule of Congress in many states of India and tried to bring out 'Total Revolution' under the leadership of Jayprakash Narayan, Civil society has been gaining new dynamism. Since then civil society came to be viewed as substitute for the "power hungry" state and the "profit driven" market. The reason for this is obvious: tremendous disenchantment with the "overreach" of the state in the advanced capitalist, the erstwhile socialist and the developing world. The revolution "from above" in the form of the interventionist state—welfare, developmental, Keynesian, even socialist has done nothing but strengthen the *status quoism* and unhindered pursuit of power, giving scant regard and attention to the overall interests of citizens. The revolution "from below" in the form of freedom struggle in the colonized had petered off (*ibid*).

In India and other democratic countries the civil society has been initiating "several mass-based political movements and grassroot activism" since 1980s such as anti-caste movement, the struggle for gender justice, for civil liberties, for the environment, for food security, for the right to work, for the right to education, movement against mega development projects, child labour, bonded labour, etc. (*ibid*). By the year 2000, an estimated 20,000 to 30,000 grassroot movements, social movements, non-party political formations, social actions groups, movement groups, were raising issues of political significance (Sheth, 2004; 45). But these grassroot activism and politico-social movements have not been able to bring out any substantial and sustainable change. Whatever change and breakthrough these managed to wrest out have relapsed in *status quoism*. Nevertheless, in many instances it has been found that while collective voice has died down, the wider problems still persist. (Tandon and Mohanty, *op. cit*).

However, there is a limit to civil society which emanates from its very constitution and socio-economic conditions it has to operate The civil society and its actors are not in a position to emancipate people from poverty, exploitation, deprivation and injustice as they do not have requisite resources and wherewithal. Neither can they, through NGOs, implement agenda of redistributive justice which involves mammoth efforts transferring resources form affluent to poor; nor can they establish and strengthen the institutions that can implement social policy (Chandhoke, 1995). Moreover, the emancipatory and democratic agenda of civil society is constantly being threatened by the exclusionary politics perpetrated through the reinvention of particularistic loyalties of caste, language, region and religion. (Tandon and Mohanty, *op. cit*)

However, it does not absolve the state of its primary responsibility towards citizen. Without being given a choice, we are assigned a role in the collective life of particular society. The society makes us responsible for its acts, which are taken in our name and on which, in a democracy we may even have some influence; and it holds us responsible for obeying its norms; thereby supporting the institutions through which advantages and disadvantages are created and distributed. (Nagel, 2005).

As the state in a democracy is organized and structured in the name of people, citizens have right to challenge the 'arbitrary inequalities produced and reproduced by the economic, the social, and the political order.' However, we have no realistic prospect of taking direct control of the political process in any large-scale contemporary state. Nevertheless, there are many areas of public life, short of directly controlling the actions of the executive, where greater public participation might serve to improve the accountability of our representatives, if only by pressurizing them into taking greater account of the actual beliefs and aspirations of a majority of the citizens (Skinner, 1992).

However, this participation has been limited to periodic election which has become more of ritual or a winning game than an effective tool of participation and control over governance. And for winning election one does not need majority of votes as is the case now-a-days in almost all democracies around the world. The representatives are getting elected on less than one third of majority votes and the government is being formed with the support of 30 to 36 per cent of the votes (Election Commission Report, 2004; Election Commission, 2009). This has been due to faulty voting system of the 'first-past-the post' which ensures victory to those candidates who get more votes than others in the race irrespective of getting majority of the votes or not.

Problem of Participation and Representation

Herein come the problems of participation and representation which are getting weaker and diluted due to various factors. The foremost among these is the belief among stakeholders of democracy that voting and elections are 'sufficient for democratic involvement.' "Recent liberal theorists of freedom and citizenship (theoretical family of Democracy) have generally been content to assume that the act of voting constitutes a sufficient degree of democratic involvement and that our civic liberties are best secured not only by involving ourselves in politics but rather by erecting around ourselves a cordon of rights beyond which our rulers must not trespass.. None of this is thought to vitiate the democratic character of our politics, partly because our rulers are still obliged to seek election, and partly because it is also said (though generally with less assurance) that they remain accountable at all times to those who have elected them...[8]

Democracy is a regime of number, resting on majorities. If it sets no limit on the scope of activity that numbers might legitimate, then democracy may be subject to degeneration that theorists from Plato and Aristotle to Walter Lippmann or Leo Strauss predicted. If liberal ground rules are not protected by institutional safeguards, then unscrupulous demagogues could mobilize popular will for repressive ends. This had been the situation under Fascism and Communism. Could it again emerge as a result of rising ethnocentrism and xenophobia, as the former national structures broke apart in Eastern Europe or migrants encroached on supposedly homogeneous societies? Majorities could become intolerant. On the other hand, the force of numbers, the appeal to public opinion, and the direct persuasiveness of the gifted orators remained central to the underlying strength of democratic regimes. (*ibid*)

The Indian democracy came to such precipice when the demagogy and majoritarianism was about to transform it into a fascist state during fag end of 90s and beginning of new millennia. But hats off to Indian electorates (derided by their western counterparts for lack of cultural and political experience on micro level, while on macro level they are sneered for their lack of education and literacy) for their wisdom and discretion in seeing the truth of fascism in majoritarianism, and calling their bluffs. It is quite ironic while the democracies world over are tightening their migration laws, citizenship rules, honing up their economic and cultural nationalism, Indian democracy is going in opposite direction. While other democracies are being afraid of the towering minarets, community shops and eateries, veil and other activities of religious and linguistic minorities, Indian democracy is opening its arms for multiculturalism to set its foot firmly and then spread to four corners of the world.

It is another matter that these are being done for garnering votes or being used as vote bank politics. It is majoritarianism in reverse or it is minoritism in perverted form that is waiting for the majoritarianism to explode, demagogy again to take center stage and it is open invitation for fascism. It is boon or bane for democracy depending on the way democracy is conducted. The way democracy is treated by the leaders and the growing tribe of 'iron law of Oligarchy' can be classified as one represented by the Western democracy and other one by the Indian democracy. Both do not bode well for the future and health of democracy as form of government, way of conducting social, economic, cultural and other activities.

"And the advent of democracy in Soviet Union, in Czechoslovakia (erstwhile) indeed in East Germany, did suggest that at crucial moments the major recourse of democratic initiatives remained as in 1789, the crowd. Sheer numbers provided the legitimation of democracy. In Western Europe and North Africa during the 1960s, younger 'radicals' had suggested that democracy had atrophied into bureaucratic decision rules. But the upheavals of 1989 (more than the revolts of 1968) confirmed the potential of participation. Instituting democracy required, most problematically, the mobilization of the crowd. Mass protest remained irreplaceable—frightening occasionally, but also inspiring as in the Soviet defense of recent liberties. Even when repression succeeded, democracy presupposed the crowd as in Tiananmen Square... Democracy in its earlier sense required a continuous public commitment, a willingness to discuss and think about what the populace wanted. Such an acceptance of crowd passions provided the dangers, but also the vitality.[9]

Recent popular upsurge in North African countries of Egypt, Tunisia, Libya and other Arab countries where democratic aspirations of the people have been kept in abeyance for decades reinforces this potential of mass protest as guarantor of democracy. However, this mass aspiration for democracy may soon be "atrophied in bureaucratic decision rules" or slide into political skullduggery or brinkmanship as it is happening in most democracies of the world, including Indian one. It is mere tactical strategy on the part of elected governments that critical mass of popular upsurge is kept in abeyance by doling out nominal welfare relieves or playing one class or section against other. The "danger" of popular upsurge remains lurking in not a distant horizon, though it may infuse "vitality" in democracy.

However, it is like walking on razor's edge, when it can enter the "danger" zone, nothing can be predicted, despite all the number game and claptraps of distributive justice being trotted out world over. The democratized PA and its institutionalization is required to infuse some vitality in democracies world over in general and in India in particular, as expanding 'rule of Oligarchy', the advent of TV and Internet blunting the importance of oratory, interpersonal communication, direct address to crowd and gatherings. The most lamentable aspect of the current democracy is falling participation and loosing interests of the people in conduct of their affairs. Moreover, the people are loosing control over their representatives and institutions that are meant to serve them.

Democracy was ending the century as the most demanding form of regime: it required continuous discussion, lest it degenerates into mere accolade. It did not make a good spectator sport, although television often threatens to transform it into one. It required restraint: majorities had to deny themselves total power. They had to place key resources of political and social pressure beyond their own control, lest civil war and repression result. But democracy also seemed to require some aspects of charisma—not to redress the bureaucratic encroachment that Max Webber believed to threaten political decision-making, but to engage mass opinion (*ibid*, p 150)

Hence, democratic vitality was renewed through moments of high drama—even at the cost of stability. It involved great contests for public spaces. As one of the fiercest critics, Vilfred Pareto, had observed, democratic regimes tended to operate cyclically. To remain vigorous, democracy required periodic efforts to include those hitherto left out of political and cultural and economic entitlement (*ibid*). It is another thing this inclusion of left out people creates fresh demand and pulls and pressures in society and system. But it gives vitality to democratic system which is vital for its survival. At least it gives hope to pent up feelings and simmering discontentment to translate into tangible entitlement. It strengthens democracy, notwithstanding the fact this fresh demands and pulls and pressures present some challenges. It is better to face these challenges arising out of the 'circulation of elite' or cyclical effects than the prospect of civil war and revolts.

The democratized PA and its institutionalization would certainly infuse vitality in democracy that has been reduced to number game, winning election and "spectator sports" through television, internet and other media of mass communication.

Problem of Representation

The problem of representation has been one of the most daunting problems of democracy that has drawn the attention of many scholars and thinkers. The main aspect of the representation that has engaged the stakeholders of democracy is the type of voting theory that would give representation to the constituency in real sense of the term. As democracy is based on representation and representatives are elected by citizens in election based on certain voting system such as first-past-the-post, which is also known as plurality voting, proportional representation, cumulative voting, etc. While the plurality voting is widely prevalent in most democracies of the world, the proportional representation is being followed in some countries with smaller population. The former system is easy in putting into practice, but it does not give adequate representation to the constituency as it is based on first-past-the-post method. The latter, though gives representation in proportion to the population or number, it is difficult to follow in a constituency with larger population. [0]

The British elections (like Indian ones or for that matter for all democracies where the elections are conducted on plural or first-past-the-post basis) are won and lost not across the country as a whole, but with 100 or so marginal seats where the parties are more evenly matched, the majorities are smaller and seats are therefore the most vulnerable (Weir and Beethan, *op. cit.*) Thus electoral battles are targeted on marginal constituencies and swing voters. Such tactical voting and targeting of votes diminish the quality of democracy. "The parties are fighting the real election, the one counts, and unless you are a swing voter in a marginal constituency, you are not part of it all – this is where the election will be won and lost and where the parties long ago dug themselves in" (The Guardian, 1997).

Hence, representation in real sense of term does not seem to be possible. And democracy being based on representation, particularly indirect one which is being followed in most of the countries, adds to our problem. The prevalent way of electing representative, that is 'first-past-the-post' or 'winners-take-all' is not based on majority voting, the representatives world over are being elected on less than one third of total votes. In such case how can they be accountable to the general people knowing that they can win by serving the interest of one third or even less than of the people? This problem of representation leads to formation of minority government who serves the interest only of those who have elected them, leaving rest to fend for themselves. In such a scenario, how can it be expected that government thus formed would be accountable and transparent?

As Madison has maintained that men and women in government and politics are to be trusted only if they are properly accountable, if they act under the law and if their conduct is open to scrutiny (Madison: 1788). Today's men and women in politics seem to be neither accountable nor open to scrutiny nor do they always act under the law. It is a fact they are not to be trusted? But what can be done and even if something must be done who would do it and how? The civil society has its limitations; the opposition seems to be acting more as government-in-waiting and the media and judiciary has its own boundaries beyond which it cannot go?

Then what is the way out? Should we wait for 'crowd power' like what is happening in North African and Arab countries where people have risen in revolt against autocratic regimes? It must not be forgotten that reliance on 'crowd power' may throw out the baby (democracy) along with proverbial bathing water? Herein comes the need of the democratized political auditing with institutionalized mechanism so that elected representatives or people's representatives cannot object that unelected audit group has no popular mandate, to scrutinize popularly elected government and its different agencies. Moreover, this political audit must have some teeth or punitive power to do the required course correction in democracy and its institutions.

The democratized political auditing and its institutionalization would be based on the principle that James Madison propounded when democracy was in its infancy: "In framing a government which is to be administered by men over men the great difficulty lies in this: you must first enable the government to control the governed; and in the next place oblige it to control itself. A dependence on the people is, no doubt, the primary control on government; but experience has taught mankind the necessity of auxiliary precaution" (James Madison, In Federalist Paper No. 51, 1788). It is on this "auxiliary precaution" that democratized PA and institutionalization would work to regain some sort of popular control over political actors that has been lost over the years.

The democratized PA and it institutionalization would act as bulwark against any further deviation from democratic principles and values. In fact, it would endeavour to resort to course corrections of democracy that has been hijacked by vested interests. It would act as a watch dog for all parts of the systems: the executive, legislature, judiciary, bureaucracy, economy, media, NGOs sector, political parties, foreign policy and other such sub-systems would come within its purview. All the public offices, government funded institutions, private business, education system and any other such entities that have some sort of public dealings or avail the public facilities or utilities. All these are suffering from the same maladies as the politics—these are going farther away from their charter of duties and mandate, and whatever works and achievements are being claimed are more a chaff than grains or may be an exercise in public relations or mere propaganda.

III

Democratized Political Auditing: Institutionalization and Popular Control

The political auditing is a mammoth project involving whole polity of a country, comprising all institutions and organizations, systems and sub-systems. 'Any audit process (whether political or otherwise) involves at least four distinct stages. You must first identify the criterion appropriate for assessment, which help define and select what is to be assessed. The second stage is to determine the standards of good or the best practices, which provide a bench-mark for the assessment. Third and the most time consuming is to assemble the relevant evidence both from the formal rules of a given institution and its informal practices, to enable a judgment to be made... the final stage is to review the evidence in the light of audit criteria and defined standards so that a systematic assessment can be reached. To do this across the whole range of a country's political life is a huge undertaking' (Weir and Beethan, *op.cit*).

Nevertheless, it can be done and what is important is its institutionalization and democratization of political auditing so that it becomes a permanent mechanism to ensure popular control and participation, accountability and transparency. If the political auditing mechanism is decentralized, democratized and institutionalized, it would revolutionize democracy, grounding it to its real moorings—that is rule by, for and of the people in real sense of the term. It may seem a very 'difficult task', but it can be done as any sort of auditing requires a bench mark or the standardized good or the best practices. In democracy, it is there in the form of constitutional mandate, rule of law, powers and functions as mentioned in the Constitution or convention and customs, party manifesto, promises made during elections, etc.

What is required is that these have to be matched or assessed by the real performance by the political actors, government and its agencies, executive, legislature and even the judiciary. So far as developing the criteria on which political auditing would be done, it can be done with the help of professional auditors and those already working in this field. Random sampling method can be used to make assessment scientific and error-free. In respect of political auditing, it would not pose much problem as there is clear cut demarcation of power and function, responsibility and well-established democratic values and ideals. These have to be matched with decisions, acts, deliberations and overall act of governance.

Then comes the question of who would do it? The political auditors would be obvious answer who would be trained to do so as per fixed norms and criteria of assessment. The acts, decision, policy making, decision-making and their implementations are there and these have to be assessed and auditing result would thus be obtained. But the main problem is under whose leadership it would be done and what would be the credential of the assessing authority that would be accepted by the popularly elected political actors, government and legislator, constitutionally appointed authority such as judiciary, etc.?

Political auditing would be done or get done by those candidates of popular House or Lok Sabha or House of Representatives or Lower House who could not win despite having substantial popular support. At the state and district or Panchayats level, those candidates who could not make to state legislative body and district or Municipal or Panchayati Raj popular bodies despite having substantial popular support would be undertaking auditing work. These political auditors would be selected in such a way that their aggregate votes would exceed that of winning candidates, for example if a successful candidate of a Parliamentary or State or Municipal or Panchayati body gets 30 per cent of total votes, two or three candidates whose total number of votes exceed that of the winning candidates would be selected, forming the panel of auditors.

To check any bias in political auditing undertaken by these unsuccessful candidates, there would be another panel of unsuccessful candidates down the line whose aggregate of votes would exceed that of primary auditors. These secondary political auditors would review any bias in the report and their opinion would have overriding power. To make it further bias proof and scientific, random sampling method can be used as add-on exercise making it credible and scientific. Moreover, to remove any bias and vendetta arising out of their inability to make to home, there would be well-laid down criteria and guidelines for auditing. The points of assessment will be as per mandate, Charter of duties and constitutional authorization or the publicly proclaimed policies and objectives.

Such mechanism would make political auditing democratic as it would be done by the people having popular support. The political actors would not find alibi that these political auditors have no popular base and hence, they could not pass judgments on their performance. In addition to it, it would do away the anomalies of representation inherent in 'the first-past-the-post' or 'winners-take-it-all' voting system, on which elections in the most of the democracies, including India are based. It would increase the representation and participation by giving these unsuccessful candidates with substantial popular support a say in governance, thus grounding democracy.

Every branch of government – Executive, Legislature and even judiciary – would be subjected to PA. Any adverse report on any act or performance of the executive or legislature or judiciary would lead to some sort of punitive action such as removal of the concerned minister or head of department or outright dismissal if such omission and commission or any deviation from set rules and conduct is repeated. The follow-up action should be so harsh that it would have deterring effect on each and every part of the political actor. Even the fourth state of democracy – media – would be subjected to PA. The adverse report would lose their accreditation and if they persist in their deviations, they would be subjected to censure and closure. Even bureaucracy would be subject to the political auditing in respect of the implementation of the government decisions. Project wise auditing should be done in addition to financial auditing being done under the Comptroller and Auditor General of India as per constitutional mandate.

The PA would be done on programmes and assurances of political parties that they have put forward to contest and win election. Once in power, whether they have fulfilled these or not, a PA would be done. If they have failed in fulfilling their promises and assurances, which has been mentioned in their respective manifestos, then they may be barred from contesting election or some other sort of penalty should be imposed. In respect of political auditing of the political parties, the auditors may be constituted from the elected representatives of trade unions, associations of professional organizations and services, cultural and art bodies, association of NGOs, industry and business chambers, and the elected representatives of religious, linguistic and other organizations of the civil society.

If some government functionaries or ministers or departments or political parties are found to be lacking in fulfilling their respective mandates or the charter of duties or manifestos on which parties contested election, they should be forced to resign. If there is more than certain frequency, to be decided later on, of breaching the trust of the people or democratic mandate, the government should resign and the department should face budgetary constraint or if it keeps on violating, it should be closed down. However, the continuity of the government or concerned branch or ministry should be maintained with some back-up mechanism.

Even opposition in popular house should be put to some sort of popular control as they are government-in-waiting. The political auditors may be constituted from the elected representatives of the media bodies, the educational and academic institutions, think-tank organizations and other associations of civil society. The exact mechanism may be developed later on. The economy would also be put to some sort of PA at macro and micro level. The public sector and private sector both would be covered under the ambit of the PA. The auditing may be done in respect to corruption, unfair practices detrimental to overall economy, security and safety of the people and nation, cartelization, etc.

The auditing may be done annually or half annually, followed by prompt corrective and punitive action. There should be two or three panels of political auditors, so that any allegation of corruption whether proved or otherwise would remove the concerned auditor from a particular audit project and any confirmation or proven act of corruption would lead to the outright dismissal, forfeiture of property and further bar from public life. His or her position would be taken by the next in panel. The methodology will be objective and empirical, and random sampling method can be used. If there is any substantial question of stability of the government or the matter may involve the bigger question, the sample size may consist whole universe. Initially, there might be some problem to find the professional. But the help of market research group, general and professional auditors may be taken.

Secrecy, uncertainty, and unpredictability would characterize the working of PA to ward off the possibility of influence or undue pressure exerted on their functioning. Once team is selected, they will be cut off from outside world. They will be kept under strict surveillance and their freedom and liberty would be restricted until they finish their assigned work. It should be a people's democratic weapon for safeguarding their liberty, freedom and rights from overt or covert alliances of vested interests.

Such democratic political auditing would not only do away into the representational deficit arising out of the 'first-past-the-post' or 'winners-take-all' but also act as force multiplier in boosting political participation which has lately plummeted down to its lowest in real sense of the term. The whole structure of democratic political auditing is based in the twin premise of removing representation deficit and ensuring greater popular participation. This popular participation would further act as check and balance that has been eroded by the systemic imbalance and consistent efforts by the vested interests consisting of oligarchy, to perpetuate their hold on power and pelf.

IV

Civil Society Initiative

Political auditing can be operational and effective only when it is institutionalized. For it constitutional amendment will be required, which is further dependent on the will power of political actors. It is difficult to presume that political actors across the democracies of world, including India would muster enough political courage to bring such mammoth or rather revolutionary change. This doubt on part of political actors emanate from their reluctance to introduce even minor systemic change such as Ombudsman or Lokpal (there is no political will to bring the higher offices such as Prime Minister under its ambit) or Women Reservation Bill.

The initiative in this regard will have to be taken by the civil society and its stakeholders. Only mass mobilization on this issue can force the political actors to institutionalize political auditing by amending the constitution or law of the country. Meanwhile, the stakeholders of the civil society will have to undertake their own initiative to do the political auditing by forming the political audit group, at least at central level or state level or unit level, with the help of the political actors who despite having substantial support could not find any say in the governance. The result thus obtained can be articulated through mass media and public meetings, building pressure on the political actors.

Later on, this process of political auditing should also cover the world body and International organizations such as United Nations, and its Auxiliaries, regional bodies, organizations, etc. and the conduct of foreign nation should also be covered under the ambit of political auditing to the extent that it affects the world peace and stability. The same mode and pattern of selection of political auditors should be followed as in the case of national politics. The candidates who could not make it to world bodies such as Security Council, World Health Organization, General Assembly, etc. would form the panel of auditors.

Even religious, linguistic, social bodies, charitable institutions, and other non-governmental bodies, Non-Governmental Organizations (NGOs) should also be brought forth under the ambit of political auditing.

Endnotes

1 *Daily Yomiuri* Online

2 Cameron, Charles M, Segal, Jeffery A and Songer, Donald, "Strategic Auditing in a Political Hierarchy: An Informational Model of the Supreme Court's Certiorari Decision", *American Political Science Review*, vol 94 no.1. March, 2000 .

3 Weir, Stuart & David Beetham (2001): *Political Power and Democratic Control in Britain: The Democratic Audit of United Kingdom*, London: Routledge

4 Cueller, Mariaano-Florentino, "Auditing Executive Discretion", *Notre Dame Law Review*, 82, November, 2006.

5 Sharkansky, Ira, 'Political Auditing', *International Journal of Public Administration*, Vol 28, No1.

6 Sharkansky, Ira. 'Political Auditing', *International Journal of Public Administration*, (Internet search)

7 "Kenryoku to chi ('Pouvoir et saoir')", *Dits et ecritis*, vol. 3, p. 404 as quoted in Michel Foucault's "*Society Must be Defended*" New York: Picador, 2003

8 Maier, *op. cit* page no149

9 Maier, (1992), *ibid*, page no149

10 Amy, Douglas J, "How Proportional Representation Elections Work" PR Library

References

Blanning, T.C.W (1998) *The French Revolution: Class War or Culture Clash*, New York: St. Martin's Press.

Chatterjee, Partha (1983): "More on the Modes of Power and the Peasantry" in R Guha (ed.), *Subaltern Studies II* (Delhi: OUP)

--------------- – (1984): "Gandhi and the Critique of Civil Society" in R. Guha (ed.), *Subaltern Studies III* (Delhi: OUP)

--------------- – (ed.) 1998. *Wages of Freedom: Fifty Years of the Indian Nation-State.* New Delhi: Oxford India.

--------------- – (2003): "Beyond the Nation? Or Within?" in C M Elliot (ed.), *Civil Society and Democracy: A Reader* (Delhi: OUP)

--------------- – (2004): *The Politics of the Governed: Reflections on Popular Politics in most of the World.* Delhi: Permanent Black

--------------- – (2008). "Democracy and Economic Transformation in India", *Economic and Political Weekly*, Vol 43, No 16, April.

Chandhoke, Neera (1995): *State and Civil Society: Explorations in Political theory*, New Delhi: Sage

.... (2009): 'Putting Civil Society in Its Place', *Economic and Political Weekly*, Feb 14, Vol. XLIV No. 7

Crick, David, (1980): *George Orwell: A Biography*, London

Dasgupta, Satadal (1986): *Caste Kinship and Community: Social System of A Bengal Caste*, Madras University Press

Dutta A, R. C. Arora, and P C Sharma, (2011) 'Analysis of Problems related to Forensic Examination in Offences against Human Body and need for Auditing' *Indian Police Journal*, Vol. LVII, No. 3

Edgar, Andrew (2005) *The Philosophy of Habermas*, Montreal: McGill-Queen's UP

Flyvbjerg, Bent (1998) "Habermas and Foucault: Thinkers for Civil Society?", *British Journal of Sociology*, Vol. 49, no. 2, June 1998, pp 209-213.

Foucault, Michel (2003) "*Society Must be Defended*" Lectures at the College De France 1975-76, New York: Picador

Gouldner, Alvin (1980) "Civil Society in Capitalism and Socialism" in *The Two Marxisms: Contradictions and Anomalies in the Development of theory*, London: Macmillan

Habermas, Jugen (1989): *The public Sphere: An Inquiry into a category of Bourgeois Society*, Polity Press

Jaffrelot, Christopher (2003): *India's Silent Revolution: The Rise of Low Castes in North Indian Politics,* Delhi: Permanent Black.

Kaviraj, Sudipta (2001): "In Search of Civil Society" in S Kaviraj and S Khilnani (ed.), *Civil Society: History and Possibilities*, Cambridge University Press

Kothari, Rajni (1970) *Politics in India*. New Delhi: Orient Longman

Kritzman, Lawrence D, Ed. (1988) *Michel Foucault: Politics, Philosophy, Culture: Interviews and Other Writings*, 1977-1984, New York and London: Rutledge

Madison, James (1788) Federalist Paper No 15

Mukherjee, Sanjeeb (2010): "Civil Society in the East, and the Prospect of Political Society", *Economic and Political Weekly*, Vol. XLV No 5, January

Nagel, Thomas (2005): "The Problem of Global Justice", *Philosophy and Public Affairs*, Vol 33 pp. 113-47.

Sanyal, Kalyan (2007): *Rethinking Capitalist Development: Primitive Accumulation, Governmentality and Post-colonial Capitalism,* London: Routledge.

Sheth, D. L. (2004) "Globalization and New Politics of Micro-Movements", *Economic and Political Weekly*, Vol. 39, No 1, pp. 45-48

Skinner, Quentin. 1992. "*On Justice, the Common Good and the Priority of Liberty*" in Chantal Mouffe (ed.), Dimensions of Radical Democracy: Pluralism, Citizenship, Community, London: Verso.

Skinner, Quentin (1992, 'The Italian City Republics', in John Dunn, (ed) "*Democracy: The Unfinished Journey – 508BC to AD 1993*. Oxford University Press, London.)

Tandon, Rajesh and Ranjita Mohanty (2002): *Civil Society and Governance*, New Delhi: PRIA

General References

Beasley, Mark, Frank Buckless, Steven Glover, Douglas Prawitt (2008) *Auditing Cases An Interactive Learning Approach: International Edition*,

Cutting, Thomas (January 12, 2008). "How to Survive an Audit". PM Hut. http://www.pmhut.com/how-to-survive-an-audit. Retrieved December 13, 2010

Davies, Marlene, John Aston (2010) *Auditing Fundamentals*

Dunn, John (1996) *Auditing Theory and Practice*, 2nd Edition

Hayes, Rick, Roger Dassen, Arnold Schilder, Philip Wallage (2004) *Principles of Auditing: An Introduction to International Standards on Auditing*

Soltani, Bahram (2007) *Auditing: An International Approach*

International Standard on Auditing 315 Understanding the Entity and its Environment and Assessing the Risks of Misstatement

Section Six

Epilogue: Ocean vs. River

"It is out of the past that the future is molded. It is the past that becomes the future."

Swami Vivekananda

"The further backward you look, the further forward you can see."

Winston Churchill

India is a wounded civilization and she has been shrinking[1] – spatially, geo-strategically, politically, culturally, and militarily. There is no need to illustrate it as Indian boundaries in ancient and mediaeval time extended up to Southeast Asia and West Asia. Our cultural boundaries extended well beyond Japan, China, Egypt and Greece. Since then we have been shrinking slowly and steadily. There should be historical-political auditing in this regard so that further shrinkage is prevented and at least we can reclaim our cultural boundaries.

The partition, which was a result of our overambitious leaders' desperation to grab the pie of power and pelf,[2] wedged further erosion in our geo-strategic strength when sizeable chunk of its territory was lost. Moreover, it created permanent hatred between two communities. The millions of people from both communities were left to marauding frenzy of communal and sectarian violence. Why did not leaders from both sides provide adequate security to the millions of people as happened in case of Greece and Cyprus where respective communities were escorted safely. There should be historical-political audit in this regard.

After partition, we might have been thinking that this is our limit. But poaching on our geographical boundaries started no sooner than we got Independence. First it was Pakistan when it occupied half of Kashmir, what is now called Pak-Occupied Kashmir in 1948 piggy riding the weakness and myopic world view of an idealist leader with personal world ambition.

Then it was turn of China when the same effete leader gifted Tibet to China in 1959 and did not get anything in return, defying all the norms and etiquettes of world diplomacy. Emboldened with this generosity by India which was misunderstood as weakness by China, the Dragon invaded us in 1962. It took away the size of Arunachal Pradesh which is called Aksai in western sector, and there is a Parliamentary resolution which calls for reclaiming the area from China by all available means. As if it were not enough, our enemies are busy in their nefarious design to 'bleed us profusely by thousand cuts'[3] and their chimerical dream of 'breaking India into twenty-thirty parts'.[4] As per an official report, 'The area along Line of Actual Control with China has "shrunk" over the years and India is clearly "withdrawing".[5] There should be politico-strategic auditing in this regard as to why not counter-strategic measure is being taken?

However, the pride in our civilization has been inflating in direct proportion to our shrinkage. The more pain, wounds, bondage and subjugation, conquests, defeats we have had, the more pontification, the more urge to cover up our defeats, not accepting the bitter reality, going for 'Ostrich like approach'. The superiority in our cultural and civilizational history, pride in our philosophical, spiritual and religious heritage has been a cover up for our desperate urge to rationalize our defeats and subjugation.

It has been a sort of vicious circle. The more defeats, conquests and bondage that we have been subject to, the more insulating, inward looking and compromising as a nation we have become. Instead of looking into our weaknesses, accepting our vulnerabilities, dissecting the nearsightedness, pettymindedness, xenophobic and lopsided views and acts of our erstwhile rulers, kings, and leaders, there has been deliberate attempt to justify our defeats and subjugation. With sole purpose of covering up the fault lines of our leaders, kings, Rajas, Maharajas, princes and other of their ilk.

Instead of accepting of our past, doing justice, learning lesson from it, we have been putting these under the carpet of collective amnesia and totting up the hollow theory of peace, non-violence and tolerance. Instead of learning from the mistakes of history, we have hitherto indulged into escapist or defeatist tendency of creating secular, leftist and jingoist or communal view of history, and teaching our successive generations these rubbishes. Instead of pouncing on our external and internal enemies, our weaknesses and vulnerabilities, we have been beating our chest and hanging our heads in convenient inevitability of destiny instead of accepting the hard reality.

"For us, at least over the last two millennia, there is no invasion we have foiled, no war that we have really won. The Independence that Gandhi won is a failure too. Dissensions and internecine strife of every kind mark our temporal span seen politically. If there are lessons on how a country should not be run, India has learnt and practiced all."[6] We have been taking pain of defeat and shrinkage, subjugation, exploitation, invasions of all sorts, yet our history book is queer mixture of defeatism, escapism, and collective myopia. Instead of accepting the bitter truth, we have been basking in the hollow glory of past feats, peace, tolerance, and so-called peaceful nature of our people. If one contrasts the volume of violence and hoariness of crimes that our present society is beset with, the theory of peacefulness of the people would fall flat.

To bury this bitter memories and hurts of defeats and invasions, we have been developing 'defeatist view' of history. In this great escapade, the vested imperialist and non-imperialist interests *et la* have been aiding in this rather suicidal and farcical endeavour. The apologists for imperialism and neo-imperialism and other vested interests invented the chimera of 'Aryan Invasion', just to rationalize and intellectualize their loot, inhuman rule, exploitation, plunder and pilferage.[7]

They simply wanted to prove that India is land of invaders right from Aryans to British who have been invading it. While some, such as so-called Aryans, Huns, Shaka, and Mughal settled on their loot, others British, France, and Dutch fled away after fleecing us to the hilt.

The underlying message is: since it is land of invaders and looters wherein everyone is or has been invader or looter of one or another ilk, so there is no wrong in looting and plundering the land and its resources. Even now this loot and plunder is going on unabated, albeit in different form, by proxy of democracy and development and growth, and by different players and actors, and what not. Earlier it was Persian, Mongol, Mughal and British, now it is their descendants, self-proclaimed inheritors of colonial legacies, apologists and collaborators of British Raj or Raj's lackeys and hanger-on kings, princes, Rajas, Maharajas and their progenies are taking forward this legacy of loot and plunder.

The only difference is that now this loot and plunder is being done in the garb of democracy, freedom, liberalism, capitalism and globalization. Famous Hindi poet and critic, Late Shri Muktibodh has recognized this psychology of loot in 1970s when he underlined 'the growing power of unity of loot.'[8] It is unabated, and its intensity and reach is getting bigger day by day. Ironically, this loot and plunder is being carried on the same basis, same rules and regulation, same criminal and judicial code, same administrative infrastructure as created by our colonial rulers. Imperialism is dead. Long live neo-imperialism! Colonialism is dead, long live neo-colonialism!

They are in government, legislature is dominated by such elements, and they have free run over media, industries, trade and civil society. Since we have not learnt our lesson from past, the past has become present and past perfect present perfect, present continuous and future and future continuous. Only time the world around us seems to have changed, we have remained stuck up in past mode of escapism, powered by destiny and messiah complex. The burgeoning middle class, lollypop of market hungry 'market states',[9] is another buffer that believes in status quo as it has and is being benefited immensely by this great loot.

According to unpublished study,[10] approximately 66 percent of the politicians, 68 percent of top bureaucrats (IAS, IPS, IFS and other All India services) 80 percent of industry and business houses, 65 percent of media are monopolized by the descendents and progenies whose father and grandfathers were with British Raj, directly or indirectly. It is really an irony that while sons of the soil continue to wallow in grinding poverty, exploitation, injustice, and inequality even if their forefathers forced the invaders and subjugators to flee the country and won freedom with their blood and sweat, the sons and daughters and inheritors of those who sided with colonial powers are ruling the roost with same 'white men's attitude', ruthlessness of aliens, same imperial approach and inhuman way, with same sets of rules, regulations and system. 'India is a natural superpower kept under leash by colonial control through native leaders…'.[11]

This "colonial control" and a sort of vicious circle can be broken not with violence, army rule or dictatorship, forceful seizure, or benevolent dictatorship. This can be achieved by Political Auditing, through democratic means. It will not only strengthen the foundation of democracy, but take our democracy to new heights of freedom, prosperity and rights. And this would be worth emulating for other democratic nations as well.

The civil society of all the democracies, quasi-democracies, semi-democracies, farce-democracies and even non-democracies are urged to form democratized Political Auditing Group and do the political auditing, and mobilize masses to institutionalize it. So that democracy is not again highjacked by 'Iron Law of Oligarchy' after freeing it from the clutches of the rule by few people, for the few people and of the few people again.

Endnotes

1 Naipaul, V.S. (1977) *India: A Wounded Civilization*, Harmondsworth, p 10

2 Singh, Jaswant , (2009) *Jinnah – India, Partition, Independence*, Rupa Publications, New Delhi

3 ISI's Policy paper as featured in Indian newspapers over the years.

4 Report in Quasi Official Chinese paper *Global Times*, September (2010)

5 "Substantial" loss of land to China, admits report', *The Times of India*, dated 11.01.2010.

6 Pillai, P.V., *Perspectives on Power: India and China : An analysis of attitudes towards political power in the two countries between seventh and second centuries*, South Asia Books: New Delhi, 1977

7 Dr. Ambedkar, Baba Saheb, " *In search of Shoodras (Low castes)*".

8 Vajpayee, Ashok, *Jansatta*, 20 Sep. 2009. Diary of Muktibodh, published by Gyanpeth Prakashan in Hindi, New Delhi, 1986

9 Bobbit, Philip, *op.cit.*

10 Yadav Arihant, *Imperialism is Dead, Long Live Imperialism!*

11 Mukhopadhyaya, Amol Kumar, *op.cit*, p54.

APPENDIX

ABCD OF DEMOCRACY: AN OVERVIEW

Democracy is a very broad concept, and used freely for legitimizing one's illegitimate rule or even by those ideologies and regimes that are anti-democratic. Democracy is not only a form of government wherein ends and means are people itself, but it is associated with a way of life also. Democracy is the guiding principle in almost all walks of human activities – political, economic, social, cultural and what not. In fact, it is a way of life.

Included in it is not only democratic political system, but also social and economic systems. The social system in a democracy stands for general social welfare through the fullest development of human personality. It is possible only when freedom and liberty are granted. Democracy provides these ideals.

During twentieth century particularly, democracy became the predominant form of government not only in Europe and other developed countries, but it also found favour with most of newly independent countries of Asia, Africa and Latin America. It became the right form of government for most of the newly freed countries that were faced with the gigantic task of development and emancipation of the people from hunger and poverty.

The social system in a democracy stands for general social welfare through the fullest development of human personality. It is possible only when freedom and liberty are granted. Democracy provides these ideals. Apart from it, it also stands for economic freedom. Everyone is provided with equal opportunity to make a living. Thus, democracy is based on three basic ideals: individual rights, liberty and equality. A democratic government ensures the enjoyment of individual rights, liberty and equality through various mechanisms.

Democracy does not discriminate people on the grounds of caste, religion, language, region and gender. In order to ensure individual rights and liberty on the basis of equality, it is based on the principal of universal participation of people in the workings of government. Universal adult franchise is the most direct form of popular participation. It is through this mechanism that government is selected and their representatives are elected.

Justification

Democracy is justified on the ground that it has some intrinsic or instrumental value like equality, wide participation etc. The people through direct or indirect elections, held at regular interval, constitute a democratic government. Once the government is elected, it holds power till the people or people's representatives have faith on it. The government is responsible and accountable to the people through elected representatives.

Democracy may have instrumental value but its intrinsic value is derived from its having moral superiority as compared to other forms of government. Majority rule is the main feature of a democratic government. As Thomas Jefferson has observed, the true principle of democracy is that the will of the majority should prevail. This principle of majority rule operates at various levels. The government is elected by majority of votes. The person or party getting majority of votes is invited to form the government. The government, in turn, holds the power till it has confidence of majority of people i.e. majority of elected members. The view or law getting maximum number of supports, whether directly or through elected representatives is accepted or adopted.

Moreover, democratic government accommodates minority view as well. Everyone has right to dissent, and opposition views are respected, tolerated and sometimes included in the majority view. Once the law is passed or view is accepted, the minority view or dissenting notes become majority. The administration is run on the basis of fixed rule. There is a rule of law that is superior. It is applicable to all and nobody is above it or beyond it. Moreover, the rules and regulations regarding working of government, its election and selection and various other aspects are fixed in the form of a written or unwritten constitution. Democratic government is based on justice. Everyone is entitled to get justice in social, economic and political sphere. In a democratic government, citizens are provided with fundamental rights. No part or organ of government can touch or tamper it. This right is protected by judicial review.

Finally, a democratic government ensures smooth change of regime. The method of election and procedures of installation of a new government is fixed and mentioned in constitution. Under ordinary circumstances, none can tamper with these. Thus, it ensures smooth transfer of power, without any armed rebellion or violent and forceful takeovers.

Procedural and Substantial

The democratic government is based on direct link between ruler and ruled, government and governed, and people and government. The government is elected directly or indirectly by people. People exercise control over government indirectly through their representatives or directly through other democratic processes – procession, protest. Or in direct democracy it is done through recall.

Even in direct democracy, the government can be voted out if it does not care for the people. This gives people confidence that government is dependent upon them. This feeling makes government acceptable to the people. The people give habitual obedience to government which begets it natural legitimacy.

Secondly, democracy puts emphasis on equality among individuals. It provides equal opportunities to people in every respect. This leads to healthy and balanced development of the people, which in turn provides stability to the system. Thirdly, the democratic form of government provides liberty to people. These liberty – freedom of speech, freedom of expression, religion, worship, movement etc. – create a bonding between people and government. This makes their mutual relationship more beneficial and stable. It reconciles liberty of people with the authority of state.

It is based on public opinion. The government is guided by public opinion. Public opinion keeps a tab on government, not allowing it to stray from the path of common good and welfare. It provides stable and responsible government. The election at regular interval keeps the government on its toes, making it stable and responsible. It imparts political education to the common people. The elections to local self-government and legislature are held regularly. During elections, many political activities like public meeting, political speech, demonstration, campaigning through multi-media occur. These make people politically aware and conscious. Their knowledge of different issues get widened. Thus it makes people aware of political culture, values and tradition.

As the democracy is based on popular government elected by people at regular interval, the new ideas and people keep on circulating. When one party comes to power, replacing another, its hopes and aspirations are reflected in administration. It brings forth changes in the system. Thus it keeps on changing with changing times. This removes any possibility of revolution or violent take-over. With elections held at regular interval and amendment process clearly mentioned, democracy ensures smooth and peaceful power transfer or regime change.

It gives rise to unity and patriotism among the people. It induces feeling of unity and patriotism among the masses. They feel themselves related with the government, as they choose the government and latter is accountable and responsible to them.

JS Mill has clearly highlighted this aspect of democracy: "Democracy strengthens the love of country because citizens feel that government is their own creation and the magistrates are their servants rather than masters. It promotes patriotism by making the citizens feel that they are an integral part of the government and the welfare of the state is their welfare".

Democracy plays vital role in character building. As Bryce has aptly said: "The manhood of the individual is dignified by his political enfranchisement and this usually gets elevated to the higher level by the sense of duty which it throws upon him. The character of people get enriched through participation in various political activities. Finally, democracy is open system of government. It is not closed system. That is why there is a lot of scope of reform in political and social process".

Despite many strengths or advantages, democracy has some inherent weaknesses, which is worth mentioning. Firstly, it fails to recognize individual talents. It is based on faulty assumption that an ordinary man has enough knowledge and intelligence to give opinion on public matters. But in reality the position is strikingly different. The common man has neither political intelligence nor sufficient education. Masses are normally ignorant, disinterested and passive to the socio-political problem. That is why Sir Henry Maine has termed democracy as government by ignorant and unintellectual which is detrimental to modern civilization.

Secondly, it puts more emphasis on quantity rather than on quality. It goes by number. If certain issue is in the interest of society and nation and majority of people does not think so, the issue would be put on backburner. Because the requisite number is required to put that issue on government agenda. Thirdly, democracy is such a system that is liable to be influenced by pressures and counter pressure in society. Different sections of people are constantly craving for different things. They use all types of techniques to pressurize government. In such a situation, it becomes very difficult for the government to work in desired direction. Even if it thinks that certain issue is of utmost importance to society and nation, it may be helpless if majority of people do not endorse its view. Moreover the interests and preferences of different section of society may vary and may be antagonistic to each other. In such a situation, decision taken by government may not find acceptance among all the sections of society.

Fourthly, the government is susceptible to be swayed by populism. The government might try to please all sections of society. In that process, vital national interests may suffer, putting the very safety and integrity of nation in danger. Fifthly, democratic government is based on faulty election process. Though every one is equal, and equal weightage is given to his or her votes, this may not be so in reality. The concept of political equality falters on many grounds. Complete equality is not possible. There are different kinds of inequalities which adversely affect election process and ultimately the formation of government.

The poor might be sidelined and their preferences might be overshadowed by those of the rich. Economic, social, religious, racial and gender related inequality might subvert the election process to the extent that it would not be possible to conduct free and fair election. In such situation, some sections may get prominence over others. Moreover, election process might stoop to such level as to invoking religious, casteist, regional and linguistic sentiment, as happens during election time in India. This may create division in society, weakening its foundations and structure. Sixthly, it is a government by rich, strong and resourceful persons. Elections are so costly and extravagant that average man or masses cannot afford it. Consequently, rich and musclemen might dominate the government, subverting and perverting lofty goals of democracy. It also puts burden on common man. As the parties spend huge amount on election which is funded by different business houses, they pass on their burden on common man by increasing the prices of goods and services. The government may also levy some additional taxes to mop up the expenses during election.

Seventhly, there is adverse effect on public character and morality due to bad effects of political parties. Political parties often stoop to such a low level that it could badly affect public morality. Their deception, Machiavellian techniques, gap between promise and reality, their opportunism and their pandering to sectarian loyalties like caste, religion, language and region generally weaken the social fabric. Eighthly, most people do not take interest in election and other political processes. Their disinterest may create a political vacuum which might be filled up by some anti-social and anti-national elements.

Ninthly, democracy has been criticized for dictatorship of majority. The brute majority might suppress the minority and dissenting views, creating further division in society. It might give rise to simmering discontentment and pent-up feelings. This is not beneficial for any society. Creativity and innovation is the first victim of majority dictatorship. Finally, democratic government is weak and unstable. The non-stop power game being played by different parties results into weak government. Sometimes situation becomes very fluid, with one government being replaced by another one at great speed. This may hamper the developmental process.

Despite all these weaknesses, democracy is the most popular and viable form of government. It accommodates the minority view, it provides opportunities to individuals to hone up and develop their personalities. By providing liberty and equality, it lays the foundation of an equalitarian society.

That is why JS Mill has said, "Giving full weight to all that appeared to me well against the arguments of democracy, I unhesitatingly give my decision in its favour". CD Burns has also highlighted the indispensability of democracy as a form of government when he maintains: "No one denies that existing representative assemblies are defective, but even if an automobile does not work well, it is foolish to go back into farm car...".

Types of Democracy

Representative Democracy

In modern times, democracy is viewed as the rule by people through elected representatives; it is based on the majoritarian principles. A small group of people is elected by the people to rule on their behalf, and this is called the system of representation. Democracy as understood in modern times can function successfully only under certain conditions.

The first and foremost condition for successful working of democracy is the enlightened citizenship. The citizens must be enlightened enough to know their rights and duties. They should be politically aware of their rights and duties. While they should be protective and assertive about their rights, they should also be keen to perform their duties.

Secondly, education is must for the successful working of a democracy. Democracy implies that people would take part in governmental activities. They should choose such representative who can fulfill their personal, regional and national aspirations. And they can do these things only when they are educated. That is why much emphasis is placed on education in a democracy.

Thirdly, the administration must be decentralized and principle of local self-government should be followed in the true sense of the term. The local self-government – Panchayat, Municipal Committee, Zila Parishad, Municipal Corporation etc. takes care of people's needs and demands at grassroot level. They also satisfy their participatory urge by providing them opportunities to take active part in local bodies. It gives rise to bonding with democratic system as well as with fellow citizens. As Bryce has observed without the existence of local self-government institutions, people cannot develop the spirit of independence.

Fourthly, the fundamental rights of people must be protected. These rights ensure the balanced development of human personalities, which makes the foundation of democracy stronger. There must be social, economic and political equality in the society. These provide the foundations on which a strong democratic government rests. People must have high moral character. If people have high moral character, they would elect good and visionary man to position of power and administration. And such administrator would certainly make the foundations of democracy strong.

Moreover, a free and independent press is essential for the successful working of democracy. A free press highlights the omission and commissions of government or a public figure. It brings forth the strength and weakness of government to public view. It informs the people about deeds and misdeeds of elected representatives. By doing this it keeps the administration on its toes. Thus it helps in bringing transparency, openness, responsibility and accountability in the government. There must be spirit of tolerance among people. Well-organized political parties are another condition for successful working of democracy. It imparts stability to the system by educating people and making them aware of their different issues. It makes them alert politically.

Other conditions for successful working of democracy are: Able and honest leaders, supremacy of civilian rule over army, law and order, independent judiciary and written constitution.

Participatory Democracy

In ancient times, Greek city state had such form of participatory or direct democracy. Such type of direct rule was prevalent in the village republics of ancient India. Direct democracy or some of its features were prevalent in ancient republics of Vaishali, Lichchavi etc. All the people residing in the Republic were member of government and used to take part in its deliberations.

In modern times though it has lost its ancient glory, it is still operational in some form or other. It is still being used to find people's verdict in solving the modern problems. It proved helpful, for example, when the issue of joining the European Union community became insoluble, with sharp division existing among countries of Europe. Particularly in Britain, it became very complicated with public opinion sharply divided between those who supported it and those who opposed it. The issue was settled by resorting to referendum – one of the tools of direct democracy. Same thing happened in case of Eritrea. Eritrea wanted to be independent from Ethiopia. But latter was not willing to grant independence to former. Finally the problem was solved in 1991 through plebiscite – another tool of direct democracy. Then there is mechanism of direct popular verdicts on important issues. Such mechanism is widely used in Switzerland and some states of USA. Direct popular verdict is used to solve the major problem befacing these states.

There are four well known forms of direct democracy – Referendum, Initiative, Recall and Plebiscite. Referendum is a procedure or mechanism whereby an important issue or controversial issue is placed before the people for their verdict. It is also used when some important decision has been taken by the legislative. But that decision does not become law unless people have given their verdict. This procedure is also applicable to constitutional amendment.

Referendum is widely used in Switzerland and some states of USA. In Switzerland the constitution provides for referendum on matters or issues important for the country. It is generally used on the issues affecting the constitution. Under this provision majority view of people as well as the majority of canton are taken into consideration. Referendum can also be held on any matter related with legislation or law making when 30,000 voters or at least eight cantons ask for it. Treaties and agreements with foreign countries are also placed before the people for popular referendum.

Initiative is another device of direct democracy. It is a mechanism whereby certain group may propose a law or even constitutional amendment. It should be supported by the signatures of certain number of people. In some cases the proposal is first placed before the legislature. If legislature agrees to make law on this issue, then the matter is closed. If it does not give consent to the proposal of law making on a particular issue, then this proposal is placed before entire electorate. If the majority of electorates endorse the view that law should be framed on particular issue, then legislature is obliged to make such law. In Switzerland, one lac voters can demand law making on any subject.

Recall refers to procedure when a certain number of electorates may demand the removal of an elected representative. The elected representative can be removed from the office if majority of electorates gives consent to the removal of that representative. A new person can also be elected. This process of recall keeps the elected representative on his or her toes. Generally, a person is elected for a fixed term. But he might indulge in such activities going against the popular mandate. Or he or she might indulge in some acts of omission and commission. The people can remove such elected persons from the office through recall. This system is operational in Switzerland and some states of USA

Plebiscite is another procedure whereby direct popular vote is sought on important matters. Plebiscite is generally used in case of creating some permanent or temporary political structure or condition. Plebiscite differs from other methods of direct democracy – recall, initiative and referendum. While plebiscite is a one time affair, recall, initiative and referendum are used frequently. Plebiscite was first used by Napoleon Bonaparte in 1799 and then again in 1802 and 1804. It was used to decide Napoleon's position in French political system. Many countries that became free after First World War opted for plebiscite to decide their respective forms of government.

The working of direct democracy and it various mechanism has underlined its limitation. The first and foremost limitation of it is that it is suitable for small states like Switzerland or Greek city state or village republic in ancient India. It is not suitable for modern states having large territory and population. Even in the states where it is in operation i.e. Switzerland or some states of USA, very few participate in the political process. Generally most of the population do not take much interest.

Moreover, direct democracy finds it very difficult to handle the critical or emergency situations like war and natural calamities on large scale. These emergency or crisis like situation demands speedy decision and follow up. This is not possible in direct democracy.

Social Democracy

Democracy is not only the form of government wherein ends and means are people itself, but it is associated with a way of life also. Included in it is not only democratic political system, but also social and economic systems. The social system in a democracy stands for general social welfare through the fullest development of human personality. It is possible only when freedom and liberty are granted. Democracy provides these ideals.

Apart from this, it also stands for economic freedom. Everyone is provided with equal opportunity to make a living. Thus, democracy is based on three basic ideals: individual rights, liberty and equality. A democratic government ensures the enjoyment of individual rights, liberty and equality through various mechanisms.

Democracy does not discriminate people on the grounds of caste, religion, language, region and gender. In order to ensure individual rights and liberty on the basis of equality, it is based on the principle of universal participation of people in the workings of government. And the universal adult franchise is the most direct form of popular participation. It is through this mechanism that government is selected and their representatives are elected.

Deliberative Democracy

Deliberative democracy stands for the open and public deliberation on the common issues, concerning all. Though it believes in the autonomous existence of the individuals, yet autonomy does not presume that there are no clash and conflict of relationships and interests. The advocates of the deliberative democracy have faith in persuasion as the best basis for political power and governance. It also delegates some power and control to the individuals on some matters and believes in political accountability. Unlike participatory democracy, it allows some division of political power between people and the professional politicians.

Cosmopolitan Democracy

Cosmopolitan democracy has been contrived in the context of globalization. With the emergence of the supranational organizations like European Union, and other regional association, democracy has acquired the cosmopolitan character. Despite the absence of a single global governance apparatus like nation state, the theory of the cosmopolitan democracy veers towards the creation of global civil society consequent upon the rise of 'globalization from below'.

The new cosmopolitan realities have also brightened the prospects of the global citizenship. The global civil society is inching in this direction with rise of the global movements for environmentalism, women rights and campaign against terrorism. However, the cosmopolitan democracy is in its infancy, and its growth would depend, as what shape the globalization would take.

Gandhiji on Democracy

Gandhi was very critical of Western civilization. He believed that Western civilization was based on 'calculated rational self-interest'. This was, in his view, destruction of human relations. He was sure that the conflict in the society would increase if the pursuit of self-interest in the form of material interest were given free hand. He believed in the ancient idea of simple, moral and pious life.

The political democracy as it was prevailing in the western countries did not find favour with Gandhi. He declared liberal democracy as 'fish market' in which people indulge in the free for all competition for self-interest. He did not like the number game of democracy. It was prevalent in Britain and other countries where one who got 51 per cent of votes he would rule. Gandhi was against this farce played in the name of democracy. Gandhi was for true democracy where the weakest had the same opportunities as the strongest. He also did not like the trend of party rule in democracy.

Earlier, Gandhi had taken negative view of democracy. He was very skeptical of the role of parliament, law-court, police, science, technology etc. He believed that these institutions of modern civilization were bereft of morality. He was fond of 'the tendency of Indian civilization to elevate the moral being'. In pursuance of this line of thinking, he presented an alternative ideal of 'real home rule or self-rule and self control.' This self-rule was to be based on spiritual values, non-violence and self-discipline. However, he changed his extreme views on the institutions of modern world later. The experiences during Freedom Movement changed his negative ideas on the pillars of modern world. Instead of discarding these as he had done earlier, Gandhi included these in his 'pardonable program for the attainment of parliamentary Swaraj'. He mooted the concept of the 'Parliamentary Swaraj'. It was to be village-based and decentralized in nature. This was a version of parliamentary democracy. In such a system, every post was to be held by the elected person.

Gandhi's view on State

Gandhi's concept of the state is based on an ideal state, *Ram Rajya*. The basic tenet of this ideal state is the Indian tradition of morality and ethics. It is to be based on the ideals of non-violence and truth. The guiding principles for the state activities are decentralization and self-sufficiency. Gandhi stood for a stateless society as he considered the traditional state as a necessary evil and wanted to do away with it slowly and gradually. He was skeptical of military, police, jail and other coercive machinery of the state because these were based on violence. He also wanted the state to restrict its activities to the minimum.

Like Thoreau, he wanted a state that governs least. His state was to be organized in such a way as to give importance and primacy to village and

Panchayat. The justice and police administrations as well as the economic activities were to execute by these villages and Panchayat, which were to be self-sufficient units. He stood for a secular state.

The Gandhian concept of the state has been criticized for its lop-sided view of the state and its activities. The State is not an evil. It protects the weak and checks the stronger one. It also undertakes welfare activities. Violence is not the basis of the state. Functions of the state cannot be restricted to bare minimum as it may lead to the decline of the state and downfall of the society. State is a natural institution like family that has evolved out of the mankind's quest for the good and organized life. The state cannot be abolished as it would lead back to the state of nature where 'Might is right' used to be the governing principle. The ideal state as propounded by Gandhiji cannot be realized, as it is not practical.

Gandhi like Marx was against property. He considered it as an obstacle in the realization of good life or spiritual life. However, he conceded that if property were acquired in the right manner, then it was required to be protected.

Gandhi put emphasis on labour. He like Marx believed that labour is the real creator of wealth. As he maintained, "the real owner of wealth is one who puts in certain amount of labour with a conscious production". He was of the opinion that one should not have even a single bite of meal without doing some type of labour. This would not only make everyone economically independent but also help in making our country prosperous and self-dependent.

'Trusteeship'

He put forward the idea of trusteeship in the realm of economic activities. He called upon the capitalists and landlords (Zamindars) to become trustee. The capitalists and landlords should regard workers and peasants as co-proprietors. They should hold their businesses or Zamindaris in trust for workers and tenants. He conceded that absolute trusteeship is not possible. Nevertheless, some sort of trusteeship would lead to better production, and equality in the society.

He was against any sort of state ownership as he maintains "if the state suppressed capitalism by violence, it will be caught in the coils of violence itself and will fail to develop non-violence at any time. But if the capitalists or Zamindars refused to become trustees, the state ownership became unavoidable, he would support a minimum of state ownership."

INDEX